Fiscal Interactions in a Metropolitan Area

Kenneth V. Greene
State University of New York
at Binghamton

William B. Neenan
University of Michigan

Claudia D. Scott
University of Auckland

Lexington Books
D.C. Heath and Company
Lexington, Massachusetts
Toronto   London

Library of Congress Cataloging in Publication Data

Greene, Kenneth V
    Fiscal interactions in a metropolitan area.

    Includes bibliographical references.
    1. Finance, Public—Washington metropolitan area. 2. Taxation—
Washington metropolitan area. 3. Washington metropolitan area—
Appropriations and expenditures.
I. Neenan, William B., 1929-   II. Scott, Claudia Devita, joint author.
III. Title.
HJ9215.G73   336.753   74-300
ISBN 0-669-91454-1

Published simultaneously in Canada.

Printed in the United States of America.

International Standard Book Number: 0-669-91454-1

Library of Congress Catalog Card Number: 74-300

Contents

List of Figures   vii

List of Tables   ix

Foreword
Harold M. Hochman   xiii

Acknowledgments   xvii

Chapter 1
Metropolitan Fiscal Flows   1

Chapter 2
Public Sector Exchanges in a Metropolitan Area   13

Chapter 3
Measurement of Benefits from Government Services   27

Chapter 4
Optimal Supply of Public Output in a Metropolitan Area   51

Chapter 5
Estimates of Benefit Incidence of State and Local Expenditures
in the Washington Metropolitan Area   61

Chapter 6
Estimates of Incidence of State and Local Revenues in the
Washington Metropolitan Area   113

Chapter 7
Interjurisdictional Fiscal Flows in Metropolitan Washington   145

Chapter 8
Fiscal Incidence of State and Local Public Sectors   157

Chapter 9
Discussion of the Results   169

Appendix A
Documentation of the Revenue and Expenditure Data for the
Washington Metropolitan Area   189

Appendix B
Expenditure Incidence Assumptions   201

Appendix C
Tax Incidence Assumptions   213

Notes   239

Index   261

About the Authors   265

List of Figures

2-1	Marginal Evaluation of a Public Service	24
2-2	Marginal Substitution Between a Private and a Public Good	24
4-1	Optimal Supply of a Public Good	52
4-2	Unitary Elasticity of Demand and Optimal Provision of a Public Good	53
4-3	An Elastic Demand for a Public Good with Suboptimal Provision	55
4-4	Source-of-Income Effects on Outlay	56
4-5	Effect of Political Fragmentation on Provision of a Public Good	59
5-1	Total Elementary and Secondary Education Benefits as a Percentage of Money Income by Income Class and by Jurisdiction: Cost-of-Service Basis	70
5-2	Total Elementary and Secondary Education Benefits as a Percentage of Money Income by Income Class and by Jurisdiction: Welfare Basis	70
5-3	Total Higher Education Benefits as a Percentage of Money Income by Income Class and by Jurisdiction: Cost-of-Service Basis	76
5-4	Total Higher Education Benefits as a Percentage of Money Income by Income Class and by Jurisdiction: Welfare Basis	76
5-5	Total Police and Fire Benefits as a Percentage of Money Income by Income Class and by Jurisdiction: Cost-of-Service Basis	84
5-6	Total Police and Fire Benefits as a Percentage of Money Income by Income Class and by Jurisdiction: Welfare Basis	84
5-7	Total Health Service Benefits as a Percentage of Money Income by Income Class and by Jurisdiction: Cost-of-Service Basis	85
5-8	Total Health Service Benefits as a Percentage of Money Income by Income Class and by Jurisdiction: Welfare Basis	85
5-9	Total Welfare Service Benefits as a Percentage of Money Income by Income Class and by Jurisdiction: Cost-of-Service Basis	91
5-10	Total Welfare Service Benefits as a Percentage of Money Income by Income Class and by Jurisdiction: Welfare Basis	91
5-11	Total Benefits from "All Other" Expenditures as a Percentage of Money Income by Income Class and by Jurisdiction: Cost-of-Service Basis	102

5-12   Total Benefits from "All Other" Expenditures as a Percentage
        of Money Income by Income Class and by Jurisdiction: Welfare
        Basis   102
5-13   Total Benefits as a Percentage of Money Income by Income
        Class and by Jurisdiction: Cost-of-Service Basis   110
5-14   Total Benefits as a Percentage of Money Income by Income
        Class and by Jurisdiction: Welfare Basis   110
6-1   Incidence of Property Taxes Paid by Maryland Residents:
        Partial Forward Shifting   119
6-2   Incidence of Property Taxes Paid by Maryland Residents:
        Full Forward Shifting   119
6-3   Effective Tax Rates of Individual Income Tax Before Offset   122
6-4   Effective Tax Rates of Individual Income Tax After Offset   122
6-5   Effective Sales Tax Rates Before Offset   124
6-6   Effective Sales Tax Rates After Offset   124
6-7   Business Cost Effective Tax Rates   130
6-8   Effective Tax Rates of Other Taxes Before Offset   137
6-9   Effective Tax Rates of Other Taxes After Offset   137
6-10   Effective Tax Rates for Total Taxes: Partial Shifting Before
        Offset   142
6-11   Effective Tax Rates for Total Taxes: Partial Shifting After
        Offset   142
6-12   Effective Tax Rates for Total Taxes: Full Forward Shifting
        Before Offset   143
6-13   Effective Tax Rates for Total Taxes: Full Forward Shifting
        After Offset   143
8-1   Fiscal Residuals by Income Class: Cost-of-Service Estimates   162
8-2   Fiscal Residuals by Income Class: Welfare Estimates   165
9-1   Exploitation and Fiscal Residuals   174

List of Tables

1-1   Total Current and Per Capita Expenditures, District of Columbia, Suburban Maryland, and Suburban Virginia, Fiscal 1970   5

1-2   Percentage Distribution of Expenditure Categories in the District of Columbia, Suburban Maryland, and Suburban Virginia   6

1-3   Revenue Sources for Current Expenditures of all Subfederal Governments in District of Columbia, Suburban Maryland, and Suburban Virginia, Fiscal 1970   7

1-4   Percentage Distribution of Total State and Local Revenues for Current Expenditures, District of Columbia, Suburban Maryland, and Suburban Virginia, Fiscal 1970   9

3-1   Source-of-Income and Use-of-Income Benefits from Government Expenditures in Washington Metropolitan Area   41

3-2   Benefits Under Different Utility Assumptions   44

5-1   Percentage of Use-of-Income Benefits by Type from Government Expenditures in Washington Metropolitan Area   63

5-2   Distribution of Elementary and Secondary Education Benefits by Income Class and by Jurisdiction: Cost-of-Service Basis   66

5-3   Distribution of Elementary and Secondary Education Benefits by Income Class and by Jurisdiction: Welfare Basis   68

5-4   Distribution of Higher Education Benefits by Income Class and by Jurisdiction: Cost-of-Service Basis   72

5-5   Distribution of Higher Education Benefits by Income Class and by Jurisdiction: Welfare Basis   74

5-6   Distribution of Police and Fire Benefits by Income Class and by Jursidiction: Cost-of-Service Basis   80

5-7   Distribution of Police and Fire Benefits by Income Class and by Jurisdiction: Welfare Basis   82

5-8   Distribution of Health Service Benefits by Income Class and by Jurisdiction: Cost-of-Service Basis   86

5-9   Distribution of Health Service Benefits by Income Class and by Jursidiction: Welfare Basis   88

5-10   Distribution of Welfare Service Benefits by Income Class and by Jurisdiction: Cost-of-Service Basis   92

5-11   Distribution of Welfare Service Benefits by Income Class and by Jurisdiction: Welfare Basis   94

5-12   Distribution of Benefits from "All Other" Expenditures by
        Category and by Jurisdiction: Cost-of-Service Basis   96
5-13   Distribution of Benefits from "All Other" Expenditures by
        Category and by Jurisdiction: Welfare Basis   97
5-14   Distribution of Benefits from "All Other" Expenditures by
        Income Class and by Jurisdiction: Cost-of-Service Basis   98
5-15   Distribution of Benefits from "All Other" Expenditures by
        Income Class and by Jurisdiction: Welfare Basis   100
5-16   Distribution of Total Benefits by Income Class and by Jurisdic-
        tion: Cost-of-Service Basis   106
5-17   Distribution of Total Benefits by Income Class and by Jurisdic-
        tion: Welfare Basis   108
6-1   Distribution of Property Taxes by Income Class and by Jurisdic-
        tion: Partial Forward Shifting   118
6-2   Distribution of Individual Income Taxes by Income Class   121
6-3   Distribution of the Sales Tax by Income Class   125
6-4   Types of Business Cost Taxes by Jurisdiction   126
6-5   Distribution of the Business Cost Taxes by Income Class   128
6-6   Distribution of the Burden of "All Other" Taxes: Partial
        Forward Shifting   136
6-7   Yield of "All Other" Taxes, 1970   138
6-8   Distribution of the Burden of Total Taxes: Partial Forward
        Shifting   140
6-9   Distribution of Total Taxes: Full Forward Shifting   141
7-1   Fiscal Flows Between Jurisdictions   147
7-2   Tax Flows Between Jurisdictions Before Federal Tax Offset   149
7-3   Tax Flows Between Jurisdictions After Federal Tax Offset   150
7-4   Benefit Flows Between Jurisdictions on a Cost-of-Service Basis 151
7-5   Benefit Flows Between Jurisdictions on a Welfare Basis   151
7-6   Net Fiscal Flows by Income Class: Benefits Estimated on Cost-
        of-Service Basis—Taxes Before Offset   153
7-7   Net Fiscal Flows by Income Class: Benefits Estimated on Wel-
        fare Basis—Taxes Net of Offset   155
8-1   Hypothetical State Income Distributions and Fiscal Residuals   158
8-2   Net Fiscal Incidence by Income Class: Benefits Estimated on
        a Cost-of-Service Basis—Taxes Before Offset   161
8-3   Net Fiscal Incidence by Income Class: Benefits Estimated on
        a Welfare Basis—Taxes Net of Offset   164
8-4   Difference Between the Fiscal Residual in the District and the
        Fiscal Residual in the Suburbs by Income Class: Benefits
        Estimated on a Welfare Basis and Taxes Net of Offset   166
8-5   Net Fiscal Advantages by Income Class. Net Fiscal Advantage of
        Living in the District Rather Than in Maryland or Virginia   167

9-1   Use-of-Income from Metropolitan Washington Public Expendi-
       tures   175
9-2   Benefit Incidence for Washington Metropolitan Area, 1970, and
       for State and Local Governments in United States, 1960, by
       Income Class   177
9-3   Tax Incidence for Washington Metropolitan Area, 1970, and
       for All State and Local Governments in United States, 1960,
       by Income Class   179
B-1   Distributive Series Employed   202
B-2   Summary Table of Distribution of Hours Spent and Miles
       Traveled for the District of Columbia, Suburban Maryland
       and Suburban Virginia   206
B-3   Summary of Procedures Used for Computing Fire Protection
       Benefits on a Cost-of-Service Basis and on a Welfare Basis
       (After Offsets)   209
C-1   Individual Income Tax Offset Rates   213
C-2   Distributive Series Employed   214
C-3   Distribution of the Value of Income-Producing Property in
       the District of Columbia   217
C-4   Calculation of Percentage of District of Columbia Sales Tax
       Paid by Businesses, 1970   220
C-5   Tourist Expenditures and Sales Tax Payments in Washington,
       D.C., in 1967   221
C-6   Lunch Expenditures by Commuters in the District of Columbia   223
C-7   Sales Tax Payments by Commuters in the District of Columbia   225
C-8   Payments of D.C. Sales Tax   226
C-9   Customers of Business Firms of Various Jurisdictions   228
C-10   Geographic Location of Corporate Customers   230
C-11   Geographic Location of Corporate Owners   230
C-12   Sales of Liquor in the Different Jurisdictions   231
C-13   Percentage of Liquor Purchases by Residency of Purchaser   232
C-14   Distribution of Cigarette Purchases by Place of Residency   235
C-15   Percentage Distribution of Insurance Premiums by Category   235
C-16   Percentage of Bank Taxes Paid by Class of Borrower   236

Foreword

A widespread student and professional concern with a "fiscal crisis" in American cities supplied the motive force for The Urban Institute's research in public finance in the early 1970s. The immediate expression of this "fiscal crisis" was familiar. There had been a dramatic growth in local public service expenditures because of the ever-increasing demands for services and the rising costs for providing them, while at the same time the rates at which public revenues increased were disproportionately slow. The inadequacy of revenues was, in turn, attributed to deficiencies in the property tax, which is the major instrument of local finance, and to failures in both the federal and the metropolitan systems of intergovernmental relations.

Faced with these realities, and the kinds of urgencies generated in the Washington environment, it was tempting to adapt a research program to a frantic quest for solutions. It was our feeling, however, that programs and reforms produced without a deeper understanding of the causes and consequences of the urban fiscal dilemma, were likely to be transient improvisations and could, indeed, like so many well-intentioned programs in the past, prove self-defeating. Given that the focus on urban and metropolitan problems in public finance was little more than a decade old, it was our conviction that to ameliorate the fiscal plight of the cities required a more solid grasp of its causes than the state of the art then permitted, and that our resources might best be used in making some small contribution toward this end.

Upon examination, it quickly becomes apparent that the interesting issues in urban political economy are not matters of finance per se—that is, how to raise funds to maintain or initiate various public programs—but of the interaction between fiscal and political factors, as in boundary arrangements between cities and their suburbs, and the relationship between the urban growth process and residential and industrial location. That is, to deal with the dilemma, we felt that we should come to grips with the fundamental forces that shape urban communities.

Put a bit differently, it seems clear that making urban government more effective and better able to deliver the desired public services cannot be achieved through short-run palliatives grounded in insubstantial theory and intuition. What is needed, rather, are public policies that are based on a new understanding of urban fiscal problems, that are interpreted in light of the preferences which underlie the public service demands and the location decisions through which preferences are expressed, and that are capable of determining the appropriate-

ness of the alternative institutional and organizational arrangements under which such services can be provided. For this, decision makers must be able to evaluate the process of community formation in terms of valid models, and to relate the characteristics of communities and their policy problems to demographic and economic parameters. Moreover, in the metropolitan context, where inter-governmental relationships are both vertically and horizontally overarching, decision makers must be able to design institutional mechanisms that detect and restrict interjurisdictional spillovers of benefits and costs, and that take advantage of economies of scale. Indeed, there is no way in which urban performance can appropriately be assessed, or the inadequacies of urban finance remedied, without first understanding how the boundary arrangements between political jurisdictions in interdependent metropolitan areas—and the zoning practices, voting rules, and property assessment procedures which impinge upon them—relate to the urban problems that are the substance of the "fiscal crisis."

Thus, the unifying factor in our research program was the hope that something could be learned about the dynamics of urban political economy and the full range of options available to metropolitan decision makers. Any resulting insights should be capable of suggesting policies with long-lasting and beneficial effects. It is as a part of such a program focusing on the fundamental issues of metropolitan political economy that one should interpret the present study by Kenneth Greene, William Neenan, and Claudia Scott, which examines fiscal transfers among the jurisdictions of the Washington, D.C. metropolitan area. This empirical counterpart to our more theoretical inquiries evolved in response to our interest (and that of our colleagues, Peter Brown, Elliott Morss, and Thomas Muller) in the argument—which some adduced to explain the difficulties of the central cities in the late 1960s and very early 1970s and which served as their basis for recommending metropolitan consolidation and the adoption of such measures as a commuter tax—that central cities are "exploited" by their suburbs.

The term *fiscal exploitation*, as used in this context, may be given several interpretations, although in each case the focus is on the extent to which there is reciprocity between central cities and their suburbs in the interjurisdictional allocations of public service costs and in patterns of public service use. Taking this question as its point of departure, the Greene, Neenan, and Scott study presents a careful examination of benefit distributions and cost allocations under alternative incidence assumptions. While its preliminary concern is with interjurisdictional flows, it also examines the extent to which government operations, through fiscal residuals, implicitly redistribute real income among major income classes within the central city. The authors go beyond all previous studies in considering not only the direct or user benefits of services but also, following the suggestion of some recent writings, the indirect benefits attributable to external effects. They do this—particularly when they examine the incidence of welfare spending—by considering, as one alternative, the allocation

of welfare benefits according to the effective demand or willingness to pay of those who finance, rather than receive, the benefits.

It should be pointed out, however, that this study does not deal with some aspects of the exploitation thesis. It makes no effort to consider the distributional or locational implications of such nonfiscal practices as suburban zoning restrictions or of the effects of such regulations as building codes. Considerations such as these suggest that fiscal residuals, the concern of this study, are themselves at best an imperfect index of the distribution of public service burdens between the central city and its suburbs. What the study does in examining fiscal flows (taking residential and industrial location as given) is to give some indication of whether the Tiebout process has produced a neutral outcome in the Lindahl sense. But it does not tell us whether the means by which measured deviations from neutrality can be remedied are fiscal or nonfiscal.

While the initial impetus of this study was a concern with alleged "exploitation" and the preconceptions it implies, as work proceeded (under Claudia Scott's direction) the emphasis shifted to a more neutral methodological perspective. Thus, the study represents a careful attempt, based on thorough research into the labyrinth of incidence theory and significant empirical investigation, to measure and assign the costs and benefits of the public services provided by the various jurisdictions in a metropolitan area, taking account of their interactions with each other and the rest of the economy. There are, of course, precedents (as in the work of Richard Musgrave and Irwin Gillespie) for such research on incidence. But despite the fact that one cannot determine whether prevailing economic and political arrangements between jurisdictions are appropriate without measuring interjurisdictional flows, the only major effort dealing with intermetropolitan fiscal transfers prior to the present study was William Neenan's own very penetrating study of Detroit and its suburbs. ("The Suburban-Central City Exploitation Thesis: One City's Tale," *National Tax Journal*, June 1970; this article also appeared as a chapter in Neenan's *Political Economy of Urban Areas* published by Markham in 1972.) We were, therefore, fortunate that Neenan consented to spend his sabbatical leave with us at The Urban Institute where he played a major role in our study of interjurisdictional fiscal transfers in the Washington area.

Perhaps even more important than the numerical results presented in the Greene, Neenan, and Scott study is its discussion of an appropriate methodology for examining fiscal incidence, and its careful description of methods that can be applied (allowing for peculiarities of governance in the Washington area) in studies of other metropolitan areas. One cannot, of course, argue that the estimates of fiscal incidence which Greene, Neenan, and Scott present are definitive, except by demonstrating the quality of their measurements and logic. On the other hand, conceived as an exercise in sensitivity analysis, the Washington study does tell us when assumptions are crucial to numerical outcomes and, therefore, how much its results might have been expected to vary as its incidence assump-

tions were modified. In so doing, it indicates the behavioral relationships on which empirical research must concentrate if, as all of us concerned with this study believe, efforts such as this are to prove a useful basis for more informed public policy in the area of intergovernmental fiscal relationships.

Needless to say, completion of a study of this scope required the cooperation of many people. Worth Bateman, then Vice President for Operations of the Urban Institute, and Robert Goldman of the Research Applied to National Needs Division of the National Science Foundation, deserve special mention for their continuing support. Within the Urban Public Finance group, special thanks are offered to Grace Dawson, Cathy Gilson, and Linda Weisberg, all of whom served as my administrative assistants; to research assistants Lennox Berkeley, Rodney Frame, and Thomas Groendyke, who were responsible for much of the data collection; and to Pat Sachs, who did most of the typing.

Harold M. Hochman
Visiting Lecturer
University of California, Berkeley
1973–74

Mr. Hochman was director of The
Urban Institute's Studies in Urban
Public Finance from 1970 to 1973.

Acknowledgments

The number of people who deserve thanks for their help in preparing this book is undoubtedly longer than the following list of acknowledgments. First of all, we must thank our research assistants Rodney Frame, Thomas Parliment, and Lennox Berkeley for their tireless efforts in manipulating practically endless amounts of data. Thomas Muller of the Urban Institute helped us to formulate the ideas for our original research design and Harold Hochman, then Director of Studies for Urban Public Finance at the Institute, guided its fruition. We must also express gratitude to our secretaries, Patricia Sachs, Sindy Keys, and Marilyn Moore, who not only made constant revisions for us with an absolute minimum of errors, but did so with a smile. We must thank all our colleagues who honed our ideas either by criticizing the manuscript or commenting upon our methodology. They include Robin Barlow, William C. Birdsall, Harvey E. Brazer, Thomas Eapen, Lee Erickson, Harvey Galper, George E. Peterson, and Richard E. Wagner. Henry Aaron and Martin David read through the entire manuscript and provided us with detailed criticisms which proved extremely useful. We also acknowledge the support of the National Science Foundation, Grant I-36291. Of course, the views expressed in this book do not necessarily express the views of the National Science Foundation.

1

Metropolitan Fiscal Flows

Introduction

The public services provided by the many political jurisdictions within a metropolitan area vary widely both in their quality and level of provision. Such variance reflects in part differing attitudes and preferences for public goods of the residents of the various jurisdictions. But it is also attributable to the wide variation in the ease with which jurisdictions can raise public revenues.

The realization that jurisdictions have widely different fiscal capacities and responsibilities has evoked responses from several sources. State legislatures have been concerned with the question of "equalizing" the resources of different localities. Grant and revenue-sharing proposals have been adopted or expanded. Enabling legislation has in some instances been passed allowing localities to tax new sources, such as retail sales and income.

Lively controversy has also centered around the charge that the decay of our central cities has, in part, resulted from the "fiscal exploitation" of these areas by their more wealthy suburbs. The belief that suburbanites impose costs upon the cities has existed for some time. However, only recently has the exploitation hypothesis been tested using empirical estimates of flows of tax burdens and expenditure benefits between jurisdictions. These studies are critically reviewed in Chapter 2. A particularly troublesome problem in making such estimates concerns the allocation of benefits from poverty-related public services, such as health and welfare expenditures. There are both theoretical and empirical reasons to believe that suburbanites do derive benefits from expenditures made by central cities to aid their poor. The theoretical argument is based on the existence of interdependent utility functions as well as the presence of conventional externalities.[1] Empirical support lies in the expression of willingness to pay for such expenditures by high-income suburbanites.[a]

In order to provide a sound empirical foundation for reform of the fiscal structure of metropolitan areas, we need a measure of tax burdens and expenditure benefits by income groups in city and suburban jurisdictions. Such information will be of assistance in formulating new policies to correct inequities and inefficiencies.

---

[a]The evidence for this is discussed more fully in Chapters 5 and 9.

Fiscal Flows

The estimation and analysis of the fiscal flows between jurisdictions in the Washington metropolitan area is a major goal of this book. Fiscal flows are the taxes paid and benefits received by household units in the various jurisdictions resulting from the fiscal decisions of all other jurisdictions in the metropolitan area. These flows are measured both on an aggregate basis, between jurisdictions, and also by income classes within jurisdictions. Thus, for instance, we measure not only the total District of Columbia taxes paid by residents of suburban Maryland, but also the total District of Columbia taxes paid by residents of suburban Maryland who have money income between $10,000 and $15,000.[b]

A net fiscal flow to a nonresident is defined as the difference between the dollar value of expenditure benefits received and tax burdens incurred during a period of time. For the question of exploitation it is the relative sizes of the aggregates of these net fiscal flows between jurisdictions which is important. For example, if one hundred suburbanites each receives benefits worth $200 from the city and each pays city taxes of $50, then there is a net fiscal flow of $15,000 from the city to the suburban residents. But if one hundred city residents in turn receive benefits worth $100 from the suburbs and pay taxes to the suburbs amounting to $50, then there is a net fiscal flow of $5,000 from the suburbs to city residents. In the aggregate, however, there is a net transfer from city residents to suburban residents of $10,000.

Net interjurisdictional fiscal flows in the Washington, D.C. metropolitan area will be measured between the District of Columbia and the Maryland suburbs, and the District of Columbia and the Virginia suburbs. Some attention is also given to the benefit and revenue transfers among suburban jurisdictions. The flow calculations to and from the Maryland and Virginia suburbs are estimated in the aggregate.

There is general agreement that both costs imposed by nonresidents on a jurisdiction and revenue contributions they make to it must be considered. However, there is substantial disagreement as to the appropriate way in which these variables should be measured. Two distinct estimates, representing contrasting viewpoints, will be made of these flows. On the one hand, services will be evaluated at their cost and compared with the total taxes before offsets, paid by nonresidents. Primary emphasis, however, will be placed on an alternative evaluation of these flows wherein benefits are based on individual evaluations of government services and the taxes paid by nonresidents are estimated net of offsets.[c]

From this exercise we hope to determine: (1) whether there are net trans-

---

[b] The Census definition of money income is used throughout the study.

[c] The ability to use some state and local taxes as deductions when paying federal income tax burdens means that the true incremental cost of such taxes is less than unity for the taxpayer. They lower the taxpayer's federal tax bill and are in this sense offsettable.

fers between the central city and suburban areas; (2) whether particular income classes in specific areas in the Washington metropolitan area are "exploiters" or being "exploited"; and if transfers do exist, (3) to propose policies to eliminate this "exploitation." The issues implicit in this analysis are at the core of most fiscal controversies which beset metropolitan areas across the country, even though the particular point at issue varies from area to area. In Michigan, New York, New Jersey, and the District of Columbia it is manifested in controversy over central city taxation of commuters. In Anchorage, Indianapolis, Memphis, and Nashville, the question of governmental consolidation of the metropolitan area has been bitterly contested. And in the Twin Cities metropolitan area a controversial plan has been adopted for sharing increases in property tax revenue among jurisdictions in the seven county area.

In all these apparently diverse controversies, the primary question is similar. Do residents of some jurisdictions in a metropolitan area enjoy an advantageous position due to existing public sector interactions or fiscal flows? In this study we hope to be able to respond directly to this question for the Washington metropolitan area and to offer at least general guidelines for answering the question as it is posed in other metropolitan areas.

Fiscal Incidence

In addition to examining fiscal flows we shall also investigate the impact of all state and local fiscal processes by income class in the District, suburban Maryland, and suburban Virginia. To measure this total fiscal incidence the tax burdens incurred and expenditure benefits received from these areas must be aggregated. The index of the resulting budgetary incidence is the fiscal residual, that is, the difference between benefits from public services and taxes paid. The income distribution of these fiscal residuals reveals both the vertical impact of the budget as well as whether there is differential treatment of members of particular income classes across city and suburban areas. If differential treatment does exist, presumably there is a fiscal incentive for migration from one jurisdiction to another.

Washington Metropolitan Area

This study encompasses revenues and expenditures in fiscal 1970 associated with all state and local governments in the Washington metropolitan area: city, county, special district, the District of Columbia, and states.[d] Capital

---

[d]For the purposes of our study, we define the metropolitan Washington area to include: the District of Columbia; suburban Virginia, including Arlington and Fairfax

expenditures are excluded because there is no satisfactory procedure for estimating the value of the services from the capital facilities in all the jurisdictions. Since only current expenditures are considered, revenue estimates are reduced to reflect that portion of total revenues which are raised merely to finance current expenditures.[e] Since the District of Columbia provides many services usually associated with state governments, as well as city services, it is necessary to include the impact of Maryland and Virginia state revenues and expenditures on the suburban areas.

Expenditure Patterns

Total and per capita current expenditures for fiscal 1970 by all subfederal governments in the Washington metropolitan area are seen in table 1-1. The level of expenditures, both in the aggregate and per capita, are notably higher in the District than in suburban Maryland and suburban Virginia. Per capita expenditure levels are higher in the District for every expenditure category except education and transportation. The District expenditures trail suburban Maryland expenditures for these two services but are larger than in suburban Virginia. Fairly similar patterns of per capita expenditures are found in the Maryland and Virginia suburbs. The much higher levels of expenditures for health and social services in the District reflect the needs of a relatively larger lower income population residing in the District. The 1970 Census reports that the percentage of all families and unrelated individuals with incomes below $5,000 was 37 percent in the District of Columbia, which is more than twice the percentage found in either the Maryland or Virginia suburbs.

Some further comparisons of expenditure patterns can be observed from table 1-2, which shows the percentage distribution of expenditure categories in the three areas. Again, similar patterns are observed for suburban Maryland and Virginia, which in turn differ sharply from the District's. More than 60 percent of suburban total expenditures are devoted to educational services while in the District only 29 percent is allocated for education. Health and social service

---

Counties and the independent cities of Alexandria, Fairfax and Falls Church, but excluding Loudon and Prince William Counties, which are less urbanized; suburban Maryland, including Montgomery and Prince Georges Counties. Revenues and expenditures of the unincorporated and incorporated cities and towns in the suburban areas are also included as are several regional authorities, such as the Maryland National Capital Park and Planning Commission. Expenditures and revenues of Maryland and Virginia are included in so far as their incidence is within metropolitan Washington. For full documentation of the revenue and expenditure data, see Appendix A.

[e]An estimate of the value of the capital component used to provide public services in a particular year is very difficult to obtain. One possibility is to use current year's debt service as a proxy measure of the flow of capital services in a particular year. However, this procedure is not used here since there is a wide variation in the use of bond issues to finance capital expenditures in the various jurisdictions.

Table 1-1
Total Current and Per Capita Expenditures, District of Columbia, Suburban Maryland, and Suburban Virginia, Fiscal 1970

Expenditure Category	Total Expenditures			Per Capita Expenditures		
	D.C.	Maryland	Virginia	D.C.	Maryland	Virginia
Elementary & Secondary Education	$135,502,200	$234,199,514	$131,321,471	$179.11	$197.91	$169.89
Higher Education	15,975,900	48,821,301	19,877,260	21.12	41.25	25.72
Fire	25,908,600	10,952,485	9,868,043	34.25	9.25	12.77
Police	66,809,600	20,533,262	13,425,653	88.31	17.35	17.37
Health & Hospitals	82,686,600	23,213,905	10,489,701	109.30	19.62	13.57
Social Services	57,425,700	8,033,583	4,852,098	75.91	6.79	6.28
Libraries	5,542,600	5,428,449	4,431,866	7.33	4.59	5.73
Parks	8,364,000	6,915,860	2,182,612	11.06	5.84	2.82
Recreational & Cultural	10,040,500	3,373,131	2,960,123	13.27	2.85	3.83
Courts	15,502,700	4,106,789	2,386,691	20.49	3.47	3.09
Corrections	18,369,300	7,193,292	3,481,037	24.28	6.08	4.50
Refuse	18,939,200	3,118,993	3,860,231	25.04	2.64	4.99
Transportation	20,950,300	36,782,358	17,166,913	27.69	31.08	22.21
General Government	35,086,200	32,966,650	24,790,689	46.38	27.86	32.07
Total	$517,103,400	$445,639,572	$251,094,388	$683.54	$376.58	$324.84

Table 1-2
Percentage Distribution of Expenditure Categories in the District of Columbia, Suburban Maryland, and Suburban Virginia

Expenditure Category	Proportion of Total Budget		
	D.C.	Maryland	Virginia
Elementary & Secondary Education	26.20	52.55	52.30
Higher Education	3.09	10.96	7.91
Fire	5.01	2.46	3.93
Police	12.92	4.61	5.35
Health & Hospitals	15.99	5.21	4.18
Social Services	11.11	1.80	1.93
Libraries	1.07	1.22	1.76
Parks	1.62	1.55	.87
Recreation & Cultural	1.94	.76	1.18
Courts	3.00	.92	.95
Corrections	3.55	1.61	1.39
Refuse	3.66	.70	1.54
Transportation	4.05	8.25	6.84
General Government	6.79	7.40	9.87
Total	100.00	100.00	100.00

expenditures are 27 percent of total District expenditures, but only 7 percent of suburban Maryland, and 6 percent of suburban Virginia expenditures. The District devotes a much larger percentage of its budget to police and fire protection, correction and courts than do the suburban areas. The suburbs spend more on transportation services.

Revenue Patterns

The total tax revenue generated in 1970 by all the subfederal governments within metropolitan Washington is arrayed according to tax instrument in table 1-3. As can be seen in the table the District relies on an unusually wide range of these instruments. With the exception of millage rates,[f] the rates of most of the District's major taxes are generally in line with those prevailing in other large cities.[2] A similar range of tax instruments is employed in suburban Maryland and Virginia when one considers the state as well as local taxes collected in these areas. A unique feature of the District revenue structure is the federal payment, which in 1970 constituted nearly 23 percent of District revenue used for current expenditures. This federal payment may be regarded as a payment in

[f]While the District property tax rate is in line with that of surrounding suburban jurisdictions, it is somewhat lower than that of many central cities.

Table 1-3
Revenue Sources for Current Expenditures of all Subfederal Governments in District of Columbia, Suburban Maryland, and Suburban Virginia, Fiscal 1970

	Total Taxes		
	D.C.	Maryland	Virginia
Tax Category:			
Real Property	112,694,088	159,182,358	91,425,535
Individual Income	82,153,241	206,022,145	81,199,486
Sales	70,663,287	54,339,907	49,772,802
Public Utility Taxes	9,848,142	22,417,059	15,058,284
Corporate Income Tax Including Franchises and Charters	17,953,646	9,854,063	7,422,955
Personal Property	15,239,442	8,601,027	12,605,587
Business Licenses and Fees	2,996,381	3,642,434	8,805,680
Motor Fuel Excise	13,827,223	22,840,192	12,390,200
Motor Vehicle Licenses and Registration	11,753,250	11,952,066	8,544,170
Alcohol Beverage Taxes Licenses and Profits	14,440,276	4,940,975	7,731,978
Tobacco Excises and Licenses	5,422,649	7,573,253	1,996,656
Insurance Company Taxes	5,454,766	6,269,361	6,366,462
Estate and Gift Taxes	6,712,917	1,600,097	5,537,645
Bank Taxes	5,571,661	3,044,464	724,672
Motor Vehicle Excise	5,810,451	7,859,277	2,556,830
Traffic and Parking Fines and Fees	5,857,242	1,764,254	2,252,790
Other*	4,353,417	10,708,919	2,251,124
Federal Payment	115,192,066	–	–
Total	505,944,145	542,611,851	316,642,586

*These include property related taxes such as transfer taxes, personal fees and in D.C. the unincorporated business income tax, in Maryland railroad and horse racing taxes, in Virginia railroad and capitation taxes.

lieu of taxes as well as compensation for services provided by the District government because of the federal presence. In 1970, 53.5 percent of the assessed value of land and improvements in the District of Columbia was tax exempt. Of this amount 77 percent was federal property. Furthermore, certain classes of District residents, such as presidential appointees, some congressional employees, and employees of international organizations, are exempt from the District income tax. Important business categories are also absolved from the corporation and unincorporated franchise taxes.[g]

[g]Until quite recently when it was made public, the privately owned D.C. Transit Company was exempted from the real property, the personal property, retail sales, motor fuel, and the motor vehicle excise taxes.

A comparison of the expenditure totals shown in table 1-1 with the revenue totals in table 1-3 indicates that they are approximately equal for the District but that expenditures are notably smaller than revenues for both suburban Maryland and Virginia.[h] The fact that revenue collections by the two states exceed state expenditures for services directly benefiting suburban residents reflects redistribution accomplished through the state fisc from the relatively high income suburban areas to the lower income areas in the rest of Maryland and Virginia. Since the District is not part of a larger subfederal jurisdiction such redistribution is not possible.

The percentage distribution of revenues used to finance 1970 current expenditures for the District of Columbia, suburban Maryland, and suburban Virginia is shown in table 1-4. Although the property and income taxes appear relatively less significant in the District than in the suburban areas, if the federal payment is disregarded and merely tax revenues considered, the District property and income taxes approach the relative importance they enjoy in the other areas. Apart from suburban Maryland's relatively greater reliance on the income tax, which is attributable to the fact that both the state and counties impose the income tax, there is only negligible variation across the metropolitan area in the relative importance of the various tax instruments.

Is Washington "Typical"?

The Washington metropolitan area appears to have such singular characteristics that its fiscal experience may not be approximated in any other metropolitan area. It is the seat of the federal government, which is the overwhelmingly dominant employer in the area. The work of government is carried out in property that is tax exempt. The District of Columbia, the central city, is governed by a set of institutions, unique in the United States, according to which responsibility ultimately rests with the Congress rather than local citizens.[i] A federal payment finances nearly one-fourth of the District's current operating budget. The Washington metropolitan area encompasses parts of two states, with different legal and fiscal institutions, in addition to the District. There are numerous single purpose governments in the area, such as park authorities. Finally, the Washington area is a major tourist center. As such it is in a position to export a larger portion of its taxes than is a city without this attraction. For example, we estimate that nearly 25 percent of sales tax revenue collected by

---

[h]For a detailed discussion of how expenditures and revenues are allocated to the various areas see Appendix A.

[i]Members of the House and Senate District Committees have been criticized because they place their responsibility to their home constituencies above the concerns of District residents. For example, Maryland and Virginia representatives strongly opposed a reciprocal income tax proposal which would tax the income of Maryland and Virginia residents who work in the District.

Table 1-4

Percentage Distribution of Total State and Local Revenues for Current Expenditures, District of Columbia, Suburban Maryland, and Suburban Virginia, Fiscal 1970

	Total Taxes		
	D.C.	Maryland	Virginia
Tax Category:			
Real Property	22.30	29.36	28.90
Individual Income	16.25	37.99	25.67
Sales	13.97	10.02	15.72
Public Utility Taxes	1.97	4.14	4.75
Corporate Income Tax Including Franchises and Charters	3.54	1.81	2.34
Personal Property	3.01	1.58	3.98
Business Licenses and Fees	.59	.67	2.78
Motor Fuel Excise	2.73	4.20	3.91
Motor Vehicle Licenses and Registration	2.32	2.20	2.69
Alcohol Beverage Taxes Licenses and Profits	2.85	.91	2.44
Tobacco Excises and Licenses	1.07	1.39	.63
Insurance Company Taxes	1.07	1.15	2.01
Estate and Gift Taxes	1.32	.29	1.74
Bank Taxes	1.10	.56	.22
Motor Vehicle Excise	1.14	1.44	.80
Traffic and Parking Fines and Fees	1.15	.32	.71
Other *	.86	1.97	.71
Federal Payment	22.79	–	–
Total	100.00	100.00	100.00

*These include property related taxes such as transfer taxes, personal fees and in D.C. the unincorporated business income tax, in Maryland railroad and horse racing taxes, in Virginia railroad and capitation taxes.

the District is paid by tourists.[j] In the light of these observations can a study of the fiscal interactions in the Washington area provide any insights applicable to other metropolitan areas?

The Washington metropolitan area indeed can be distinguished from other metropolitan areas. On closer inspection, however, it appears that all metropolitan areas have distinctive qualities and that consequently there may be no "typical" metropolitan area, but merely areas which more or less share some broadly common attributes. Viewed in this perspective Washington may be no less "typical" than the next metropolitan area. Many large central cities have a

[j]See Appendix C.

tax base which presumably permits considerable tax-exporting, such as Detroit's heavy industry and New York's commercial and financial activity. To the extent a city does have such an exportable tax base its fiscal situation parallels the District, which can effectively export a part of its financial burden to the federal treasury through the mechanism of the federal payment. Further, just as Detroit and New York must bear certain costs because of the presence of industrial and commercial property, so the District incurs costs associated with visits of foreign dignitaries and tourists. Thus even though specifics may vary, analytically the fiscal effects are similar for Detroit, New York, and the District of Columbia to the extent revenue contributed by nonresidents exceeds the costs incurred in their behalf.

Additional parallels between Washington and other metropolitan areas can be drawn. The federal government is the dominant employer in Washington; Boston has its education-research industry; Seattle the aerospace industry; and Detroit the automobile industry. New York, Miami, and Los Angeles have tourist industries which rival Washington's. The District of Columbia was created by land transfers from Maryland and Virginia, but the Chicago, Cincinnati, Philadelphia and St. Louis metropolitan areas also extend into two states. The political structure of no two cities is identical. Some cities are contained within counties; some are coextensive with them. School districts in cities may be dependent or independent; coterminous with city boundaries or not. State support of local functions may be generous or niggardly. Indeed whether functions are state- or locally-supported varies considerably from state to state. And whereas the District of Columbia may be the "Last Colony," subject to control by congressmen elected by constituencies whose interests conflict with the District's, many cities must deal with state legislatures that are hostile to the interests of the largest cities.

Thus despite the area's peculiarities the fiscal circumstances encountered in the Washington area should at least be suggestive of the situation in other metropolitan areas. The procedures employed in estimating benefit and tax incidence in this study should be generally applicable in other areas, with the general conclusions applicable in broad outline to other politically-fragmented metropolitan areas. Of course, the precise, quantitative results of this study cannot be accepted as generally valid for other metropolitan areas.

The Chapters to Come

In Chapter 2 pertinent literature regarding the provision of public services in politically-fragmented areas will be reviewed with special attention given to what has been called the "suburban-central city exploitation" hypothesis. Six unresolved issues concerning suburban-central city fiscal interactions will be identified for resolution. The definition of benefits from local government

expenditures is considered in Chapter 3. A distinction between "use-of-income" and "source-of-income" benefits is proposed. It will be shown that the imputation of use-of-income benefits requires the specification of utility functions. A specification will be proposed and assumptions stated for imputing use-of-income benefits from government expenditures in the Washington area. A median voter model of the public fisc in a local, open economy is developed in Chapter 4 as a basis for discussing whether an optimal provision of public services is likely to be found in the Washington area. This issue must be resolved before we can say whether or not the benefits from expenditures equal total revenue or not.

In Chapters 5 and 6 the estimates of the benefit and tax incidence of state and local fiscs in the Washington area are presented under various assumptions. These estimates are given by income class for the District of Columbia, suburban Maryland, and suburban Virginia. In Chapter 7 the aggregate net fiscal flows between the District and the two suburban areas are derived from the benefit and tax incidence estimates in Chapters 5 and 6. The estimates of these flows provide data with which the suburban-central city exploitation hypothesis may be resolved. In Chapter 8 the overall net fiscal incidence of the Washington area state and local fisc is presented with an analysis of the impact of this incidence pattern on location decisions. Finally, in Chapter 9 a number of the theoretical and policy implications of the study are presented as well as an indication of the limitations inherent in this and similar studies.

There are three technical appendixes. The sources of the revenue and expenditure data used in the study are listed and the procedures employed in deriving these data are discussed in Appendix A. A detailed discussion of the procedures and assumptions employed in deriving the benefit and tax incidence estimates presented in Chapters 5 and 6 are detailed in Appendixes B and C, respectively.

2

Public Sector Exchanges in a Metropolitan Area

Introduction

In 1973 there were 267 Standard Metropolitan Statistical Areas (SMSA) in the United States and Puerto Rico. Municipal government services in the SMSAs are provided by many, often overlapping, jurisdictions. Thus a metropolitan resident, in addition to being a municipal citizen, can be a member of as many as a dozen or more different local jurisdictions. There are basically two schools of thought concerning this political fragmentation of metropolitan areas. One group of scholars following Tiebout's classical analysis, believes that at least some political fragmentation in metropolitan areas is a necessary condition for the full articulation of citizen demand for public services. An opposing school does not look so benignly on what it regards as the "balkanization" of metropolitan areas. It judges that in most metropolitan areas greater political unification is necessary both to realize economies of scale in the provision of public services as well as to internalize externalities in the provision of services such as education and poverty-related programs as well as to counteract the segregation by income class that might be precipitated by fragmentation.

An understanding of the general issues involved in this controversy will be a useful background for the subsequent discussion of suburban-central city fiscal exploitation and other questions associated with the differential incidence of public fiscs in metropolitan areas. Therefore in this chapter we will review literature (1) standing in the Tiebout tradition as well as (2) advocating metropolitan integration. This literature is concerned with the optimal provision of public services in a metropolitan area. Since few would claim that at the present services are provided in metropolitan areas in a precisely optimal manner, there is question of how significant deviations from the optimum are and which groups bear the principal burden of this deviation. There is a growing literature which addresses this question in terms of the suburban-central city exploitation thesis. This literature will be reviewed in this chapter in some detail. Although this particular thesis has been tested in various ways over the past twenty years, the basic question it addresses has not been resolved to the satisfaction of most students of the problem. Six unresolved issues concerned with the measurement of suburban-central city fiscal interactions will be identified in the light of the literature review. These issues are briefly explicated in this chapter and will be resolved in the course of the analysis in subsequent chapters.

One or Many Jurisdictions in a
Metropolitan Area

The social and economic interactions between a central city and suburbs have been scrutinized by sociologists, political scientists, and reformers for over fifty years.[1] Only in recent years, however, have they received sustained attention from economists. Tiebout's "A Pure Theory of Local Expenditures" has been a seminal economic analysis of public sector interactions in a metropolitan area. Using such strong assumptions as (1) citizens are completely mobile, that is, they are not restricted in their residential choices by the availability of suitable job opportunities nor by legal or extralegal barriers; and (2) local public expenditures generate no interjurisdictional externalities, Tiebout attempted to show that an optimal pattern of local public services would be supplied.[2] The equilibrating mechanism in the Tiebout model is migration of citizens seeking to maximize their fiscal residuals by locating in that community which provides the most desirable package of expenditures and taxes. In its simplest terms the Tiebout model predicts that the incidence of expenditures and taxes has an impact on residential choice.

Oates has attempted to test this hypothesis by examining whether local public expenditures and taxes are capitalized in property values. Such capitalization is to be expected if, as Tiebout assumed, citizens seek to maximize their utility from local public fiscs through their residential choices. Oates has regressed the median value of owner-occupied dwellings in fifty-three northeastern New Jersey communities on several variables including the per pupil expenditures for public education and the effective tax rates in the various communities. To overcome the problem posed because both expenditures and taxes must be considered endogenous variables he uses predicted values for the expenditures and tax variables in his regression analysis. He finds that:

> . . . local property values bear a significant negative relationship to the effective tax rate and a significant positive correlation with expenditure per pupil in the public schools . . . [P]eople do appear willing to pay more to live in a community which provides a high-quality program of public services (or in a community which provides the same program of public services with lower tax rates).[3]

In the light of evidence such as this, that citizens in politically-fragmented metropolitan areas attempt to maximize their utility within the usual income and price constraints considered by economic theory, it may indeed be true that citizens in many older central cities do bear relatively greater fiscal burdens than those borne by suburban residents. This would result if central city fiscs bear a disproportionate share of the burden of financing poverty-related expenditures and services to nonresidents with no offsetting compensation, coupled with the fact that central city residents are, for one or more reasons, in practice restricted

to residential choices within the central city. Unfortunately, a question such as this cannot be fully discussed within the terms of the Tiebout model since it assumes away precisely the issues at question, interjurisdictional benefit and tax flows and all residential immobility.

A number of recent studies, however, have addressed what Baumol has called the question of the "cumulative deterioration" of central cities.[4] Baumol envisions the process of deterioration as follows: Initially several high income families, attracted, for example, by suburban open spaces, move out of the city. The average income level in the city falls slightly, its tax base is diluted, the quality of public services decline, and a hint of blight can be detected. Other well-to-do residents, taking note of these occurrences, are also persuaded to move to suburban areas, further lowering income levels in the city, diluting the tax base, and increasing blight. This process continues until, as Baumol puts it, "a chronic nadir of lethargy" is reached.[5] No mechanism exists, internal to the system, which will check the exodus of high-income residents from the central city. Meanwhile those who do remain are burdened with maintaining, out of diminished resources, public services associated with an increasingly dependent central city population. In Chapter 3 an attempt is made to establish a basis for contending that such services generate benefits for residents throughout a metropolitan area in addition to the benefits enjoyed by the direct recipients of the services.

Albin analyzes the distributional consequences of politically-fragmented metropolitan areas in terms of another Baumol model, that of "unbalanced economic growth."[6] Albin assumes that a suburb is endowed with a relatively larger "progressive" industrial sector than is the central city, with the consequence that incomes tend to grow faster in the suburbs. This changing income distribution in turn imposes two budgetary pressures on the central city. "First, public assistance expenditures will mount (relevant to the extent that these programs require local finance) and intensify the difficulty of financing services and merit goods. Second, the burden on education will be acute; particularly if we consider education to be one of the critical means of social transformation." [7] A dilemma appears, however, when means are sought for financing these increased expenditures. A progressive tax structure in the central city is called for if the burden for financing these increased expenditures is to be imposed on individuals employed in the "progressive" sector in the central city, whose incomes are increasing the most. But since individuals in this sector are the most mobile in society, such a policy may be counterproductive. As Buchanan has recently contended, in such a situation the appropriate fiscal strategy may be for a central city to adopt a neutral tax system rather than one with progressive incidence, whose principal effect may be merely to drive richer residents to other jurisdictions.[8] It has long been recognized that redistributive goals cannot be effectively pursued by local governments.

In addition to tax strategy another response sometimes proposed in the face

of cumulative deterioration is the political consolidation of metropolitan areas. The principal theoretical arguments for consolidation are that thereby economies of scale in the provision of public services can be achieved as well as externalities internalized through consolidation.[9] For example, externalities based on interpersonal utility interdependence is an especially important factor in the distribution of the benefits from the provision of elementary and secondary education and social services in the Washington metropolitan area, as is shown in Chapter 5. With the consolidation of a metropolitan area a high-income family, for example, could not escape fiscal responsibility for these interdependencies simply by moving to the outer rim of the metropolitan area, since this would be included within the same jurisdiction.

The principal form that political unification in metropolitan areas has taken is the consolidation of city-county government. Since 1947 there have been eleven such consolidations, ten of them approved by referendum and one by legislative action. In 1972 thirty-six other areas were seriously studying such consolidation.[10] Governmental consolidation has, however, also taken other forms and has been achieved under diverse circumstances for a wide range of motives.[11] Although there has been a general tendency to regard such consolidation favorably in the literature, they have been subjected to scanty systematic evaluation and a number of scholars feel they are undesirable.[12]

For several reasons metropolitan areas generally are unlikely to be politically integrated in the foreseeable future. The momentum of existing institutional arrangements is in itself enough to guarantee the maintenance of current arrangements in most areas, barring some major crisis in urban governance.[a] Residents of smaller jurisdictions in a metropolitan area often are especially opposed to consolidation, apparently perceiving they enjoy advantages from fragmentation.[13] These advantages need not be at the expense of other communities, but may result merely from a fuller articulation of their demand for public services than would be possible under a unitary metropolitan government.

Evans has shown, however, using relatively weak assumptions, that suburban residents can be expected to oppose consolidation with the central city for reasons other than a desire for public sector diversity.[14] In his model he assumes: (1) central city expenditure provides a good which is public across the whole metropolitan area whereas public expenditure in the suburb provides a good which is public within the suburb but private between suburb and city; (2) incomes are the same in city and suburb; (3) tastes are also the same; and (4) the city is larger than the suburb.[15] On the basis of these assumptions Evans shows that the central city unequivocally gains from consolidation since

---

[a]There have been some recent innovative approaches to problems posed by political fragmentation. For example, the seven county Twin City metropolitan area has adopted a tax base-sharing plan which reduces motivation for competitive fiscal zoning by the various local jurisdictions. According to this plan, which was first implemented in 1973, 40 percent of the net annual growth of commercial and industrial property values in the seven county area is assigned to the area's three hundred taxing units on the basis of the population of the unit weighted by its per capita property valuation.

the suburb would then contribute to the cost of the public good hitherto provided exclusively by the city.[b] The outcome for the suburb, however, is ambiguous. On the one hand, it would gain from the greater provision of the public good resulting from consolidation, but it would also have to pay higher taxes. Thus its welfare position after consolidation could be either better or worse than before, depending on the relative weights of the expenditure and tax effects. Under the assumption that income in the suburb is above that in the city, Evans shows that the suburb is more likely to suffer a welfare loss from consolidation. [16] Similarly the smaller the suburb the more likely suburban residents will suffer a welfare loss through consolidation since their tax burden will increase without a notable increase in the provision of the public good.[17] Evans concludes that "the central city can continue to grow by annexation or consolidation so long as it is not very much larger than adjacent suburbs. When it becomes relatively large the benefits of consolidation for any individual suburb become smaller than the cost so that annexation ceases and the large central city remains surrounded by a growing number of small suburbs. The analysis also suggests that while any single small suburb will be unwilling to be annexed by a large central city, the suburbs as a whole will be more willing to become part of a large consolidated metropolitan area. . . . Of course it will still be worth while for each individual suburb to attempt to remain independent. . . . These suburbs. are likely to be high income areas and this will strengthen their determination to remain independent."[18]

Implicit in the whole discussion of the merits of multiple public sectors versus consolidation is a cluster of questions sometimes known as the "suburban-central city exploitation thesis." Such terminology is admittedly prejudicial, since it connotes that suburbanites take unfair advantage of residents in the central city. But such an interpretation is unfortunate. Even if it should be true that in some sense suburbanites enjoy a welfare gain at the expense of the central city, this does not in itself establish suburban culpability. It could simply mean that public sector institutional arrangements are skewed in favor of suburbanites and they have responded in an economically rational manner. This question will be discussed further in Chapter 9 in the light of the estimates made of the fiscal flows in the Washington metropolitan area.

The "Suburban-Central City Exploitation Thesis"

Early Research

In a pioneer study some twenty years ago Hawley found per capita public expenditures in seventy-six central cities with 100,000 or more population to be

[b]It will be argued in Chapter 3 that social service redistributive expenditures generate "use-of-income" benefits which accrue to all in a metropolitan area even though the central city finances considerably more of them than does the suburban area.

positively correlated with the percentage of the SMSA population residing outside the central city. On the basis of this finding he concluded that residents of the central city were being exploited in the sense that they "... are carrying the financial burden of an elaborate and costly service installation, i.e., the central city, which is used daily by a noncontributing population in some instances more than twice the size of the contributing population."[19]

Margolis reports similar results from his examination of 1957 per capita payments for government payrolls for all local governments which overlay the central city in the thirty-six largest SMSAs. "It is clear that the greater the outside population relative to the residents of the central city, the greater will be the central cities' local public expenditures."[20] However, Margolis does not accept these findings as necessarily confirmatory of the exploitation thesis. He feels that these larger expenditures of the central city may well be offset by the fact that central cities have a larger industrial and commercial tax base. Further, retail sales to, and the employment of, nonresidents may generate increased property tax revenues that more than offset the higher government expenditures. For Margolis, "the argument that central cities are exploited by the non-central cities is not well established. If anything, central cities may be relatively better off."[21]

Brazer found that 1953 per capita expenditures of the overlying governments of the forty cities with over 250,000 population were negatively correlated with the ratio of the central city population to the SMSA population. Even though these results are an additional indication that suburban communities impose a burden on central city government services, Brazer likewise is not willing to conclude with certainty that the suburbs exploit the central city. Higher expenditures in themselves are not sufficient to establish exploitation. "Conceivably the suburbanite, through his contacts with the city, contributed as much or more to the latter's tax bases as is required to finance the additional expenditures he imposes upon it."[22] Brazer has also pointed out that suburbs are by no means homogeneous, some being industrial enclaves as well as the more traditional residential communities, and that it is thus entirely possible that a suburb as well as a central city can be "exploited" by suburbs.

Finally, Kee reports that changes between 1953 and 1962 in certain local public expenditures from a sample of central cities are significantly related to the extent of commutation into these cities. But since this increased burden on the central cities might be offset by increased tax contributions from the commuters, Kee also concludes that we still have no definite answer to the "... question of who is bearing a net burden. ..."[23]

Impact of Commuters on Central City

Book has attempted to estimate directly the net fiscal impact of commuters on a central city. In his analysis of commutation into New York City he divides

central city public services that affect commuters into two categories: (1) those that are collectively consumed and for which the marginal cost of provision is assumed to be zero and (2) those that are provided to commuters only at some positive marginal cost.[c] He then derives estimates for the value of the benefits from those two categories, which he views as the sum of (1) the estimated value of the services collectively consumed by commuters and (2) the marginal cost to the city of supplying services to commuters. For 1968 he estimates this sum to be at least $32 million. In that same year, commuters paid $14 million under the New York City nonresident earnings tax. Consequently, Book concludes "that commuters to New York City should be paying, in total, more than double the current amount of city nonresident or commuter taxation."[24]

Three comments can be made on Book's estimates of the net fiscal impact made by commuters on the central city. First, in addition to the nonresident earnings tax, it should be noted that commuters also bear other New York City taxes, specially the city sales tax and any business property tax that is shifted to them. Presumably the revenue contribution of commuters through these taxes should be added to the $14 million nonresident earnings tax contribution to determine the total tax contribution made by commuters in 1968. Second, Book's estimates embody the strong assumption that public goods are evaluated equally by all who consume them. It is not clear, however, by how much an evaluation of "public goods" in terms of, say, individual utility would deviate from Book's evaluation. Finally, Vincent, among others, has contended that commuters generate economic gains for a city in the form of increased property values and income which should be added to any direct tax contribution they make in order to derive the total compensation paid to a city.

In his own study, Vincent has used stepwise multiple-regression analysis of 1960 data for sixty-five SMSAs to estimate precisely these effects of commutation by suburban workers and shoppers on both central city government finance and the personal income of central city residents. He argues that personal income gains to central city residents from suburban commutation must be taken into account in a discussion of central city-suburban exploitation since, "if these commuters were not allowed to form an additional supply of labor, the productivity of central city land and capital would be lower than if commuters were present—assuming, of course, that the commuters do not simply displace a resident labor supply."[25] Vincent, by evaluating the regression coefficients at the mean, estimates the "costs" and "gains" to the central city from both worker commutation to the central cities and retail sales to suburban shoppers in central cities. On the basis of the median values for these estimated costs and gains,

---

[c]Services included in the first category are parks, custody and rehabilitation, general administrative services, administration of justice, water and air pollution control, and water supply. Services in the second category are police and fire protection, streets and highway, and street cleaning. Primary and secondary education as well as welfare expenditures are excluded from the analysis by Book on grounds that commuters neither impose any costs in these areas nor derive any benefits.

Vincent concludes that ". . . central city residents as a whole are not being exploited, particularly when the relationship of commuting to the personal incomes of central city residents is taken into account."[26]

A problem does seem to arise, however, from Vincent's asymmetrical treatment of income gains. Just as central city residents enjoy higher income due to interaction with suburbanites, so too the productivity of suburbanites presumably is higher because of their proximity to the central city.[27] Such gains to all residing in the metropolitan area are a collective good which arises from the mere fact of population concentration rather than through the public fisc. Hence, it appears invalid to consider by itself either central city income gains or suburban income gains from such concentration. Since there is no a priori reason why the gains enjoyed by one group from population concentration should be the larger, and in the absence of estimates for both groups, it would seem to be appropriate to assume they are offsetting. In this framework the question of exploitation would be resolved simply by comparing the dollar value of public sector benefits received by commuters with their total tax contributions to the central city. Even on this basis, however, Vincent's estimates indicate that most likely commuters do not exploit central cities.[28]

Smith's study of San Francisco is still a third analysis of the commuter exploitation question. He implicitly assumes that local government services are either intermediate products which serve as inputs for the private business sector or they are services which benefit residents exclusively. Intermediate products to business in turn benefit either residents or nonresidents. Thus outlays for intermediate products alone are of potential benefit to commuters. These include ". . . expenditures for general government, public safety, highways, sanitation and waste removal, the conservation of health, the municipal railway, the civil defense. Expenditures for recreation facilities are also included because of their role in attracting people to the city. . ."[29] In 1967 expenditures for these services were $105 million out of total San Francisco city and county expenditures of $331 million.

On the basis of assumptions regarding the percentage of expenditures made in behalf of commercial, industrial, and residential property, and regarding the shifting of benefits and taxes, Smith concludes that ". . . nonresidents appear to contribute from $19.7 million to $53.6 million more in the way of tax revenues than it costs the city to attract and to service them."[30] In other words, commuters do not exploit San Francisco. Indeed, as in Vincent's analysis, the opposite appears to be true.

There are some troublesome problems with Smith's analysis, however. First, the basic procedure he adopts for determining the value of the intermediate products supplied by government to business seems unreliable. As Smith himself admits, it is quite bold to assume, for example, that expenditures per acre of land in San Francisco are divided in the same proportion between commercial, industrial, and residential uses as the average of estimates in five smaller cities,

the largest of which is New Rochelle, New York, with a 1960 population of only 76,812. Second, Smith's assumption that the value of a local government service to its user is equal to its cost needs substantiation. In Chapters 3 and 5 the basis for evaluating benefits from government services in terms of individual utility will be explored. A third, more general comment is that all interjurisdictional fiscal studies that focus merely on the commuter impact on the central city are very partial. Such a narrow scope may well be legitimate for some purposes, for example, determining whether commuters *qua* commuters adequately compensate the central city for services they receive, but it leaves unresolved the question of the overall fiscal relationship between suburbs and central city. Smith recognizes the limitation implicit in his partial approach. "Just because the core city is the most likely place for ethnic minority groups, the poor, and the uneducated to congregate is no reason for the other residents of the city to alone finance welfare expenditures accompanying these groups."[31]

All Suburbanites and Central City

There have been some analyses of suburban-central city public sector interactions in terms of all metropolitan residents and not merely with reference to commuters. Banovetz has estimated fiscal flows in the Minneapolis-St. Paul metropolitan area to see whether Minneapolis, St. Paul, or one of the suburban counties, Hennepin or Ramsey, is exploited by another.[32] He assumes that "benefits," measured by cost-of-service, accrue to an area on the basis of the number of direct program recipients residing in the area. He further assumes that the incidence of the local property tax and the state income tax, the major funding sources of these programs, is the situs of their collection.

The benefits allocated to each area on this basis are paired with the area's total tax liability, under the incidence assumptions just described. If its benefits exceed its tax liability, an area is assumed to be subsidized by the other areas. On the basis of such an analysis, Banovetz reports "that no conclusive evidence can be found to support charges that either the core cities of Minneapolis and St. Paul or their suburbs in Hennepin or Ramsey Counties, respectively, are subsidizing the other to any appreciable extent."[33]

Even though this study is more comprehensive than those which address merely the impact of commuters, it too does not provide a completely satisfactory analysis of suburban-central city fiscal interactions. First, benefits from several functional categories, such as highways, police and fire protection, libraries and cultural facilities, and utility services, are not estimated in the Banovetz study. This results in the underestimation of the benefits provided by the core cities to the surrounding population.[34] Second, the costs of poverty are assumed to generate benefits only for direct program recipients. This assumption means that Minneapolis and St. Paul, with their relatively large

dependent population, are thereby assigned the bulk of benefits from poverty-related expenditures in the metropolitan area. Implicitly therefore a relatively higher tax burden is justified for the two central cities. Indeed Banovetz, as have others, allocates benefits from all public services on a cost-of-service basis rather than in terms of individual utility received from the services.

Third, the suburban areas are treated as if they were homogeneous, when in reality there is a mixture of industrial and residential suburbs, with a wide range of income levels. The relationship between residential suburbs and the central city differs substantially from that of industrial enclaves.

Neenan has estimated the public sector benefit and tax flows between Detroit and six representative suburban jurisdictions.[35] Benefit flows are estimated for the following expenditure categories: libraries, zoos, art museums, recreation and parks, streets and traffic control, poverty-related expenditures, water supply, and the tax exemption provided to certain classes of property. As done in other studies, Neenan first allocates benefits on the basis of the cost incurred in behalf of direct recipients. However, he then adjusts this benefit incidence by a willingness-to-pay index which purports to reflect the utility received from the public services by citizens in various income classes. Tax exporting and the federal offset are introduced into the tax incidence calculations. Finally, the revenue flows between Detroit and the six suburbs through state revenue sharing and the municipal nonresident income tax imposed by Detroit and one of the six suburbs are also estimated. From this analysis Neenan concludes ". . . that six suburban communities in the Detroit SMSA enjoy a considerable welfare gain through the public sector from Detroit. For a family of four this welfare gain ranges from over $4.00 to nearly $22.00 a year."[36]

Three critical comments on Neenan's study can be noted. First public education is omitted from his analysis. Even though this service is provided through independent school districts in the Detroit SMSA rather than by municipal governments, presumably it generates notable externalities and should therefore be included in a comprehensive study of suburban-central city fiscal interactions.

Second, Neenan's adjustment of benefits to a willingness-to-pay basis has been challenged by Ramsey, and Auld and Cook. Ramsey contends that the cost-of-service estimates of benefits are more appropriate since, ". . . from the point of view of the unit undertaking an activity, what is relevant is their cost not the valuation placed on it by residents in other units."[37] For Ramsey,

> . . . exploitation of central city residents by suburban residents exists
> if the following sum is negative: central city revenue collections
> generated by suburban residents less the cost of services provided by
> the central city and used by suburban residents plus the cost of
> services provided by the suburbs and used by central city residents less
> the suburb's revenue collections generated by central city residents.[38]

This issue of the cost-of-service versus individual utility evaluation of public services is addressed in Chapter 3.

Auld and Cook find that Neenan's use of voter data and attitude surveys to establish a generalized willingness-to-pay index is deficient.

> To derive willingness-to-pay multipliers for all public goods and services from voting responses by consumers to a referendum on a particular expenditure item would be inappropriate. The voter response studies cited by Neenan were concerned mainly with welfare programs and goods of a redistributive nature. The implication that these results could be applied to all goods and services would be dangerous.[39]

Third, Bradford and Oates contend that Neenan's procedure of estimating willingness-to-pay benefits is biased toward finding exploitation of the central city. Their criticism focuses on Neenan's willingness-to-pay index whereby public sector benefits are evaluated proportional to income. In figure 2-1, $D_Y =$ 100 refers to a poor individual's demand curve and D_Y = 200 refers to a demand curve of an individual with twice as much income.

> If output is assumed to be G_1 [as shown in fig. 2-1], a doubling of income leads to considerably less than a doubling of total valuation (as measured by the areas under the demand curves). As a little experimentation should convince the reader, as long as we are operating in a region in which the lower-income citizen positively values increments in G (i.e., to the left of G_2) *no* income elasticity would be large enough to produce a doubling of total valuation with a doubling of income, if the underlying demand curves are linear.[40]

This particular criticism of Neenan seems to rest, however, on a confusion of total evaluation with value in exchange.[d] Bradford and Oates show that total evaluation of a government outlay, that is, the total area under the demand curve, cannot be expected to double as income doubles. However, what is at question here is not total evaluation in this sense but the total evaluation which is the analogue of the private market value in exchange, namely, the benefits from a government outlay evaluated in terms of the value of the marginal unit. Assume, for example, that the indifference curves U_A and U_B, shown in figure 2-2, describe the marginal rates of substitution (MRS) between private goods (expressed in dollars) and a public good for two individuals, A and B. Assume further that B has twice the income of A and that B's MRS at G_1 is twice that of A's. The value in exchange of G_1 for B is BB'; which is twice as large as AA', the value in exchange of G_1 for A. This result follows from the fact that the total

---

[d]Moreover, it assumed that the marginal evaluation of the first unit is the same.

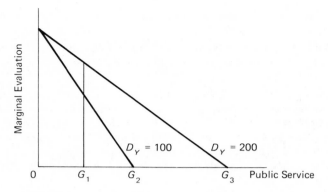

Figure 2-1. Marginal Evaluation of a Public Service.

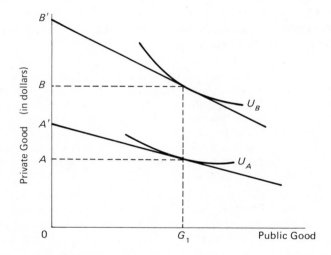

Figure 2-2. Marginal Substitution Between a Private and Public Good.

value in exchange for both A and B is their respective MRS evaluated at G_1 times G_1 units of output.

There is some evidence from voting and survey data that citizen evaluation of public output rises proportionately with income, as can be illustrated by this example. Assume there are two citizens A and B with \$10,000 and \$20,000 income, respectively, both living in a jurisdiction with a proportional tax system. If both A and B tend to support proposals for additional public outlays with the same intensity despite the fact that B's tax liability is twice that of A's, we may well have the situation depicted in figure 2-2 with B's MRS twice as large as A's.

Unfortunately relevant empirical analyses of citizen attitudes toward public service provision are too scanty to allow definitive statements about the relationship between income and such attitudes even though we can, with some confidence, define the general nature of this relation. This important topic is addressed in Chapters 3 and 9.

Issues Outstanding

Previous research concerning suburban-central city fiscal interactions has at least served to focus attention on a narrowing spectrum of significant issues. From the review of this research six major issues emerge that must be resolved in any comprehensive evaluation of the interjurisdictional fiscal relationships in a metropolitan area.

1. The final incidence of all taxes imposed in the metropolitan area must be determined. Thus taxes paid by all metropolitan residents, both commuters and others, must be estimated and their final incidence determined. In the case of the Washington metropolitan area this means that the incidence of income, property, sales taxes, and a whole array of minor taxes, with due allowance for shifting, must be estimated. The results of this task are detailed in Chapter 6.

2. A similarly comprehensive effort must be made to identify the beneficiaries of all public services financed within the metropolitan area. Thus all beneficiaries in the metropolitan area, and not merely commuters, must be included in the analysis, and all services which generate benefits to metropolitan residents must be evaluated. To the extent that education and poverty-related programs generate benefits for nonresidents, they must be included in the analysis. The question of allocating increased income and property values that result from agglomeration to one or other jurisdiction is fraught with theoretical as well as computational difficulties and will not be undertaken in this study. These gains seem to be a collective good which arise simply from population concentration and interaction rather than primarily as a consequence of public action. It would, of course, be of interest to know if one group or the other in the metropolitan area shared disproportionately in this gain.

3. The issue of evaluating benefits of public services either in terms of the direct cost incurred in behalf of a clientele or in terms of the utility provided to individuals must be joined and resolved. This issue is discussed in Chapter 3 and, despite the admitted difficulties of operationalizing the concept, it is concluded that individual welfare rather than cost of service is the theoretically preferable basis for determining benefit incidence.

However, cost-of-service estimates of benefits are useful for some purposes. They are the more traditional method of measuring benefits and since they can be computed with weaker assumptions they may appear to be more objective and command greater attention. For these reasons, and fully admitting the

problems inherent in such estimates, they are provided in Chapter 5 and form the basis for one set of the fiscal flow and fiscal incidence estimates presented in Chapters 7 and 8, respectively.

4. The benefit incidence from metropolitan expenditures estimated in terms of individual utility analogous to the value in exchange of the private market is also estimated. Even though this procedure is judged to be theoretically superior, it requires a number of strong assumptions if it is to be implemented. Some of these assumptions are operative in the benefit assignment between private, public nonredistributive, and public redistributive discussed in Chapter 3. On the other hand since these welfare benefits are intended to represent behavioral values, testable hypotheses capable of refutation can be inferred from the pattern of benefit incidence based on individual utility which is reported in Chapter 5 and which forms the basis for the other set of estimated fiscal flows and fiscal incidence presented in Chapters 7 and 8, respectively.

5. The fact remains, however, that the major problem in establishing value-in-exchange estimates for public output is that citizen attitudes must be known. And since there exists no market test for public outcomes, we must largely rely on information derived from the political process and attitude surveys to determine such attitudes. We do not possess a quantitatively precise evaluation of particular public services and hence the benefit estimates based on what knowledge we do possess are accurate only within a range of values. In Chapter 3 and again in Chapter 9 the problem of basing individual evaluations on empirical data is discussed.

6. It is possible that the differential impact of the various metropolitan public sectors, both by area and income class, may in the final analysis either be negligible or offset by some factor such as capitalized property values. If so, the suburban-central city exploitation question may indeed be answerable but uninteresting. In Chapters 7 and 8 we shall see, however, that fiscal incidence varies notably across income classes and geographical areas in the Washington metropolitan area. In Chapter 9 the significance and the limitations of these findings is discussed.

3

Measurement of Benefits from Government Services

Introduction

The analysis of government expenditures which proceeds on the assumption that expenditures provide satisfaction to individuals and that such satisfaction should be the basis for assessing tax liability has developed notably in the past two decades. Many theoretical and empirical questions remain to be resolved, however, before we possess a generally acceptable technique for estimating the benefit incidence of government expenditures. Some of the major problems associated with identifying, measuring, and imputing expenditure benefits will be addressed in this chapter in the context of subfederal government expenditures in the politically-fragmented Washington metropolitan area. Specifically, four points will be considered.

1. It will be shown that government expenditures affect income at its source both through an impact on factor earnings as well as through in-kind and money transfers. Such benefits will be called source-of-income benefits.
2. On the other hand, government expenditures generate the consumer-type benefits considered in traditional Musgrave-Samuelson public-good analysis. They will be called use-of-income benefits. There are three mutually exclusive use-of-income benefits, each of which gives rise to tax liability under a benefit tax regime: private, public nonredistributive, and public redistributive use-of-income benefits.
3. The imputation of use-of-income benefits requires the specification of utility functions in terms of which the dollar value of these benefits can be evaluated. There have been several recent theoretical discussions of individual utility functions containing government expenditures as arguments and some empirical estimations of the marginal utility of income. From this literature a technique will be devised for estimating the dollar value of the use-of-income benefits from government expenditures across income classes.
4. Finally, there is a brief discussion, continued in Chapter 5, of how the use-of-income benefits generated by government expenditures in the Washington metropolitan area should be apportioned between the three categories, private, public nonredistributive, and public redistributive.

The welfare gains generated by government outlays have received considerable attention in the literature dealing with the economic theory of public
finance. Only recently, however, have incidence studies appeared which attempt
to allocate the benefits from government expenditures in a manner symmetrical
to the distribution of tax burdens in the more numerous tax incidence studies.[1]

A separate development, but one which has considerable significance for
the manner in which benefit incidence is to be measured, is the analysis based on
the hypothesis that the individual, rather than some collectivity, is the appropriate frame of reference for economic analysis. Buchanan succinctly contrasts
this individualistic approach with the contrary collectivist position:

> The state has its origin in, and depends for its continuance upon the
> desires of individuals to fulfill a certain portion of their wants collec-
> tively. The state has no ends other than those of its individual members
> and is not a separate decision-making unit. State decisions are, in the
> final analysis, the collectivity decisions of individuals.[2]

In other words, government outlays are assumed to generate benefits for
individuals and Say's dictum, "the value paid to government by the taxpayer is
given without equivalent or return,"[3] is rejected as being generally untrue.
Just as individuals satisfy certain wants through their purchase of goods and
services in the market, it is contended that individual wants are also satisfied
through the provision of public services.

Even though public expenditure analysis has been at least formally integrated into the framework of economic methodology, with problems pertaining
to the provision of public services discussed in terms of individual utility maximization, there remain many conceptual and empirical questions to be resolved
before the benefits from government expenditures in a metropolitan area can be
evaluated in a manner comparable to the national income measurements of
private goods and services. The range of these outstanding problems can be
inferred from the following cluster of queries which will be addressed in this
chapter.

1.   Is it not true that school teachers as well as students and childless bachelors
     benefit from educational expenditures? Don't both stockholders in Port-
     land cement companies and highway construction workers as well as users
     of highway services benefit from the interstate highway program? Don't
     social workers benefit from social welfare programs as well as welfare
     clients?
2.   How should the dollar value of these "non-consumer" benefits be esti-
     mated? Are not at least some of these source-of-income gains resulting
     from government expenditures offset by income losses to other members
     of society? When should the net income gains from an outlay, whether

in money or in kind, be added to consumer benefits from the outlay in order to estimate society's total benefits from the outlay?

3. Individuals, in addition to receiving source-of-income benefits, also receive utility from the consumption of public services. How should we distinguish between the consumer, or use-of-income, benefits received by direct recipients of public services and externalities or spillover consumer benefits received by others? What is the dollar value of the benefits received, for example, by a school child and a childless bachelor from expenditures for elementary education?

4. And are there not other services, such as general government, fire protection, and the availability of health services, that, once available, yield benefits to the whole citizenry? Do these "collective" goods generate benefits which are evaluated in equal dollar terms by all citizens? If not, how should they be evaluated?

5. If indeed the consumer, or use-of-income, benefits from all government services should be imputed on the basis of individual evaluation, can we say that this evaluation varies systematically with the marginal utility of income? If so, how should the marginal utility of income be measured empirically?

6. Is the welfare of some individuals in society a function of others' well-being? If so, is it not true that some citizens must be said to receive benefits from, say, public assistance expenditures or from education even though neither they nor their families actually receive any of the services provided to children in poor families?[4] How should such redistributive benefits be evaluated? If they do increase the welfare of some in society, either for benevolent or malevolent reasons, then must they not also be considered use-of-income benefits which, like other such benefits, are grounds for assigning tax liability under a benefit-tax regime? The answers which we propose for resolving these questions in connection with the imputation of benefits from Washington area public expenditures will become evident from the subsequent discussion in this chapter.

Government expenditures alter the welfare of individuals in society in two ways: (1) by affecting their sources of income and/or (2) by providing consumer, that is, use-of-income satisfaction. Individuals' sources of income are affected either as a direct intent of programs, as in the case of public assistance payments and veterans' bonuses; or as a consequence of a program's execution, as in the case of salaries for public school teachers and mail clerks. Use-of-income benefits, on the other hand, are the basis of the effective demand for public outlays. They are either (1) private benefits received by direct recipients of a service, (2) spillover benefits appropriated by those other than direct recipients, or (3) redistributive benefits resulting from a redistributional effect in favor of

some other group in society. Some examples of these three use-of-income benefits are, respectively, the benefits received by (1) public school students, (2) citizens who are protected because others have received polio immunization, and (3) persons whose utility is enhanced because school lunches are provided gratis to poor children.

Government outlays are either exhaustive expenditures made to factors of production or money transfers to individuals. Both generate increased income for individuals, that is, source-of-income benefits. Exhaustive expenditures can generate increased income through general equilibrium adjustments initiated by the purchase of factors of production and through in-kind transfers. Of course, money transfers directly increase the personal income of the transferees. These three source-of-income benefits will be examined in turn with a view to determining appropriate procedures for their estimation in the context of a politically-fragmented metropolitan area.

Factor Payments

Payments made to factors of production, such as the salaries paid to teachers, refuse collectors, and police officers, are entered in the national accounts as personal income. Presumably, however, these payments overestimate the net gain for public employees from these outlays. If resources are assumed to be fully employed, then it follows that, say, a police officer would have been employed in the absence of the outlay for police salaries, even though he might then have received a somewhat lower real wage. Only the difference between his wage, given the actual outlay, and what he would have received without the public outlay can be properly called his source-of-income benefit. Further, assuming full employment, the police officer can enjoy increased income only at the expense of others whose real income must be necessarily reduced. Any complete enumeration of source-of-income benefits must thus include both these losses as well as gains. In the full employment case, the losses must equal the gains across the citizenry.

Under the assumption of less than full employment, however, the increased income attributable to an outlay may well be greater since wages paid those employed by the government program must be weighted by some value less than one to allow for the possibility that the resources would otherwise be unemployed. In this instance the net benefit to any public employee is the difference between his actual wage and his expected wage weighted by the probability of his being employed in the absence of the government outlay.[5] Societal net benefits in the unemployment case will be greater than zero though necessarily less than the dollar value of factor payments, except in the limiting case of total unemployment.

Interest payments on government debt similarly generate source-of-income

benefits which appear as personal income in the national accounts. Bondholders benefit to the extent that a government debt issue has raised interest rates by increasing the demand for loanable funds. As in the case of salaries, however, it would be incorrect to consider total interest payments simply as a net source-of-income gain to bondholders.[6] Only the difference between these interest payments and what interest payments would have been in the absence of the debt issue is properly a source-of-income benefit to bondholders. From society's viewpoint, however, there is no net source-of-income benefit since the gain to lenders is achieved only at the expense of borrowers.[a]

In-kind Transfers

Exhaustive expenditures are sometimes used to achieve redistributive goals. This occurs when citizens are explicitly exempted from any liability to finance these services. When such a redistributive intent governs the provision of a particular service, the exhaustive expenditure can be said to generate a source-of-income benefit equal to the value of the in-kind transfer. There is no inherent reason why one particular public service rather than another should be used to provide these transfers. Social policy, however, does seem consistently to have charged certain programs more than others with a redistributive mission. Public housing, health care, as well as public education and recreational programs for the poor have often been identified as instruments of redistribution.

To the extent services are explicitly provided gratis to a certain group they cannot logically be imputed to the same group as use-of-income benefits. However, these services do generate use-of-income benefits for those citizens who have an effective demand for them, that is, for those who are willing and able to support them through taxation. The total benefits generated by a redistributive program are thus the sum of its source- and use-of-income benefits.[7]

The valuation of source-of-income benefits poses a troublesome measurement problem. The most commonly used procedure has been simply to impute to the recipients the dollar value of the cost of in-kind transfers.[8] In the case of money transfers the dollar value indeed serves as an unequivocal measure of the welfare gain to the recipient. But the cost of an in-kind transfer is not necessarily an accurate index of the welfare gain it provides to the recipient. Recipients may well not be indifferent between money and in-kind transfers of equal market value since the in-kind transfer may impose a constraint on consumption choices not imposed by a money transfer.

Schmundt, Smolensky, and Stiefel have proposed that the cost of in-kind transfers can be transformed into a benefit-equivalent cash transfer by the use

---

[a]Keynesian multiplier analysis provides a final source-of-income benefit from government expenditures. With unemployed resources, exhaustive expenditures and transfers generate income directly as well as through subsequent rounds of induced spending.

of a "benefit weight," which is the ratio of the "recipient's evaluation of his benefits . . . and the market value of that transfer. . . ."[9] This ratio will be one for money transfers but, at least conceptually, may range from less than zero to greater than one for in-kind transfers. Normally, however, the range should be from zero to one. "Benefit weights in the neighborhood of unity may not be unlikely for a considerable number of recipient groups . . ." since restrictions imposed on consumer behavior are weakened insofar as many low-income citizens participate in a number of in-kind transfer programs, for example, food stamps, subsidized housing, and medicaid.[10]

Thus even though recipients undoubtedly value in-kind transfers at something less than their cost, in some instances the evaluation may be close to cost.[11] Since currently there exists no body of empirical research which would justify adjusting in-kind benefits to money equivalents by specific benefit weights, in this study we will impute in-kind benefits to recipients on the basis of their cost. This procedure will be used with the caveat that the value of in-kind benefits will thereby be overestimated, but with some assurance that the order of magnitude of this error may not be too significant.

Money Transfers

The full value of money transfers have typically been attributed to the transferees as benefits in previous benefit-incidence studies. Transfer payments are indeed source-of-income benefits and it is correct to include them under this rubric in allocating benefits from government expenditures. However, just as it is the income differential induced by a government expenditure that is properly a source-of-income benefit to the employed factors, so it is the difference between the value of the transfer payment plus the value of the possibly increased leisure time and the income that would have been earned in the absence of the transfer which theoretically is the net source-of-income benefit to transferees. As conceptually sound as this adjustment may be, there are seemingly insurmountable practical difficulties in deriving estimates for it. Hence just as in-kind transfers will be allocated to their recipients on the basis of their cost, so the full value of money transfers will be assigned to transferees.

Finally, even though as the discussion above indicated, public employees do enjoy some source-of-income advantage from government outlays, no attempt will be made to estimate this gain from subfederal government expenditures in the Washington area. It may generally be presumed, however, that at least the primary intent of most subfederal expenditures is not to generate increased income for those on the public payroll. This is in contrast with the explicit intent of programs providing either in-kind or money transfers to offer source-of-income benefits to a specified clientele.[12] The argument that other subfederal expenditures may create little source-of-income benefits is bolstered

by the likelihood that many factors of production will be in fairly elastic supply to any single locality. Therefore, our inability to pinpoint these source of income benefits should not notably affect the quantitative results.

Use-of-Income Benefits

Individuals can satisfy wants either through their activity in private markets or through collective action via the political process. But since in both instances wants of individuals are satisfied it follows that both privately and publicly financed commodities must be entered as arguments in individual utility functions as generating individual benefits.[13] As Musgrave puts it, "The utility of defense along with that of door locks and ice cream is included in the individual's preference function, and both goods should be provided in relation thereto."[14]

Some public services are distinguishable from market services primarily by the fact of government provision. In these instances beneficiaries are limited principally to the direct recipients of the service. Most public services, however, generate external benefits enjoyed by others than the direct program clientele. But whether the benefits of a public service are appropriated largely by direct consumers or are more widely diffused across society, it remains true that all benefits from public services are received by individuals. This individualistic nature of benefits from government services is implied in the traditional utility function containing pure private and public goods:

$$u^i(x^i_1, \ldots, x^i_n; x_{n+1}, \ldots, x_{n+m}) \qquad (3\text{-}1)$$

where $x^i_1, \ldots, x^i_n$ are n private goods and the total amounts of private goods consumed in an economy of s individuals are

$$\sum_{i=1}^{s} x^i_1, \ldots, \sum_{i=1}^{s} x^i_n; \qquad (3\text{-}2)$$

and $x_{n+1}, \ldots, x_{n+m}$ are m public goods and the total amounts of public goods consumed in the economy are

$$x_{n+1}, \ldots, x_{n+m} \qquad (3\text{-}3)$$

Since a pure private commodity generates benefits only for the individual consuming it, the total consumption of such a commodity is derived by summing quantities across all individuals, as shown in equation (3-2). The benefits from a purely public commodity, however, cannot be appropriated by one or other

individual but are spread across all members of the relevant society, as implied
in equation (3-3). In actuality all major public services generate benefits in a
more or less ill-defined manner for the population at large even though some
services, say public education, also provide benefits for an identifiable group.
Thus all public services properly fall within the domain of Samuelson's recent
definition of a public good as "one that enters two or more person's utility."[15]

    The socially optimal output of private commodities is defined as the quan-
tity whose marginal cost is equal to the price consumers are willing to pay for
the marginal unit, given the usual convexity conditions. This situation is contained as a particular case in the more generally defined optimality for a public
commodity. The necessary and sufficient condition for the socially optimal output of a public commodity is that the marginal evaluations of the public commodity summed across all individuals equals its marginal cost. Thus for the
$n + k$th public commodity in a society with s individuals we have:

$$\sum_{i=1}^{s} u_{n+k}^{i} = MC_{n+k} \qquad\qquad (3\text{-}4)$$

    In the case of a pure private commodity, u_{n+k}^{i} will be positive for only one
individual, its consumer. For publicly provided services, however, presumably
u_{n+k}^{i} will be positive for various groups of citizens receiving use-of-income benefits: (1) those receiving private benefits as well as (2) those receiving either a
nonredistributive or redistributive external benefit from a service provided to
others. From the optimality condition in equation (3-4) we can infer that if
public output is socially optimal the value of that output, evaluated at the
margin, must equal total expenditures if unit costs are assumed to be constant.
Whether the actual provision of public services in the Washington or any metropolitan area is indeed optimal, or whether it is more likely to be suboptimal or
superoptimal, will be discussed in Chapter 4.

Use-of-Income Benefits from
Redistributive Programs

    Nonredistributive and redistributive benefits are two forms of external bene-
fits both of which constitute bases for the effective demand for public services.
Nonredistributive external benefits are generated by such services as elementary
and secondary education, whose external benefit, say, the improved cultural
tone of society, is the consequence of the service provided to a specific subset
of the population. Under an optimal tax regime those enjoying such an external
benefit would be assessed a tax liability equal to their marginal evaluation of it.

Redistributive external benefits, on the other hand, arise from gratuitous in-kind or monetary transfers in favor of certain members of society. A necessary condition distinguishing redistributive from nonredistributive benefits is that redistributive benefits arise only if the recipients *qua* recipients of the transfer do not thereby incur any tax liability. Thus transfer recipients are not included among the beneficiaries of the transfer program judged to have effective demand for the program and therefore, under an optimal tax regime, to be assessed to support the program. The transferee admittedly enjoys increased welfare from his transfer, but this increased welfare does not constitute a basis for tax liability under a benefit-tax regime grounded on effective demand.

Thus the consumer of use-of-income benefits generated by programs which are redistributive in intent should be attributed to those other than the trans-ferees. Such benefits are reflected in the public-good arguments in individual utility functions, as shown in equation 1 above, as well as in the marginal evaluations in equation (3–4). MacRae objects to using phraseology in the man-ner which suggests

> that when wealthier individuals voluntarily transfer income to the poor, the redistribution is "beneficial" to them or their "welfare" has been increased. To say that is so merely because the transfer is voluntary, runs counter to the ordinary meaning of "benefit" or "welfare" which cannot legitimately be altered in this way to fit the terminology of economics.[16]

In what sense, if any, is it valid then to say that higher income citizens benefit from redistribution programs? Do they benefit from these programs in the same way they benefit from schools that educate their children and from parks they frequent?

Despite MacRae's objection, it does seem to be true at least within the framework of traditional economic analysis that citizens must be said to benefit from redistributive services, if they willingly finance them. Anomalies, such as "redistributive benefits for the rich can always be increased if only the number of the poor is increased," can be dispelled if it is recognized that benefit evalua-tion is always made in a particular context with such variables as total output, population, income distribution, and the expectations of the citizenry, all given. In any specific context citizens will have particular marginal rates of substitution between private consumption and such government programs as public assis-tance, schools, and parks. If some of these general parameters should change, for example, per capita income decline, the absolute income level of the poor fall, and the income level of the rich remain unchanged with the gap between the poor and the rich thus increased, then we might expect the marginal rates of substitution of the rich to shift in favor of the public assistance program relative to educational and park outlays. If such a displacement were to occur then the

benefits enjoyed by the rich from government expenditures would be maximized by increasing redistributive outlays relative to education and parks. It would also be true to say that the rich received increased dollar benefits from redistributive services. Such an outcome would not at all be inconsistent with the total welfare of the rich as well as that of the poor being lower in the second state than in the first.[b]

In recent years the theory and measurement of income distribution has been receiving increased attention.[17] The private and public "grants economy," market exchange versus personal transfers, Kantian altruism, "cooling out" or "buying off" the poor, and Pareto-optimal income redistribution have all been topics of recent and lively debate. A common denominator more or less easily inferred from these various discussions is the recognition that redistributive use-of-income, or consumer, benefits are generated by at least some government programs.

Four of the reasons why individuals may wish to finance redistributive programs are: (1) to institute a "silent trade," (2) philanthropy, (3) a compulsive desire to "do good," and (4) control of the poor. Boulding distinguishes between reciprocal transfers, or exchange, and philanthropy, which is a unilateral transfer. What appears to be philanthropy, however, may at times involve a "silent trade," that is, a gift offered with the mutual implicit expectation of a return gift. "In our society the exchange of gifts at Christmas is perhaps a case in point. Even though it is supposed to be more blessed to give than to receive, most of us probably find that if our gifts strikingly exceed our receipts, or the reverse, we feel a little uncomfortable."[18] Intergenerational exchange affords another example of a silent trade. "The young are supported by the middle-aged in the hope that when the middle-aged are old, the young, who will then be middle-aged, will then support them."[19] Thus the existence of a silent trade may be at least partial explanation for the greater effective demand for such programs as Social Security and unemployment compensation compared with, say, AFDC. Most taxpayers can at least imagine themselves in need of support during retirement or a period of unemployment, whereas they may not be able to visualize themselves as falling within the AFDC risk population. If this surmise is valid, a quid pro quo may be operative in support of the former programs that is lacking for the more purely redistributive AFDC program.

Unilateral transfers, on the other hand, or philanthropy, are motivated by a sense of community. "It is because 'no man is an island,' because the very realization of our own identity implies in some sense that there is a common

---

[b]Examples analogous to this can be supplied from the private sphere. Thus if a person has an automobile accident he may derive relatively high utility from getting his car repaired, as can be indicated by his not choosing to take a vacation in order to finance the repairs. Consequently it would be true to say that, given the accident, he derives benefits from the car repair even though presumably his total welfare is less than it would have been without the accident. Thus benefit analysis depends crucially on the context within which it is undertaken.

identity in humanity, that we are willing to 'socialize' our substance and to share with the afflicted."[20] Thus Boulding sees real altruism with no implied quid pro quo as a potential motivational source for transfers. Such altruism, or empathy with others, may be reduced as others' welfare increases relative to one's own. Thus "as he gets more and we get less, we rejoice indeed in his affluence, but at some point our dissatisfaction with our own penury is likely to exceed this vicarious enjoyment. Once we admit this fact, exchange reestablishes itself."[21]

Ireland has discussed what he calls a "Kantian motive." It can serve as still a third basis for the effective demand for redistributive programs. This motive, growing out of a Kantian categorical imperative to "do good," is satisfied by the desire to do a "good" act quite independently of whether anyone is actually benefited by it. "The goal of a Kantian act is *act utility*, not the utility of the result the act brings about. What the individual derives satisfaction from is the *act* of doing the 'good' deed of providing the funds."[22] Presumably it is some such motivation that Banfield has in mind when he asserts that the political involvement of many "affluent liberals" is concerned more with satisfying a categorical imperative to "do good" than with actually relieving the privations of the poor.[23]

From the discussion to this point it might be inferred that benevolence or at least a certain benign disregard of the poor necessarily characterizes all motivation for redistribution. But as can be adequately documented by the history of mankind and introspection, malevolence sometimes serves as a motivating force in human events. Piven and Cloward specifically contend that welfare programs are designed by the dominant economic classes for the purpose of managing and controlling the lower classes. Thus, rather than being a response to a categorical imperative, or a desire to help others, public welfare programs are seen as basically a self-interested use of income extracted only under duress.

> Historical evidence suggests that relief arrangements are initiated or
> expanded during the occasional outbreaks of civil disorder produced
> by mass unemployment, and are then abolished or contracted when
> political stability is restored. We shall argue that expansive relief policies
> are designed to mute civil disorders, and restrictive ones to reinforce
> work norms.[24]

Thus for Piven and Cloward what taxpayers envision they are receiving in return for welfare expenditures is the maintenance of their privileged positions.

Intensity of Support for Redistribution

The intensity of attitudes concerning redistribution are affected in many subtle ways by a person's social context. Thus, what may be called the "United

Fund" motivation may influence a person's willingness to finance not only redistribution but also any public enterprise. Support for a program may depend heavily on whether or not people judge others are contributing their "fair share."[25] Similarly one's concern for others may turn heavily on the question of income ranking. There are indications that a person's sense of well-being may depend as much on whether he feels that his relative position is being maintained as he is that his absolute standard of living is not being eroded.[26] To the extent this is true people may be more willing to assist others if they perceive that their own relative position is not threatened thereby.

If such interdependencies do affect a person's willingness to support redistributive programs then we may infer that the particular fiscal institutions which finance redistribution, as well as both the variance of the income distribution and the spatial distribution of rich and poor in a metropolitan area, will help determine the magnitude of the use-of-income, consumer benefits generated by redistributional programs. If, for example, the tax liability for such programs is evenly spread over the whole area rather than falling more heavily on central-city residents, these residents are less likely to feel they are bearing more than their "fair" share of the costs. Further, the greater is the dispersion of income and thus the smaller the chance of the income rank order being altered by redistributional programs, the greater should be the use-of-income benefits perceived by the higher income residents.[27] Finally, if charity indeed does begin at home and is attenuated by distance, it may be that support for redistribution is stronger if the transferees are visible members of one's local community rather than merely anonymous residents of the larger metropolitan society.[28] Alternatively, however, it can be argued that with the poor nearby they may be judged to be "pushy" and thus not "deserving" of assistance. But, as Piven and Cloward contend, such feelings might result in support for redistributive programs to "buy off" the poor. There may be therefore some optimal geographic configuration of residence, place of employment, and recreational locale which balances these contrary influences and maximizes metropolitan support for redistribution.[29]

Three general inferences can be drawn from this brief discussion of social influences on attitudes toward redistribution. (1) Individuals are expected to be more willing to support redistribution insofar as they perceive that their peers bear similar assessments in support of redistribution. (2) They will be more apt to support redistribution the higher is their absolute level of income and insofar as the rank order of income is not notably altered nor the absolute income difference between themselves and transferees notably reduced by redistributive efforts. (3) Intensity of support for redistribution, finally, is likely to be a function of psychological attitudes toward the poor derived from the extent and quality of contact with the poor.

Distinction between Redistributive and
Nonredistributive Programs

The practical significance of distinguishing between programs that are redistributive in intent and those that are not can be seen from an illustration used by Hochman and Rodgers. They have contended that transfers may be required by the Pareto criterion since ". . . the utility of individuals with higher incomes depends upon and is positively related to the incomes of persons lower in the distributive scale . . ."[30] Their analysis proceeds on the assumptions that (1) all individuals have marginal utilities of income for own-consumption greater than zero; (2) all transfers must be Pareto-optimal, that is, they must at least not reduce the welfare of those financing the transfers; and (3) transfers must flow only from persons with higher income to those with lower.[31]

Hochman and Rodgers calculate an illustrative response to the question, "Under what assumptions about utility interdependence would the actual fiscal structure be Pareto-optimal?"[32] They use Gillespie's fiscal incidence estimates of federal, state, and local expenditures and taxes in the United States for 1960 as the measure of the actual redistribution carried out through the fisc in a given year. By assuming that the positive fiscal residuals for the lower-income classes and the negative fiscal residuals (for the higher-income classes, generally) derived from the Gillespie analysis reflect the actual redistribution required by the Pareto criterion, they infer values for the willingness of individuals at various income levels to transfer income to those with lower incomes. On this basis they conclude that "utility interdependence increases in significance as income increases and becomes really significant only when income reaches a level of $10,000 or more."[33]

These results, however, are based on two strong assumptions. First, all government expenditures, including even defense outlays, are assumed to be vehicles for redistribution. Second, benefits from collective outlays are implicitly assumed to generate merely use-of-income consumer benefits, which are assigned in proportion to income.[c] Since it is implausible that citizens regard all government outlays indiscriminately as vehicles for redistribution, it is necessary to determine which services do indeed carry a redistributive intent and which do not. Only with this distinction in mind can we proceed to allocate use-of-income benefits, which are the basis for assigning tax liability in a benefit-tax regime, and source-of-income benefits, which do not give rise to tax liability since they are precisely the vehicle for redistribution. To meet these difficulties, in the next

---

[c]Because there is no recognition of use-of-income consumer benefits being received by higher income citizens from redistribution as such, we would have to conclude from the Gillespie estimates that a disequilibrium situation exists, with higher-income citizens generally acquiescing in a massive welfare loss through budgetary action.

section benefits stemming from the subfederal expenditures in the Washington area will be classified as either use- or source-of-income benefits, with use-of-income benefits further divided into private, public nonredistributive, and public redistributive. In the final section of this chapter the question of the allocation of benefits by income class will be discussed and a technique adopted for allocating benefits by income class in the Washington area.

Benefits from Washington Area Expenditures

Five expenditure categories, elementary and secondary education, higher education, health, recreation, and welfare, are assumed to generate some source-of-income benefits for low-income recipients in the Washington area as a consequence of a redistributive design. The general justification for this assignment is twofold: (1) voting and survey data indicate that there is willingness on the part of some to finance these services for low-income citizens and discussion in the various media indicates that these expenditures are designed to achieve at least some redistribution and (2) these functions do in effect provide direct services gratis to low-income citizens in the Washington area. There is a more detailed discussion of particular features of these Washington area programs in Chapter 5. To the extent that these expenditures are expressly redistributive and are provided to the margin where benefits equal tax costs, the dollar value of the source-of-income benefits must equal use-of-income benefits received by those willing and able to finance them. In addition to the redistributive source-of-income benefits from these five expenditures there is the pattern of gains and losses in factor income generated by all government outlays. Even though gains in factor income are listed as source-of-income benefits in table 3-1, no attempt will be made to estimate the incidence of these benefits.

The three categories of use-of-income benefits, private, public nonredistributive, and public redistributive, all serve as a basis for assigning tax liability under a benefit-tax regime. The private benefits from government outlays are received directly by specific, identifiable recipients of a public service. Six Washington area services, to be discussed in more detail in Chapter 5, are assumed to generate private use-of-income benefits:

1.   elementary and secondary education and libraries
2.   higher education
3.   fire, police, and corrections
4.   health
5.   recreation
6.   transportation

Table 3-1

Source-of-Income and Use-of-Income Benefits from Government Expenditures in Washington Metropolitan Area

Government Expenditures	Source-of-Income Benefits	Use-of-Income Benefits
Courts	Increase in Factor Income	Public Nonredistributive
Elementary and Secondary Education & Libraries	Increase in Factor Income In-kind Transfers	Private Public Nonredistributive Public Redistributive
Higher Education	Increase in Factor Income In-kind Transfers	Private Public Nonredistributive Public Redistributive
Fire, Police, and Corrections	Increase in Factor Income	Private Public Nonredistributive
General Government	Increase in Factor Income	Public Nonredistributive
Health	Increase in Factor Income In-kind Transfers	Private Public Redistributive
Public Works	Increase in Factor Income	Public Nonredistributive
Recreation	Increase in Factor Income In-kind Transfers	Private Public Redistributive
Transportation	Increase in Factor Income	Private
Welfare	Increase in Factor Income Money Transfers	Public Redistributive

These services are provided through the public sector even though there are close market substitutes.

The six services generating public nonredistributive benefits are included in most inventories of local government collective goods:

1. courts
2. elementary and secondary education and libraries
3. higher education
4. fire, police, and corrections
5. general government
6. public works

Public nonredistributive benefits, as distinct from private benefits, are associated in the first instance with certain necessary characteristics of a viable society such as the promotion of justice, a sense of security in person and property, and the maintenance of public amenities. Universal education has long been promoted as

essential to democratic institutions. Since services such as these which generate public nonredistributive benefits also provide private benefits that can be appropriated by an identifiable clientele, it is necessary to apportion the total benefits from such services between these categories. Further, since education in addition is designed to achieve redistributive goals it is necessary to apportion benefits from this particular service among all three use-of-income categories. This troublesome task is undertaken in Chapter 5 with the results summarized in table 5-1.

Public redistributive use-of-income benefits are the opposite side of the redistributive coin to source-of-income benefits. Whereas source-of-income benefits are received by lower-income citizens, redistributive use-of-income benefits are attributable to those higher-income citizens both willing and able to finance redistributive programs. Assuming an optimal provision of such programs, the total value of money plus in-kind transfers must equal the total use-of-income redistributive benefits. But while the former are attributed to the transfer recipients, the latter are assigned to the nonpoor population. Five Washington area services are assumed to generate some use-of-income redistributive benefits:

1. elementary and secondary education and libraries
2. higher education
3. health
4. recreation
5. welfare

Imputation of Use-of-Income Benefits by Income Class

Benefits have generally been allocated by income class in previous incidence studies according to two procedures: (1) Benefits from services that can be associated with a specific clientele have been allocated on the basis of the cost incurred in behalf of a group. Thus benefits from public education, for example, are allocated to families on the basis of the per student cost of education. In this procedure it is therefore implicitly assumed that only the direct recipients of a service benefit from it with no allowance made for externalities. (2) Benefits that are not so easily identified with a specific clientele have usually been allocated by income class according to one rule or another, usually chosen quite arbitrarily with no theoretical justification.

Aaron and McGuire have recently shown that benefit incidence results crucially depend on assumptions made concerning the value of individual utility functions.[34] The essential points of their analysis can be illustrated by an example. Assume (1) there are two individuals, A and B, with $1,000 and $2,000 income, respectively; (2) both have the same separable utility functions for private and public goods; and (3) G_1 units of a public good are provided. This

example is illustrated in figure 2-2. Both A and B consume the same quantity of the public good, G_1 units, but their evaluation of the G_1^{th} unit differs because their incomes differ. The value to A of G_1 units is AA' and to B it is BB', as shown in figure 2-2. These values are the product of A's and B's marginal rates of substitution (MRS) between private and public goods (the slopes of the indifference curves) at G_1 times G_1 units. In this way a "value in exchange" for the public good is generated which is the analogue of the national accounts evaluation of market goods.

This procedure for evaluating public goods may be summarized in notational form:

$$(MRS^A)(G) + (MRS^B)(G) = E,$$ (3-5)

where E is the dollar outlay for the public good.[d] With identical additive and separable utility functions, the partial derivatives of U^A and U^B with respect to G are equal:

$$\frac{\delta U^A}{\delta G} = \frac{\delta U^B}{\delta G} = C$$ (3-6)

Hence

$$\frac{MRS^A}{MRS^B} = \frac{\dfrac{\delta U^A/\delta G}{MU_Y^A}}{\dfrac{\delta U^B/\delta G}{MU_Y^B}}$$ (3-7)

where MU_Y^A and MU_Y^B are the partial derivatives of U^A and U^B with respect to personal income (Y).

Rearranging

$$(MRS^A)(MU_Y^A) = (MRS^B)(MU_Y^B) = C$$ (3-8)

and

a. $MRS^A = \dfrac{C}{MU_Y^A}$ (3-9)

b. $MRS^B = \dfrac{C}{MU_Y^B}$

[d]The reasonableness of this formulation which implies the optimal provision of the public good is examined in Chapter 4.

Substituting (3–9) into (3–5) we have:

$$\left(\frac{C}{MU_Y^A}\right)G + \left(\frac{C}{MU_Y^B}\right)G = E \tag{3-10}$$

$$V_A + V_B = E \tag{3-11}$$

where V_A and V_B are the values of the public good consumed by A and B. In other words, the dollar benefits of public goods are imputed to individuals in inverse proportion to their marginal utility of income. Thus if utility functions can be specified and, knowing the outlay for a public good, its dollar value can be imputed to individuals by income class.

This procedure for evaluating public output is illustrated by a simple example in table 3–2. Assume that a public expenditure of $500 evaluated at the margin generates a total of $500 use-of-income benefits for two individuals having $1,000 and $2,000 income, respectively. Assume further that the two have identical separable utility functions. The individual evaluations of the public outlay depends on the form of the utility function. Assume, for illustrative purposes, three different utility functions with the following implicit marginal utilities of income:

Assumption A: $MU_Y = K$

Assumption B: $MU_Y = \dfrac{K}{Y}$

Assumption C: $MU_Y = \dfrac{K}{Y^2}$

By substituting values for MU_Y^A and MU_Y^B in equation (3–10) the value in exchange of the $500 public outlay can be computed for the two individuals.

Under Assumption A, with the marginal utility of income constant over all incomes, benefits are equal for the two individuals, as shown in table 3–2. Under Assumption B, with marginal utility declining proportionately with income, the

Table 3–2
Benefits Under Different Utility Assumptions

Income of Individuals	Benefits		
	Assumption A $MU_Y = K$	Assumption B $MU_Y = K/Y$	Assumption C $MU_Y = K/Y^2$
$1,000	$250.00	$166.67	$100.00
$2,000	$250.00	$333.33	$400.00

marginal utility for an individual with $2,000 income is one-half that of an individual with $1,000 income. Consequently, the dollar value of benefits for the higher income person will be twice that for the lower-income one. Given the constraint that the sum of individual evaluations must equal the dollar value of the outlay, the higher-income person is imputed benefits of $333.33 and the lower income person benefits of $166.67. Under Assumption C, with marginal utility declining as the square of income, marginal utility for the higher-income person is one-fourth that of the lower-income person with the dollar value of his benefits consequently $400, or four times larger than for the lower-income person.

Thus Aaron and McGuire have demonstrated that the imputation of benefits across income classes is extremely sensitive to the form of the utility function that is chosen either explicitly, or as has most often been the case, implicitly. If benefits are allocated on a cost of service basis, as is often done in benefit incidence studies, it is implicitly assumed that the marginal utility of income is constant across income classes. The consequences of such a strong assumption for benefit incidence analysis are considerable. Larger dollar benefits, for example, are imputed to lower-income classes and the total incidence of the budget will appear more "pro-poor" than if it were assumed that the marginal utility of income declined even slightly with income, as can be easily inferred from the simple illustration in table 3-2. But the mere identification of a strong assumption carries no guarantee that another assumption is preferable. The critical problem remains: Which specification of utility functions is most appropriate for allocating benefits from public outlays? Or, in other words, can evidence be marshalled to support one particular index of the income elasticity of marginal utility?

Maital has recently addressed precisely this question and offers evidence to support one particular estimate of the marginal utility of income, which, in turn, he proposes for allocating benefits from public outlays.[35] With some modifications Maital's approach will be adopted for allocating benefits from Washington area government outlays to the various income classes.

Maital proposes this general functional form for the marginal utility of income:

$$MU(Y) = KY^{-\phi}$$

where ϕ is the elasticity of marginal utility with respect to income as well as the inverse of the elasticity of substitution between goods.

In terms of the illustration shown in table 3-2, if $\phi = 0$, $MU_Y = K$; if $\phi = 1$, $MU_Y = (K/Y)$; and if $\phi = 2$, $MU_Y = (K/Y^2)$. Sato has shown that if a function such as $MU(Y)^{-\phi}$ is regarded as the canonical form of a constant elasticity of substitution ordinal utility function the strong, cardinal utility assumption need not be made.[36] Further, on the grounds that ϕ can be interpreted as the

inverse of the weighted average of elasticity of substitution among goods, Maital derives values for ϕ from international estimates of the elasticities of substitution.[37] The estimated values of ϕ for twelve developed countries range from a low of 1.04 in the United Kingdom to a high of 3.84 in the Netherlands. Interestingly, three different studies report a value of 1.50 for the United States.[38] If the elasticity of marginal utility with respect to income in the United States is 1.50, or even greater than 1.0, then we may infer that the marginal utility of income declines more than proportionately with income and the dollar value of benefits from a given public outlay must rise more than proportionately with income. Such a conclusion, as Maital points out, is contrary to

> ... the widely held view that government budgets significantly redistribute incomes. If public good benefits are indeed distributed as regressively (that is, pro rich) as suggested in this paper, it would take a substantial increase in the progressivity of tax-transfer systems in the U.S. and Canada (and probably other countries) to achieve in *fact* the redistribution believed to be affected now.[39]

Maital thus provides both a theoretical rationale as well as a specific estimate of a crucial variable for imputing the dollar value of benefits to citizens across income classes. His estimation of the elasticity of marginal utility with respect to income should serve at least to narrow the acceptable range of values for this variable. There remain reasons however, why 1.50 may not be a completely accurate measurement. Even though three studies do provide identical, independent estimates of ϕ for the United States, two of these studies rest on the assumption of separable utility functions and use private market rather than public sector data,[40] and the third study employs the unlikely assumption that Congress has designed the federal income tax structure to extract an equal absolute sacrifice from each taxpayer.[41]

   By assuming separable utility functions, the inverse of the elasticity of substitution between goods can be understood as the elasticity of marginal utility with respect to income. If two goods are neither complements nor substitutes, then as the consumption of one is increased, the marginal utility of the other remains unchanged, and any decrease in the value of the inverse of the marginal rate of substitution between these goods measures the reduced marginal utility of additional real income. If, however, the goods should be complements (substitutes), then as the consumption of one is increased the marginal utility of the other increases (decreases), and any change in the inverse of the marginal rate of substitution cannot be considered an unequivocal measure of the change in the marginal utility of the increased real income. In the case of a complementary good this procedure would overestimate any decrease in the marginal utility of income; and for substitutes it would underestimate any decrease.

   If it is true that on balance subfederal public services tend to complement rather than substitute for market commodities, we would expect the value of ϕ,

or the inverse of the elasticity of substitution between goods, to be somewhat less than 1.50 when used to evaluate public output. Indeed this inference is supported by an estimation of ϕ which is based on Fellner's analysis complemented by survey and voting data. As will be shown shortly this estimation procedure indicates that the value of ϕ when evaluated in terms of public output is close to one. The benefit incidence pattern which follows from using 1.0 will show fewer benefits attributed to higher income classes than would occur if 1.50 were used. However, notably more benefits will be allocated to the higher income classes than would occur following the cost-of-service technique, assuming as it does the constant marginal utility of income.

Fellner has shown that the marginal utility of income can be estimated by first stating the first order condition for individual utility maximization:

$$\frac{\delta U/\delta X_1}{P_1} = \lambda$$

where

X_1 = a commodity

P_1 = price of commodity

λ = MU_Y

The consumer is confronted successively with a low and high price for X_1. Then we may explore how much more income he requires in order to induce him to buy the same amount of X_1 as he purchased at the low price. Since the marginal utility of X_1 must be the same in both price situations, and if prices have gone up k percent, we can infer from the first order condition that "the marginal utility of income . . . in the high-income situation is k percent lower than in the low-income situation."[42] And if the decline of marginal utility over an income range is known, the elasticity of marginal utility with respect to income can be easily computed.

This result may be applied to the public sector in order to derive an estimate of the income elasticity of marginal utility for evaluating public output. Assume the same first order condition as for private commodities, with X_1 now a public good and P_1 the appropriate tax-price for an individual citizen. Assume further that an individual's tax-price is doubled. We can infer the elasticity of marginal utility with respect to income if we can determine how much we must increase his income to induce him willingly to finance the same level of public service as before his tax increase. Considerable evidence has been adduced indicating we would have to double his income to bring this about.[43] In other words, with a doubling of tax-price it appears that the same quantity of public output will be demanded if a person's income is doubled. Since we may infer from the first

order condition that, at this new level of income, the marginal utility of income will be one-half its value at the lower income level, the elasticity of marginal utility with respect to income will be one.

Summary of Procedures for Benefit
Measurement and Imputation

The discussion of this chapter can be summarized in five statements describing the procedures that will be used for estimating benefits from Washington area government expenditures and for their imputation by income class.

1. Source-of-income benefits from redistributive expenditures, whether in the form of money or in-kind transfers, will be imputed to recipients on the basis of their cost. No attempt will be made to estimate any source-of-income benefits and losses due to the impact of government expenditures on factor earnings.

2. The use-of-income benefits from the various expenditures will first be divided into three classes, private, public nonredistributive, and public redistributive benefits. These three classes of benefits are additive for any given service, with their sum equaling the total use-of-income benefits generated by each expenditure category. The assumption that the dollar value of use-of-income benefits equals total expenditures will be examined in Chapter 4.

3. Private benefits will first be assigned to the specific clientele which is assumed to derive market-like benefits from the service in question, for example, families whose children directly benefit from public elementary and secondary education. These private benefits will also then be allocated across income classes on the assumption that the income elasticity of marginal utility is unitary.

4. Public nonredistributive benefits will first be allocated on a cost basis to all citizens within a benefit area rather than merely to a specific clientele. Then, like private benefits, they will be allocated across income classes on the assumption that the income elasticity of marginal utility is unitary.

5. Public redistributive benefits will be allocated to those income classes that are assumed to have an effective demand for providing transfers to others. It will be assumed that all families with an income of $5,000 and over have some effective demand for these programs. Since families with income below $5,000 are likely to be recipients of redistributive services, we must conclude that, according to social policy, they should be exempt from tax liability to finance these services. The public redistributive benefits will be allocated across those in income classes above $5,000, again using the assumption that the income elasticity of marginal utility is unitary.

One important question remains to be addressed before benefits from government expenditures in the Washington metropolitan area can be allocated by income class: What is the total value of the use-of-income benefits generated by

these expenditures? Does their value equal, or is it greater than, or less than, the dollar value of the expenditures? This question can be resolved only after some determination has been made concerning the likelihood of an optimal supply of public output being provided in the metropolitan area. This topic is the subject of Chapter 4. In Chapter 5 the specific assumptions made concerning the various expenditure categories will be discussed, and benefits will be allocated by income class and geographic area.

4

Optimal Supply of Public Output in a Metropolitan Area

Introduction

The value of private sector output in the national accounts is calculated on the basis of value in exchange. In theory, value in exchange equals price times quantity, where price is the marginal rate of substitution between a numeraire and the good in question. Hence no attempt is made to estimate the consumer surplus generated by private output. Public sector output, on the other hand, is entered in the national accounts on the basis of cost rather than the value in exchange. Further, most benefit incidence studies have assumed that the value of public services to individuals is either identical with the cost incurred in providing a service [1] or is some fraction of total expenditure which is determined by some arbitrary rule-of-thumb. The theoretical deficiencies of such benefit measurements have been discussed in Chapter 3.

Procedures were proposed in Chapter 3 for evaluating public sector use-of-income benefits in a manner analogous to the national accounting measurement of market output. In the absence of market evaluation it was proposed that the marginal rate of substitution between income and public services be used to evaluate public output. Since this procedure is based on the marginal evaluation of public services, the total value computed is comparable to the market value in exchange and thus, as in the market case, does not include consumer surplus.

One major theoretical problem, however, remains to be resolved before public sector benefits can be allocated across income classes in the Washington metropolitan area. We must first determine what is the relationship between the total dollar value of use-of-income benefits and total government outlay. A priori it cannot be determined whether the benefits are (1) equal to, (2) greater than, or (3) less than the expenditures. Only if it is assumed both that the marginal cost of service provision is constant and that there is an optimal provision of public services, will total expenditures equal the total marginal benefits received by citizens.[2]

The optimal level of public good output is that for which the sum of the marginal rates of substitution across all citizens equals the marginal cost of the public good:

$$\Sigma MRS_i = MC$$

This condition is illustrated in figure 4-1. If we assume: (1) a three-person

51

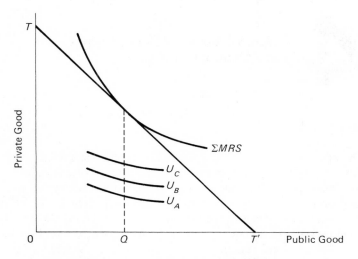

Figure 4-1. Optimal Supply of a Public Good.

community; (2) that indiduals A, B, and C are to be maintained on utility levels indicated by the indifference curves U_A, U_B, and U_C, respectively; and (3) that TT^1 reflects the production transformation curve between market and public output with marginal cost equal to average cost, then Q is the socially optimal production of the public good. At this output the summed marginal rates of substitution of A, B, and C equal the marginal cost of the public output in terms of the private good numeraire. Only with Q output does the value of the public output evaluated at the margin equal the product of Q units times the marginal cost of the Qth unit (slope of TT'). For output less than Q, the summed marginal rates of substitution are greater than marginal cost and thus total benefits are greater than total costs. For output greater than Q, the summed marginal rates of substitution are less than marginal cost, and total benefits are less than total costs.

In this chapter one model of the political decision-making process will be employed to derive some hypotheses concerning the likelihood that the actual expenditure level chosen by a community is optimal. The model employed is a purely democratic, individualistic, majority-voting-rule model. This model will first be used to derive certain predictions about the effect of tax institutions and variation in the income elasticity of demand on the likelihood that the level chosen will deviate from the optimal. Then we will focus on the consideration that local public expenditures may lead to increased factor earnings for some voters. The implications of this outcome for an optimal service level are then examined. In the final section the impact of political fragmentation on the expenditure levels of local governments is explored.

Elasticities of Tax Schedules and
Marginal Evaluations

Assume that an isolated or fully consolidated local government is determining its level of provision for a single purely public good.[3] Assume also that there are only three individuals and that the political decision-making process is purely democratic and employs a majority decision-making rule. In this case, the wishes of the median voter will prevail.

Let us assume that the good in question has unitary income elasticity of demand and that the tax structure levies taxes in proportion to income. Individual C is assumed to have twice as much income as individual B, who in turn has twice as much as individual A. This means that the slope of A's budget line between public and private goods is twice that of B's and B's is twice that of C's. Moreover, along any vertical line the slope of A's indifference curve between private and public goods is twice that of B's and B's is twice that of C's. This is shown in figure 4–2. [4]

In this situation each individual has the same level of preferred output, Q_0. At this level of output, the summed individual marginal evaluations, or the social marginal benefit, equal the summed marginal costs, or summed tax prices. Individual A pays $Y_A A$ in taxes, B pays $Y_B B$ and C pays $Y_C C$.

Now let us try to predict the consequences of altering the tax institution. Suppose we assume that the tax structure, instead of being proportional, is regressive, as is likely to be the case for local governments. What are the consequences for the level of output chosen and its relationship with the social optimum? First, ambiguity regarding the meaning of a "more regressive tax structure" must be removed. A "more regressive tax structure" does not neces-

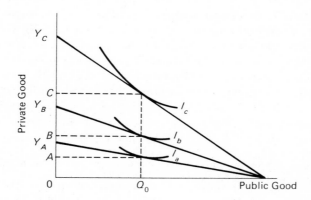

Figure 4–2. Unitary Elasticity of Demand and Optimal Provision of a Public Good.

sarily define the tax share paid by the median voter. Our assumption that benefits are proportional to income implies that the proportion of total benefits for any output level received by B is $Y_B(Y_A + Y_B + Y_C)^{-1}$. With a proportional tax structure his share of taxes is the same. The introduction of a regressive tax structure must mean that A's share of taxes will increase and C's will decrease so that A will demand less than the socially optimal output level and C will demand more. But B's share of taxes *may* remain the same. If it does, he would continue to choose the socially optimum output level of Q_0.[5]

Suppose, however, we interpret a change to a more regressive tax structure to mean that those with more than the mean income pay less and those with less than the mean income pay more than under a proportional tax structure. Since income distributions tend to be skewed toward the right, the mean income is typically greater than the median. This implies that the median voter, given our assumptions about price elasticities of demand for services, will face a higher proportion of the tax bill. Regressivity, understood in this sense, would tend to make him choose less than Q_0 with the consequence that the level of provision would be suboptimal. Summed marginal evaluations would in this instance exceed the costs of providing the service. Conversely, a move from a proportional tax structure toward progressivity would imply that the level of output chosen will be greater than the optimal.[6] Since most studies indicate that local tax structures are regressive, the implication is that this institution tends to foster suboptimal levels of provision.[a]

The situation wherein the income elasticity of demand for public services is greater than one and the tax structure is proportional is depicted in figure 4–3. For income levels above those of the median voter, tax prices increase proportionally with income, but marginal evaluations increase more than proportionally. Individual A, whose income is less than the median voter's, has a negative marginal fiscal residual at the level of output, Q_B, chosen by the median voter. The tax structure is proportional as depicted in figure 4–3. For income levels above those of the median voter, tax prices increase proportionally with income, but marginal evaluations increase more than proportionally. Individual A, whose income is less than the median voter's, has a negative marginal fiscal residual at the level of output, Q_B, chosen by the median voter. His negative marginal fiscal residual is equal to the difference between the slope of this indifference curve and budget line at Q_B. Individual C, on the other hand, has a positive fiscal residual at output level Q_B, which is in turn equal to the difference between the slope of his indifference curve and his budget line at Q_B.

---

[a]If there are other reasons why local governments might provide suboptimal levels of provision, such as benefit spillouts uncompensated for by tax spillins or grants-in-aid, an efficiency basis may exist for progressive local tax structures. On the other hand, it should be noted that the perception of tax burdens under a regressive tax structure dominated by the property tax may be such as to lead to overprovision. If the lowest income classes are basically renters and if they do not perceive any burden from the property tax, then they might consider their tax price to be virtually zero. The high-income group would then contain the median voter and a superoptimal level of provision might be chosen.

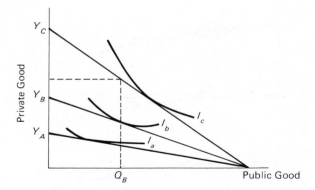

Figure 4-3. An Elastic Demand for a Public Good with Suboptimal Provision.

If C's income is higher than B's by the same proportion that B's is higher than A's, then the summed marginal evaluations would again equal the total tax price and marginal cost of the public service. But since the median voter's income is likely to be less than the mean income, the rich individual's excess of marginal evaluation over tax price is likely to be greater than the poor individual's excess of tax price over marginal evaluation. Consequently a socially suboptimal provision of services will be chosen. From this analysis we can infer that publicly provided goods with high income elasticities of demand, such as libraries and recreation services, will tend to be underprovided. Those with low income elasticities, on the other hand, such as sanitary services and highways will tend to be overprovided.[7]

The Effect of Changes in Sources of Income

We have assumed so far in this chapter that effective demand for local public services derives only from those who enjoy increased welfare through consuming public services. But, as was discussed in Chapter 3, government outlays also have an impact on sources of income. If it is assumed that public and private goods require relatively different factor proportions in their production, then the expansion of the public sector at the expense of private output will increase the ratio of the marginal revenue productivity of those factors used more intensively in the public sector to the marginal revenue productivity of the factors more intensively employed in the private sector.[8] To the extent that this occurs, the income distributional pattern is altered by public outlays. This situation is illustrated in figure 4-4 in terms of the median voter model.

If we assume that the tax structure is proportional and that marginal evaluations are proportional to income and if source-of-income benefits are ignored,

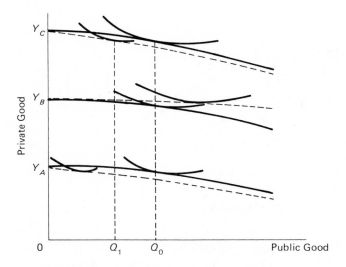

Figure 4-4. Source-of-Income Effects on Outlay.

A, B, and C will each prefer the same level of output, Q_0, and the sum of their marginal evaluations equals the sum of their tax prices. But now assume, for instance, that B derives all of his income from his salary as a public school teacher and that A and C derive income entirely from private sector employment, with public education the service represented on the horizontal axis in figure 4-4. Income effects, or source-of-income benefits, are introduced into the analysis by pivoting the budget lines on the points Y_A, Y_B, and Y_C. Thus, as public school outlays increase, drawing resources from the private sector, the marginal revenue productivity of B increases relative to A's and C's marginal revenue productivity in the private sector. Relative factor-prices consequently shift in favor of B and against A and C. The new budget lines that allow for these source-of-income displacements are shown in figure 4-4 by the slashed lines. The source-of-income budget line for B rises above the simple tax-price budget line and for A and C it falls below that line, with the gain to B equal to the combined loss suffered by A and C.

   If the three individuals are aware of these source-of-income benefits they will all be in disequilibrium with Q_0 units of public school services. Since A and C would then want to reduce output below Q_0 and only B would want to expand it, we would conclude from the median voter model that output would be reduced toward Q_1, as shown in figure 4-4. At Q_1 individual C would be the median voter forming a majority with B in favor of reducing output to Q_1. In this event output would be less than the socially optimum output, Q_0, and total marginal benefits would be greater than total marginal costs.

   Two considerations, however, suggest that a greater than socially optimal

output may be indicated by the introduction of source-of-income benefits into the analysis. First, the source-of-income decrement suffered individually by A and C may be so indirect and negligible as to be essentially unnoticed by them whereas B's gain may be a significant fraction of his income. If so, the relevant budget lines for A and C in a voting model would be their simple tax-price lines, whereas it would be the source-of-income budget line for B. The median voter in this instance would still favor Q_0 units of output but there would be pressure from B to expand beyond this level.

Second, most decisions concerning public sector output levels are in the first instance made by government agencies and legislative bodies which are subject only to periodic review by voters who usually do not focus exclusively on the question of the level of expenditures. Thus it may be worthwhile for a minority that stands to gain significantly from a particular program (i.e., B) to organize and lobby strenuously in favor of expanding output so as to increase factor returns. The returns to organization and lobbying might be expected to exceed their costs. In a general equilibrium model others would necessarily suffer an offsetting loss in income but since this loss would be spread over many (i.e., A and C) it might be difficult to organize this latent group into active opposition. Although each would have an interest in organizing, this interest might be dominated by the free rider phenomenon. If so, output might be greater than the social optimum, Q_0. The precise outcome in any instance will be determined by the interaction of such factors as the concentration of the gains in factor income, the diffuseness of the income losses, and the responsiveness of output decisions to organized pressure groups rather than to the total citizenry.[9]

How important are such source-of-income effects on the local level of services? No doubt federal government expenditures on defense, for example, create significant economic rents for those who own, say, uranium deposits. But the same may not be as true for public school teachers hired by local school districts since source-of-income effects are dampened if local governments must hire personnel in competitive, national markets. If teachers are available to a community in highly elastic supply from a national pool, then an increased school personnel budget in any one district will be translated primarily into the hiring of more teachers rather than increased salaries for employed teachers.

Our argument implies that lobbying for increased public service levels will be strongest and most effective where some of the taxpayer-voters perceive a gain to themselves in the form of increased income.[10] We would expect a tendency for a relatively greater provision of those local services that are labor- and land-intensive since these factors are more immobile than capital and are most likely to be owned by local residents. Relatively less of those services using factors of production primarily owned by those outside the jurisdiction should be employed. For example, we would expect that the ratio of teachers to audio-visual aids and the ratio of policemen to police cars should tend to be greater than is efficiently indicated.

The source-of-income effects of transfer programs can also be analyzed in terms of the median voter model.[b] Recipients of income transfers have an obvious stake in expanding the funding of these transfers, which is reflected in the overwhelming support of low-income families for these programs. In terms of the discussion concerning figure 4-4, we would therefore expect transfer programs to be superoptimal. The drive of transfer recipients to expand these programs, however, is countered by a phenomenon that may not be present for other programs. There seems to be more intense opposition to social welfare activities and especially to AFDC, for example, than to other government activities.[11] It may be that some citizens judge, mistakenly, that a major fraction of their taxes go to finance welfare programs and that, therefore, these transfers are greater than they actually are. If such a "transfer" illusion does exist there will be voter pressure to cut back transfers, with the consequence that they will be less generously funded than they would be if voters were accurately apprised of their magnitude.

Effect of Political Fragmentation

An important aspect of reality, so far left unaccounted for in the discussion of this chapter, is the political fragmentation found in most metropolitan areas. There has been a considerable debate whether spillovers between communities necessarily lead to suboptimal provision levels.[12] Much of this discussion concerns interactions between communities. Here our concern is much simpler. Abstracting from the problems of strategic behavior created by intercommunity spillovers and assuming only a one-directional flow of benefits out of a community, we wish to consider whether fragmentation increases the likelihood that the summed marginal benefits from the provision of local government services exceed their marginal cost.

In figure 4-5 each individual is assumed to face a tax price and possess a marginal evaluation that is proportional to his income, with A, B, and C each preferring the level of output, Q_0, which is chosen. The positive evaluation of the single surburbanite(s) is ignored for the moment.

In such a situation it has generally been concluded that there would be an underprovision of public services. This follows from the fact that some benefits to society are ignored by the decisionmakers, who are residents of the locality. The level of output chosen must, therefore, be less than where society's marginal benefit equals the marginal cost of service provision. This necessarily follows, however, only if nonresidents pay none of the cost of service provision. But the

---

[b]Welfare programs generate income effects for personnel administering the programs as well as for program recipients. Thus welfare expenditures affect factor payments to social workers, for example, in much the same way as educational expenditures affect teacher income.

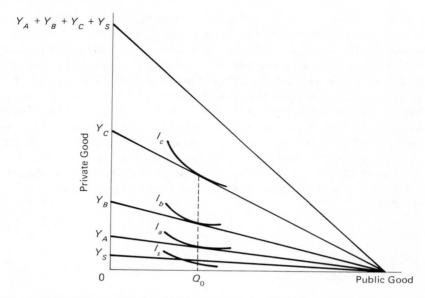

Figure 4-5. Effect of Political Fragmentation on Provision of a Public Good.

situation may be as we have depicted in figure 4-5, where the sum of the slopes of the budget lines facing the city residents is less than the slope of the total budget line, which is the total marginal cost of the service. Thus, even though at the level of output chosen by city residents, Q_0, the sum of their evaluations falls short of total social evaluation, their costs are less than total social costs. If, as pictured, the suburbanite's share of the city tax burden is greater than his share of marginal benefits, then a superoptimal level of provision will be chosen. Thus, fragmentation per se need not imply underprovision of public services.

Conclusion

The median voter model has allowed us to derive certain hypotheses concerning the optimal provision of public services by local governments. From the analysis of this chapter we cannot conclude, however, that in general the provision of public services tends to be optimal or more or less than optimal.[c] Even less are we in a position to make a certain judgment concerning the level of expenditures in the Washington metropolitan area. To do so we would need to know (1) both the income elasticities of the tax structure and of the demand

---

[c]This question is discussed further in Chapter 9 in terms of the values estimated for the Washington area.

for the public service, (2) the economic rent received by residents from local government expenditures, and (3) the tax contributions made by nonresidents to the local fisc as well as benefits they receive from it. In addition the implications of the strong assumptions underlying the median voter model would have to be explored. Specifically, the impact of the magnitude and distribution of decision-making costs would have to be determined. Despite these major unknowns, we nonetheless feel that the analysis of this chapter allows us at least to conclude that there is no major influence which necessarily biases output to be superoptimal or suboptimal and that thus we may with some assurance assume there is a tendency for outlays to cluster around the social optimum. This assumption will allow us in Chapter 5 to distribute benefits which are equal in dollar value to total subfederal Washington area government expenditures.

5

Estimates of Benefit Incidence of State
and Local Expenditures in the
Washington Metropolitan Area

Introduction

Three important conclusions emerge from the discussion of the previous chapters. First, total use-of-income marginal benefits from government services are assumed equal to their cost. Second, our measurement of source-of-income benefits is limited, for practical considerations, to income-redistributional transfers made either in money or in kind. Third, since benefits from government services generate individual utility similar to that received from market services, they should be evaluated in terms of individual welfare rather than merely the cost of providing the service. However, cost-of-service estimates are useful for some purposes. In this chapter these judgments are implemented and the benefit incidence from the subfederal government expenditures in the Washington metropolitan area is estimated on both an individual welfare and a cost-of-service basis.

Six of the most important government services are examined in detail,[a] with other government services considered in summary fashion. Benefit incidence will be estimated by income class and by geographic area in the metropolitan area (see Appendix B.1).[b] Four specific judgments must be made prior to estimating the benefit incidence:

1. It must be determined what proportion of the benefits generated by a service is private and what proportion nonredistributive and redistributive public benefits.[1] This important question is discussed in connection with each service, with the assumptions used for the various services summarized in table 5-1.
2. The geographical domain over which the public benefits accrue must be determined. It will be assumed here that the Washington metropolitan area is an economic and social unity and, for the services assumed to generate public benefits, the appropriate benefit area is coextensive with the whole metropolitan area rather than some smaller area.
3. The place of residence of those receiving private benefits must be determined.

---

[a]The services considered are: elementary and secondary education, higher education, fire, police, health, social services, libraries, parks, recreation, courts, corrections, public works, transportation, and general government.

[b]Notation [B.1] indicates that in the technical Appendix B note 1 gives further details on the procedure being discussed.

4.   The income of the private benefit recipients must also be determined. The procedures for resolving these latter two questions are outlined in the course of this chapter with a more detailed discussion of these procedures and the data sources employed found in Appendix B.

Distribution of the Benefits from Government Services

Elementary and Secondary Education

Education generates benefits in three distinct senses. First, private benefits are either currently received by a student and his family, or were received in the past and/or are anticipated in the future. These include increased earning capacity, consumption enjoyment, and benefits unrelated to the educational process, such as child-sitting services. Numerous nonredistributive external benefits have been widely recognized, for example, the benefits of living in a more educated and pluralistic society. Further, in the past decade, especially, various educational programs have been mounted with expressly redistributive goals. In terms of the benefit framework developed in Chapter 3, education, therefore, can be said to generate private, public nonredistributional, and redistributional benefits.[2]

No precise measurement exists of the private and public fractions of the total benefits from elementary and secondary educational expenditures. For the sake of illustration, Aaron and McGuire assume that zero and 70 percent of the benefits of these expenditures are public for their low and high estimates of publicness.[3] The assumptions we make fall within this range. Thus, we assume that 20 percent of the benefits of elementary and secondary education constitute nonredistributive public benefits and that 30 percent of the expenditures for the education of poor children generate redistributive public benefits. Consequently 80 percent of the benefits of the education expenditures for the nonpoor are private benefits and 20 percent are nonredistributive public benefits; while 50 percent for the poor are private benefits, 20 percent are public nonredistributive and 30 percent are public redistributive. In addition to these use-of-income benefits which equal the dollar value of expenditures, the public redistributive benefits also generate source-of-income in-kind transfers to the poor. These assumptions are shown in table 5-1.

The arbitrary nature of these assumptions must be emphasized.[4] While numerous studies have attempted to quantify the private returns from education and it has generally been admitted that there are also social returns to education, attempts to measure them have not produced definitive results. Becker, for example, suggests that social returns could range from less than zero to approximately 60 percent of total returns in the case of higher education. There have

Table 5-1
Percentage of Use-of-Income Benefits by Type from Government Expenditures in Washington Metropolitan Area

Government Expenditures	Use-of-Income Benefits		
	Private	*Public Nonredistributive*	*Public Redistributive*
Courts	0 percent	100 percent^{P} and R	0 percent
Elementary and Secondary Education and Libraries			
(a) for children with less than $5,000 income	50^{P}	20^{P} and R	30^{R}
(b) for children with $5,000 or more income	80^{R}	20^{P} and R	
Higher Education			
(a) for students with less than $5,000 income	75^{P}	0	25^{R}
(b) for students with $5,000 or more income	100^{R}	0	0
Fire, Police and Corrections	100^{P} and R	0	0
General Government	Weighted average of incidence of all benefits		
Health			
(a) for citizens with less than $5,000 income	0	0	100^{R}
(b) for citizens with $5,000 or more income	100^{R}	0	0
Recreation			
(a) for citizens with less than $5,000 income	60^{P}	0	40^{R}
(b) for citizens with $5,000 or more income	100^{R}	0	0
Refuse Collection	100^{P} and R	0	0
Transportation	100^{P} and R	0	0
Welfare	0	0	100^{R}

"P" and "R" indicate that the benefit is imputed to families with less than $5,000 income or $5,000 and over, respectively.

been no direct attempts to measure the value of use-of-income redistributive benefits from educational expenditures.

In the absence of direct measurements of the private and public returns to education we are forced to support our assumptions by a general argument that relies on the widespread contention that elementary and secondary education generate notable externalities. In point of fact for over a century such education has enjoyed public financial support in this country, usually with wide popular approval. Furthermore, in recent years public policy has emphasized the redistributional dimension of elementary and secondary education. There is evidence that this emphasis enjoys fairly widespread favor. Watts and Free, for example, find that support for increasing federal expenditures to educate low-income children is a positive function of income.[5] In their 1971 survey they find that 64.6 percent of those interviewed with income less than $5,000 preferred to see such program expenditures increase, and that support rose to 69.1 percent in the $5,000 to $10,000 range, 70.8 percent in the $10,000 to $15,000 range, and 76.7 percent in the over $15,000 income category.[6] The fact that individuals in the higher income classes favored these expenditures suggests that redistributive use-of-income benefits are generated among these classes by educational services provided to children from low-income families.

Distribution of Benefits

Since private benefits from elementary and secondary education are to be allocated to students and their families, we need to determine their jurisdiction of residence and the educational outlay for the jurisdiction. The income characteristics of these families is derived from a 25 percent sample of all Census tracts in each of our major jurisdictions. The income characteristics of school children are estimated by distributing the number of public school children in each tract according to the distribution of school age children in the various income classes in that tract[c] (see Appendix B.2).

The benefits from public elementary and secondary educational expenditures measured on a cost-of-service basis are distributed by income class and jurisdiction in table 5-2 and figure 5-1. Benefits measured in this way have a progressive incidence in all three of the jurisdictions,[d] with the degree of progres-

---

[c]Such a procedure takes into account the fact that the portion of school age children attending public schools will be lower in high income tracts. It does not take account of the fact that tracts themselves have some income diversity and that within tracts richer children are less likely to attend public schools. Thus, the resulting series is likely to slightly overestimate the use of public schools by the children of high-income families. In the absence of information regarding the income of students' families, and since, in the District of Columbia, there appears to be greater aversion to public schools by higher income families than in the nation as a whole, this procedure is preferable to using a national series on school attendance.

[d]"Progressive" benefit incidence will be used throughout to mean "pro-poor," that is, the benefit-income ratio decreases with income.

sivity highest in the District of Columbia.[7] The greater degree of progressivity in the District reflects both the family structure of high-income residents in the District and their use of private schools. Both factors imply fewer children from high-income families in public schools in the District.

The distribution of use- and source-of-income benefits from elementary and secondary educational expenditures by income class and jurisdiction is shown in table 5-3 and figure 5-2. The total values in table 5-3 are greater than in table 5-2 since they include all use-of-income benefits, which equal total expenditures, in addition to the redistributive in-kind transfers received by those with less than $5,000 income. Benefits thus estimated on a welfare basis in contrast with a cost basis drastically reduce total benefits as a percentage of money income allocated to the lower-income classes and increases this percentage for the higher-income classes. This shift results both from recognizing public nonredistributive and redistributive benefits and from adjusting the value of both private and public benefits by the declining marginal utility of income. According to the welfare measure there is a considerable interjurisdictional flow of benefits since all three areas receive public nonredistributive and redistributive use-of-income benefits from educational outlays in the other two areas. In general, it appears that those with less than $15,000 income obtain more benefits from elementary and secondary education if they live in the city, while those with the highest income receive the least benefit if they are city residents.

Higher Education

There is a general presumption among economists that public benefits are a smaller fraction of total benefits for higher education than for elementary and secondary education.[8] Many of the purported benefits of elementary and secondary education are associated with goals that promote a viable society, such as the reduction of crime and antisocial behavior, and the promotion of the minimal skills among the citizenry necessary for a functioning democracy. It is sometimes contended that society gains from the increased productivity resulting from the research activity of college-educated individuals. However, it seems likely that typically the value of such contributions can be captured in the form of higher income by those doing the research. This would not be true of instances where the research contribution constitutes a collective good that belongs to the public domain and cannot be appropriated by the initiators. However, since such situations do not appear to be all that frequent, we will assume there are no public nonredistributive benefits from higher educational expenditures which can be added to the private consumption and investment benefits appropriated by the students themselves.[9] However, since redistribution is a goal frequently identified with higher education and because society does subsidize the college education of a certain number of poor individuals, we will assume that 25 percent of the use-of-income benefits generated by higher education are public

Table 5-2
Distribution of Elementary and Secondary Education Benefits by Income Class and by Jurisdiction: Cost-of-Service Basis

Income Class	From D.C. Expenditures	From Maryland Expenditures	From Virginia Expenditures	Total Benefits as a Percentage of Money Income
Benefits to D.C. Residents				
below $3,000	20,604,400	None	None	80.0
3,000–3,999	7,710,100			30.6
4,000–5,999	21,752,200			22.2
6,000–7,499	16,632,900			14.6
7,500–9,999	22,551,600			10.4
10,000–14,999	29,173,600			6.3
15,000–24,999	12,997,400			2.3
25,000 and above	4,080,000			0.7
Total	135,502,200			
Benefits to Maryland Residents				
below $3,000	None	6,802,055	None	43.1
3,000–3,999		2,891,297		15.8
4,000–5,999		7,752,999		10.8
6,000–7,499		11,621,748		10.2
7,500–9,999		26,351,689		8.4
10,000–14,999		65,486,097		6.3
15,000–24,999		81,894,023		4.3
25,000 and above		31,399,606		1.9
Total		234,199,514		

Benefits to Virginia Residents	None	None	
below $3,000		4,522,763	42.4
3,000–3,999		1,565,558	12.2
4,000–5,999		4,787,726	9.4
6,000–7,499		6,882,002	9.4
7,500–9,999		14,687,276	7.6
10,000–14,999		34,614,152	5.6
15,000–24,999		47,650,558	3.6
25,000 and above		16,611,436	1.5
Total		131,321,471	

Table 5-3
Distribution of Elementary and Secondary Education Benefits by Income Class and by Jurisdiction: Welfare Basis

Income Class*	From D.C. Expenditures	From Maryland Expenditures	From Virginia Expenditures	Total	Total Benefits as a Percentage of Money Income
Benefits to D.C. Residents					
below $3,000	7,673,431	—	—	7,673,431	29.8
3,000–3,999	3,621,049	—	—	3,621,049	14.4
4,000–5,999	10,414,472	273,552	155,115	10,843,139	11.1
6,000–7,499	9,141,770	553,389	313,795	10,008,954	8.8
7,500–9,999	16,129,244	1,051,986	596,521	17,777,751	8.2
10,000–14,999	30,032,317	2,246,400	1,273,803	33,552,520	7.2
15,000–24,999	22,262,697	2,718,184	1,541,324	26,522,205	4.7
25,000 and above	16,536,782	2,883,624	1,635,135	21,055,541	3.5
Total	115,811,762	9,727,135	5,515,693	131,054,590	
Benefits to Maryland Residents					
below $3,000	—	2,327,970	—	2,327,970	14.8
3,000–3,999	—	1,156,109	—	1,156,109	6.3
4,000–5,999	163,328	2,705,387	121,748	2,990,463	4.2
6,000–7,499	420,870	4,246,425	313,449	4,980,744	4.4
7,500–9,999	1,161,060	12,147,402	864,243	14,172,705	4.5
10,000–14,999	3,827,211	42,649,438	2,848,496	49,325,145	4.8
15,000–24,999	6,973,691	81,100,773	5,186,981	93,261,445	5.0
25,000 and above	6,142,766	65,582,235	4,577,212	76,302,213	4.6
Total	18,688,926	211,915,739	13,912,129	244,516,794	

Benefits to Virginia Residents					
below $3,000	—	—	1,560,816	1,560,816	14.7
3,000–3,999	—	—	635,534	635,534	5.0
4,000–5,999	115,063	151,247	1,667,215	1,933,525	3.8
6,000–7,499	271,828	356,930	2,481,226	3,109,984	4.2
7,500–9,999	715,092	938,805	6,612,462	8,266,359	4.3
10,000–14,999	2,263,043	2,970,245	21,523,474	26,756,762	4.4
15,000–24,999	4,940,005	6,483,844	45,900,029	57,323,878	4.3
25,000 and above	4,207,924	5,523,144	33,970,395	43,701,463	3.8
Total	12,512,955	16,424,215	114,351,151	143,288,321	

*Includes source-of-income benefits for income classes below $5,000.

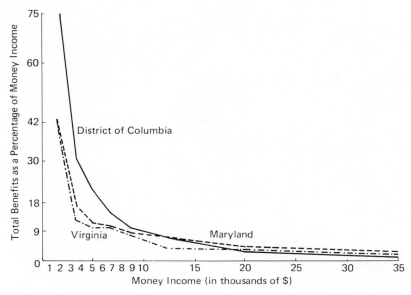

Figure 5-1. Total Elementary and Secondary Education Benefits as a Percentage of Money Income by Income Class and by Jurisdiction: Cost-of-Service Basis.

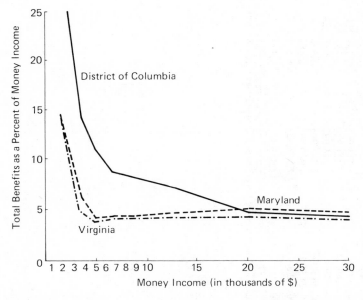

Figure 5-2. Total Elementary and Secondary Education Benefits as a Percentage of Money Income by Income Class and by Jurisdiction: Welfare Basis.

redistributive. This means that lower income college students must receive in-kind source-of-income transfers equal in value to 25 percent of higher educational expenditures.

Distribution of Benefits

Since members of one jurisdiction may attend higher educational institutions in other jurisdictions and since tuition payments do not cover the full costs, higher educational expenditures generate private benefit flows to non-residents. Thus the cost-of-service estimates of the benefits from higher educational expenditures, as shown in table 5–4 and figure 5–3, indicate some inter-jurisdictional flows, in contrast with the cost-of-service estimates for elementary and secondary educational benefits (see Appendixes B.3 and B.4). Since the public higher educational institutions in the city are frequented exclusively by those in lower-income classes, the benefit incidence of the District of Columbia expenditures is extremely progressive. A somewhat less progressive incidence pattern exists for benefits from suburban expenditures. Benefits received by those in the $7,500 and over income classes are higher in Maryland than in Virginia. This reflects the fact that the major state university is within commuting distance of many suburban Maryland residents.

Higher educational benefits estimated on a welfare basis are shown in table 5–5 and figure 5–4. These estimates allow for redistributive public benefits and source-of-income, in-kind transfers, as well as the adjustment for the greater effective demand of the higher income recipients of the benefits. The benefits are still generally progressive above the $3,000 level, but they become slightly regressive or "pro-rich" above the $15,000 level in Maryland. As in the case of elementary and secondary education, the shift from the cost-of-service to the welfare basis does not dramatically shift the absolute level of benefits attributed to the suburbs in contrast with the city. The principal difference between the two measures lies in the estimated benefit incidence by income class.

Police and Fire Protection

The benefits from protective services have generally been assumed to accrue either in proportion to income or property ownership or equally to everyone and so to be distributed on a per capita basis. Gillespie, for example, argues that expenditures for fire services are made to protect property, and that benefits therefore should be allocated to individuals and businesses in proportion to the value of their property that is protected.[10] Consequently benefits to individuals are distributed among income groups according to a weighted average of homeowners and renters. Benefits to business firms, on the other hand, are

Table 5-4
Distribution of Higher Education Benefits by Income Class and by Jurisdiction: Cost-of-Service Basis

Income Class	From D.C. Expenditures	From Maryland Expenditures	From Virginia Expenditures	Total	Total Benefits as a Percentage of Money Income
Benefits to D.C. Residents					
below $3,000	—	22,246	12,426	34,672	0.1
3,000–3,999	1,644,752	9,562	14,911	1,669,225	6.6
4,000–5,999	4,443,744	42,444	29,822	4,516,010	4.6
6,000–7,499	3,842,283	69,959	29,822	3,942,064	3.5
7,500–9,999	5,650,270	173,969	37,278	5,861,517	2.7
10,000–14,999	—	196,216	64,615	260,831	0.1
15,000–24,999	—	286,371	40,597	326,968	0.1
25,000 and above	—	174,945	19,048	193,993	0.1
Total	15,581,049	975,712	248,519	16,805,280	
Benefits to Maryland Residents					
below $3,000	—	997,892	30,038	1,027,930	6.5
3,000–3,999	20,547	428,919	36,045	485,511	2.7
4,000–5,999	55,862	1,903,873	72,090	2,031,825	2.8
6,000–7,499	66,178	3,138,108	72,090	3,276,376	2.9
7,500–9,999	141,147	7,803,691	90,112	8,034,950	2.6
10,000–14,999	—	8,801,583	156,195	8,957,778	0.9
15,000–24,999	—	12,841,672	103,986	12,945,658	0.7
25,000 and above	—	7,847,458	40,194	7,887,652	0.5
Total	283,734	43,763,196	600,750	44,647,680	

Benefits to Virginia Residents				
below $3,000	—	11,692	826,682	838,374	7.9
3,000–3,999	5,223	5,026	992,018	1,002,267	7.8
4,000–5,999	14,358	22,307	1,984,036	2,020,701	4.0
6,000–7,499	15,509	36,769	1,984,036	2,036,314	2.8
7,500–9,999	31,559	91,435	2,480,045	2,603,039	1.3
10,000–14,999	—	103,127	4,298,745	4,401,872	0.7
15,000–24,999	—	150,511	2,832,062	2,982,573	0.2
25,000 and above	—	91,947	1,136,009	1,227,956	0.1
Total	66,649	512,814	16,533,633	17,113,096	

Table 5-5
Distribution of Higher Education Benefits by Income Class and by Jurisdiction: Welfare Basis

Income Class*	From D.C. Expenditures	From Maryland Expenditures	From Virginia Expenditures	Total	Total Benefits as a Percentage of Money Income
Benefits to D.C. Residents					
below $3,000	—	6,877	4,182	11,059	0.1
3,000–3,999	1,044,510	3,708	6,733	1,054,951	4.2
4,000–5,999	3,459,394	18,430	18,163	3,495,987	3.6
6,000–7,499	3,817,145	32,338	24,872	3,874,355	3.4
7,500–9,999	7,270,946	93,728	42,597	7,407,271	3.4
10,000–14,999	42,668	158,259	99,515	300,442	0.1
15,000–24,999	51,628	336,521	107,714	495,863	0.1
25,000 and above	54,771	441,158	112,316	608,245	0.1
Total	15,741,062	1,091,019	416,092	17,248,173	
Benefits to Maryland Residents					
below $3,000	—	308,475	10,108	318,583	2.0
3,000–3,999	13,009	166,395	16,275	195,679	1.1
4,000–5,999	46,678	652,865	36,038	735,581	1.0
6,000–7,499	75,775	1,132,887	47,041	1,255,703	1.1
7,500–9,999	209,293	3,606,636	85,990	3,901,919	1.2
10,000–14,999	95,412	5,845,788	233,778	6,174,978	0.6
15,000–24,999	173,745	13,619,048	312,319	14,105,112	0.7
25,000 and above	153,269	18,851,131	274,992	19,279,392	1.2
Total	767,181	44,183,225	1,016,541	45,966,947	

Benefits to Virginia Residents				
below $3,000	—	3,682	278,107	281,789	2.6
3,000–3,999	3,306	1,950	446,623	451,879	3.5
4,000–5,999	13,767	9,574	888,924	912,265	1.8
6,000–7,499	22,074	17,861	1,047,047	1,086,982	1.5
7,500–9,999	58,155	54,313	1,683,119	1,795,587	0.9
10,000–14,999	56,416	106,601	4,179,192	4,342,209	0.7
15,000–24,999	123,153	243,035	4,461,815	4,828,003	0.4
25,000 and above	104,905	276,416	3,781,362	4,162,683	0.4
Total	381,776	713,432	16,766,189	17,861,397.	

*Includes source-of-income benefits for income classes below $5,000.

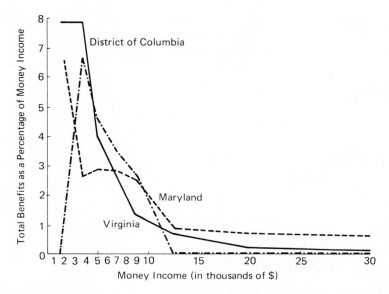

Figure 5–3. Total Higher Education Benefits as a Percentage of Money Income by Income Class and by Jurisdiction: Cost-of-Service Basis.

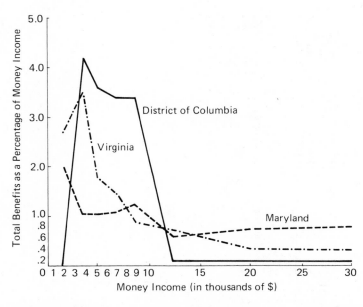

Figure 5–4. Total Higher Education Benefits as a Percentage of Money Income by Income Class and by Jurisdiction: Welfare Basis.

distributed on the basis of consumption, under the assumption that benefits are passed forward to consumers in the form of lower prices.

Eapen and Eapen, however, contend that fire protection services "are purely social goods which are jointly consumed and, by their nature, are available for consumption by all to the exclusion of no one."[11] In practice they allocate benefits from protective services to individuals in three ways: per capita, proportional to income, and one-half of the benefits on a per capita basis and one-half proportional to income. Whereas most studies employ identical assumptions to distribute benefits from both police and fire services, Gillespie assigns fire protection benefits directly to property and police protection benefits to people.

These various allocation procedures are subject to a number of criticisms. Thus if we believe that the objective of police expenditures is the prevention of crime, that police resources are allocated among areas in proportion to crime rates, and that crime rates are distributed among areas in proportion solely to the income, property or population of an area, then we may question the appropriateness of allocating police benefits according to only one or other of these measures. Even though Gillespie's contention that benefits from fire protection accrue directly to property may be plausible, his assumption that the full value of these benefits is passed forward to users of the property is open to question. Previous attempts to measure benefits from protection services have uniformly assumed that benefits from protective services are entirely appropriated by residents of the jurisdiction providing the service. This assumption is inappropriate for a metropolitan area in which substantial numbers of non-residents own property, and move across jurisdictional lines for work, shopping, and recreation.

Distribution of Benefits

We will distribute the benefits of police expenditures directly to individuals rather than property on the grounds that it is the subjective feeling of increased safety that is the most immediate benefit of police protection. Attributing benefits to individuals in proportion to the number of hours spent in a jurisdiction means that considerable benefits are attributed to nonresidents. When benefits are adjusted to a welfare basis allowance is made for the greater effective demand for police protection on the part of those with higher income[e] (see Appendix B.5).

Fire departments conceive of their objective as the "protection of life and property." In fact these two goals are so intimately intertwined that it is difficult

---

[e]Traffic-related police expenditures are considered under the transportation expenditure category and outlays for police services associated with the presence of the federal government are assumed shifted to the nation as a whole (see Appendix B.6).

to determine with any precision what portion of a department's total resources are devoted to the protection of individuals as opposed to property. However, since the benefits of superior fire protection are likely to be reflected largely in lower fire insurance premiums in the area and hence higher rental values and higher property values, we will assume that 90 percent of the benefits from fire protection services accrue to property and 10 percent to individuals.[f] Benefits attributed to individuals are initially determined by the number of hours spent in a jurisdiction. The allocation of benefits directly provided to property is a bit more complicated. First an estimate is made of the proportion of these benefits accruing to commercial as opposed to residential property. These benefits are then treated as a negative property tax on improvements.[g] Essentially, since we assume that fire service protects capital improvements rather than land 75 percent of the benefits are shifted forward to users of the commodities produced with the property and 25 percent is shifted backward to those owning the property. Allowance is made for the fire protection benefits provided federal government property both in the city and suburbs (see Appendix B.7).

The combined benefits from police and fire expenditures measured on a cost-of-service basis are displayed in table 5–6 and figure 5–5. The incidence of protective service benefits are progressive both in the District of Columbia and the suburban area. The absolute level of benefits is considerably higher in the District of Columbia, at least partially because it alone relies exclusively on public fire protection services, whereas volunteer fire departments are extensively employed both in Maryland and in Virginia.

The incidence evidence of the protective services, estimated on a welfare basis, is considerably less progressive, as can be seen in table 5–7 and figure 5–6. In fact, above the very lowest income classes the incidence pattern is more or less proportional for all these areas. While the incidence for Virginia residents remains somewhat regressive, the curve relating the effective benefit rate to income in Maryland becomes U-shaped indicating progressivity between the lowest- and middle-income classes but regressivity above the $15,000 level. As can be seen from both tables 5–6 and 5–7 there is a considerable interjurisdictional benefit flow.

Health Services

Expenditures for health services include outlays for both community health facilities as well as for general and mental hospitals. Previous benefit incidence studies have typically divided health expenditures into two categories, public health and hospital, and assumed that the former generated public benefits and

---

[f]At least on the welfare basis, neither the size of the interjurisdictional tax flows nor the incidence of the benefits by income class is very sensitive to the assumption about what proportion of the benefits go to property.

[g]For a detailed discussion of the incidence assumptions used for the positive property tax, see Chapter 6.

the latter private benefits. Indeed notable federal public health outlays are designed to control communicable diseases through research and programmatic efforts. Local public health agencies, however, do not typically support research efforts; and even though they do conduct tuberculosis control programs, much of their effort is directed toward the detection of such pathologies as hypertension, cancer, and glaucoma. They also provide services, such as tetanus shots and pre-natal care, which do not involve the typical public health externalities associated with controlling contagion. Consequently, we will assume that public health expenditures generate use-of-income, private benefits for the direct beneficiaries of the services, if they have an income of $5,000 or more. Further, since such programs are often designed to provide in-kind transfers to low-income individuals we will assume that services provided to those with less than $5,000 income generate public redistributive benefits for those with higher income.[12] We will also allocate source-of-income benefits equal to the value of the in-kind transfers to the lower income individuals.

Hospital expenditures by the state and local governments in the Washington area will be assumed to generate private benefits for direct recipients of hospitalization who have $5,000 and over income. Such services provided to the poor will be allocated to them as source-of-income transfers and to those with $5,000 and over income as public redistributive benefits [13] (see Appendix B.8).

Distribution of Benefits

Benefits from all health services measured on a cost-of-service basis and allocated by income class and geographical area, are shown in table 5-8 and figure 5-7. The incidence is sharply progressive even though there is a substantial use of these health services by the nonpoor. The level of public-health-care service provided in the District of Columbia is considerably higher than in the suburban areas.

Benefits from health services estimated on the welfare basis are shown in table 5-9 and figure 5-8. The benefits are progressive over all income classes, except at very high income levels where the incidence is proportional with a hint of regressivity in the District for the $25,000 and over income class. Even with the assumption that health services generate public redistributive benefits to the nonpoor across the metropolitan area, the total benefits received from public health services is higher in the District of Columbia than in the suburban areas.

Welfare Services

Welfare service expenditures encompass all locally financed public assistance payments as well as outlays for facilities to care for the indigent aged, abandoned children, and problem children, including the administrative costs of these pro-

Table 5-6
Distribution of Police and Fire Benefits by Income Class and by Jurisdiction: Cost-of-Service-Basis

Income Class	From D.C. Expenditures	From Maryland Expenditures	From Virginia Expenditures	Total	Total Benefits as a Percentage of Money Income
Benefits to D.C. Residents					
below $3,000	17,161,621	36,281	57,772	17,255,674	16.7
3,000–3,999	4,342,610	17,161	15,364	4,375,135	6.7
4,000–5,999	9,869,236	54,732	37,075	9,961,043	4.5
6,000–7,499	7,701,388	55,298	30,935	7,787,621	3.3
7,500–9,999	10,089,876	89,919	42,169	10,221,964	2.6
10,000–14,999	11,856,690	141,804	53,262	12,051,756	1.9
15,000–24,999	8,555,612	161,969	56,812	8,774,393	1.3
25,000 and above	4,059,432	154,134	46,212	4,259,778	0.6
Total	73,636,465	711,298	339,601	74,687,364	
Benefits to Maryland Residents					
below $3,000	780,992	1,175,370	77,697	2,034,059	3.3
3,000–3,999	214,333	410,227	21,480	646,040	1.5
4,000–5,999	478,329	1,048,528	48,820	1,575,677	1.2
6,000–7,499	477,814	1,199,964	49,378	1,727,156	1.0
7,500–9,999	896,524	2,546,304	93,803	3,536,631	0.8
10,000–14,999	1,809,417	6,368,382	193,433	8,371,232	0.7
15,000–24,999	2,155,624	9,532,413	262,196	11,950,233	0.6
25,000 and above	1,049,915	6,966,473	158,863	8,175,251	0.5
Total	7,862,948	29,247,661	905,670	38,016,279	

Benefits to Virginia Residents					
below $3,000	345,008	10,161	2,028,437	2,383,606	5.6
3,000–3,999	117,939	5,495	679,778	803,212	2.4
4,000–5,999	280,796	17,087	1,586,126	1,884,009	1.6
6,000–7,499	273,112	20,468	1,526,305	1,819,885	1.3
7,500–9,999	459,358	41,510	2,532,909	3,033,777	1.0
10,000–14,999	816,704	95,882	4,520,260	5,432,846	0.7
15,000–24,999	1,157,024	199,352	5,696,024	7,052,400	0.5
25,000 and above	607,805	165,066	2,368,067	3,140,938	0.3
Total	4,057,746	555,021	20,937,906	25,550,673	

Table 5-7
Distribution of Police and Fire Benefits by Income Class and by Jurisdiction: Welfare Basis

Income Class	From D.C. Expenditures	From Maryland Expenditures	From Virginia Expenditures	Total	Total Benefits as a Percentage of Money Income
Benefits to D.C. Residents					
below $3,000	4,121,104	10,700	14,846	4,146,650	4.0
3,000–3,999	1,961,244	5,347	6,222	1,972,813	3.0
4,000–5,999	5,602,916	19,266	18,956	5,641,138	2.5
6,000–7,499	5,580,189	22,801	19,265	5,622,255	2.4
7,500–9,999	8,921,293	42,428	30,310	8,994,031	2.3
10,000–14,999	14,071,278	85,109	47,050	14,203,437	2.2
15,000–24,999	14,960,821	138,682	58,137	15,157,640	2.2
25,000 and above	13,924,445	253,216	37,926	14,215,587	2.1
Total	69,143,290	577,549	232,712	69,953,551	
Benefits to Maryland Residents					
below $3,000	140,383	444,897	11,387	596,667	1.0
3,000–3,999	80,658	187,130	16,037	283,825	0.7
4,000–5,999	250,042	535,964	11,707	797,713	0.6
6,000–7,499	330,368	680,427	27,718	1,038,513	0.6
7,500–9,999	772,590	1,429,372	62,377	2,264,339	0.5
10,000–14,999	2,126,146	4,428,990	169,748	6,724,884	0.6
15,000–24,999	3,627,953	9,062,849	304,682	12,995,484	0.7
25,000 and above	3,084,064	12,829,376	261,820	16,175,260	0.9
Total	10,412,204	29,599,005	865,476	40,876,685	

Benefits to
Virginia Residents

below $3,000	67,030	3,885	510,685	581,600	1.4
3,000–3,999	46,164	2,112	253,830	302,106	0.9
4,000–5,999	149,913	7,219	747,837	904,969	0.8
6,000–7,499	191,247	9,724	909,618	1,110,589	0.8
7,500–9,999	396,482	21,752	1,748,717	2,166,951	0.7
10,000–14,999	947,841	60,989	4,291,531	5,300,361	0.7
15,000–24,999	1,859,903	170,103	7,390,741	9,420,747	0.7
25,000 and above	1,506,592	238,744	5,217,772	6,963,108	0.6
Total	5,165,172	514,528	21,070,731	26,750,431	

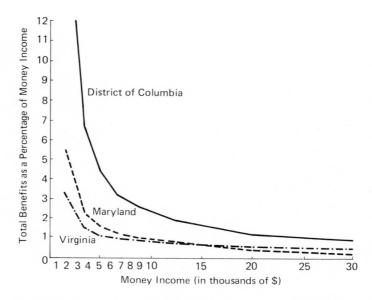

Figure 5-5. Total Police and Fire Benefits as a Percentage of Money Income by Income Class and by Jurisdiction: Cost-of-Service Basis.

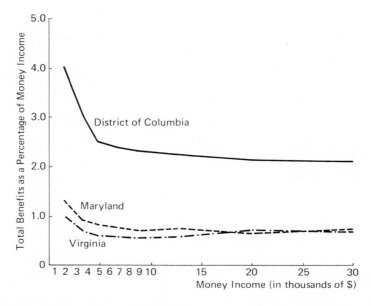

Figure 5-6. Total Police and Fire Benefits as a Percentage of Money Income by Income Class and by Jurisdiction: Welfare Basis.

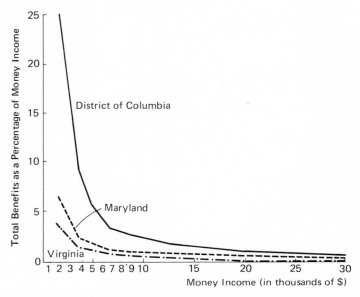

Figure 5-7. Total Health Service Benefits as a Percentage of Money Income by Income Class and by Jurisdiction: Cost-of-Service Basis.

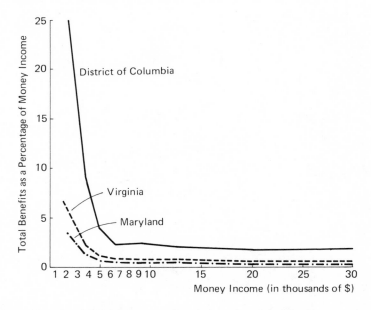

Figure 5-8. Total Health Service Benefits as a Percentage of Money Income by Income Class and by Jurisdiction: Welfare Basis.

Table 5-8
Distribution of Health Service Benefits by Income Class and by Jurisdiction: Cost-of-Service Basis

Income Class	From D.C. Expenditures	From Maryland Expenditures	From Virginia Expenditures	Total Benefits as a Percentage of Money Income
Benefits to D.C. Residents		None	None	
below $3,000	26,584,479			25.7
3,000–3,999	5,934,144			9.0
4,000–5,999	11,863,716			5.3
6,000–7,499	8,387,001			3.6
7,500–9,999	10,962,887			2.8
10,000–14,999	10,380,302			1.6
15,000–24,999	5,778,578			0.8
25,000 and above	2,795,493			0.4
Total	82,686,600			
Benefits to Maryland Residents	None		None	
below $3,000		4,055,903		6.6
3,000–3,999		984,002		2.3
4,000–5,999		1,881,045		1.4
6,000–7,499		1,667,632		0.9
7,500–9,999		3,094,718		0.7
10,000–14,999		5,062,352		0.4
15,000–24,999		4,482,780		0.2
25,000 and above		1,985,473		0.1
Total		23,213,905		

Benefits to Virginia Residents	None	None		
below $3,000			1,615,449	3.8
3,000–3,999			498,427	1.5
4,000–5,999			1,011,202	0.9
6,000–7,499			874,111	0.6
7,500–9,999			1,456,090	0.5
10,000–14,999			2,095,876	0.3
15,000–24,999			2,062,394	0.1
25,000 and above			876,152	0.1
Total			10,489,701	

Table 5-9
Distribution of Health Service Benefits by Income Class and by Jurisdiction: Welfare Basis

Income Class*	From D.C. Expenditures	From Maryland Expenditures	From Virginia Expenditures	Total	Total Benefits as a Percentage of Money Income
Benefits to D.C. Residents					
below $3,000	26,584,479	—	—	26,584,479	25.7
3,000–3,999	5,934,144	—	—	5,934,144	9.0
4,000–5,999	8,820,654	62,733	26,873	8,910,260	4.0
6,000–7,499	5,288,428	115,528	49,488	5,453,444	2.3
7,500–9,999	8,925,257	193,547	82,908	9,201,712	2.3
10,000–14,999	12,404,168	314,676	134,795	12,853,639	2.0
15,000–24,999	11,480,926	344,744	147,688	11,973,358	1.7
25,000 and above	11,951,344	330,484	141,554	12,423,382	1.9
Total	91,389,400	1,361,712	583,306	93,334,418	
Benefits to Maryland Residents					
below $3,000	—	4,055,903	—	4,055,903	6.6
3,000–3,999	—	984,002	—	984,002	2.3
4,000–5,999	250,120	1,212,878	16,765	1,479,763	1.1
6,000–7,499	554,442	772,277	37,163	1,363,882	0.8
7,500–9,999	1,319,573	1,850,979	88,447	3,258,999	0.8
10,000–14,999	3,672,565	4,415,215	246,162	8,333,942	0.7
15,000–24,999	6,196,940	6,423,024	415,365	13,035,329	0.7
25,000 and above	5,341,443	6,131,000	358,022	11,830,465	0.7
Total	17,335,083	25,845,278	1,161,924	44,342,285	

Benefits to
Virginia Residents

below $3,000	—	—	1,615,449	1,615,449	3.8
3,000–3,999	—	—	498,427	498,427	1.5
4,000–5,999	217,789	34,078	657,098	908,965	0.8
6,000–7,499	455,307	71,244	401,968	928,519	0.6
7,500–9,999	966,049	151,161	864,612	1,981,822	0.6
10,000–14,999	2,343,380	366,677	1,800,762	4,510,819	0.6
15,000–24,999	4,514,285	706,367	2,896,172	8,116,824	0.6
25,000 and above	3,685,632	576,705	2,571,751	6,834,088	0.6
Total	12,182,442	1,906,232	11,306,239	25,394,913	

*Includes source-of-income benefits for income classes below $5,000.

grams. Benefit incidence studies have uniformly assigned all benefits from these programs, including administrative costs, to direct program recipients.

Distribution of Benefits

Benefits from welfare service expenditures, estimated on a cost-of-service basis, which attribute benefits from all expenditures including administrative costs to the program recipients, are shown in table 5-10 and figure 5-9 (see Appendix B.9). Even though the benefit incidence is highly progressive, notable benefits are received by higher income classes.[h]

Benefits from welfare service expenditures allocated on the assumption that they are use-of-income public redistributive benefits to the nonpoor and source-of-income transfers to the poor are shown in table 5-11 and figure 5-10. The use-of-income benefits shown in table 5-11 equal total expenditures, or the total cost-of-service estimate of benefits, as shown in table 5-10. Because of the relative concentration of the poor population of the metropolitan area in the District a considerable shift of benefits from the District to the suburban areas occurs as we move from a procedure which allocates cost-of-service benefits to program recipients to a procedure which assumes that welfare services generate redistributive public benefits for the whole metropolitan area. Whereas total cost-of-service benefits received by the District are $57.4 million, with $8.0 and $4.8 million for suburban Maryland and Virginia, respectively, total use-of-income benefits from these same programs are only $16.0 million for the District and $31.9 and $22.4 million for suburban Maryland and Virginia, respectively. Further, instead of the preponderance of benefits being concentrated in the lowest income classes, as they are under the cost-of-service estimates, the welfare based measures attribute significant amounts to the higher-income classes.

Other Government Services

A brief discussion follows of the methods employed to allocate the benefits from the remaining state and local government expenditures in the Washington metropolitan area, as shown in tables 5-12 through 5-15 and figures 5-11 and 5-12.

Libraries

The benefits from public library services are assumed to be private, public nonredistributive, and public distributive in the same proportion as benefits from elementary and secondary education, as shown in table 5-1 (see Appendix B.10).

---

[h]Our definition of income on an annual basis makes it possible for a household unit to be recorded as nonpoor on an annual basis, but yet be eligible for welfare payments during part of a year.

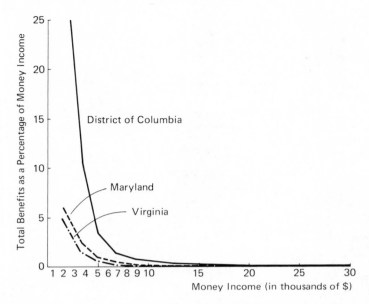

Figure 5-9. Total Welfare Service Benefits as a Percentage of Money Income by Income Class and by Jurisdiction: Cost-of-Service Basis.

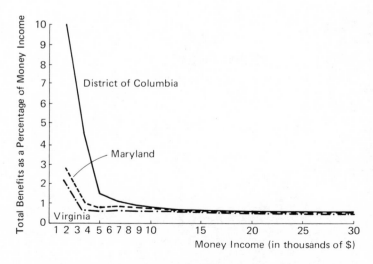

Figure 5-10. Total Welfare Service Benefits as a Percentage of Money Income by Income Class and by Jurisdiction: Welfare Basis.

Table 5-10
Distribution of Welfare Benefits by Income Class and by Jurisdiction: Cost-of-Service Basis

Income Class	From D.C. Expenditures	From Maryland Expenditures	From Virginia Expenditures	Total Benefits as a Percentage of Money Income
Benefits to D.C. Residents				
below $3,000	34,254,431	None	None	33.6
3,000–3,999	7,218,410			11.0
4,000–5,999	7,539,994			3.4
6,000–7,499	3,215,839			1.6
7,500–9,999	2,446,335			0.6
10,000–14,999	1,280,593			0.2
15,000–24,999	1,050,890			0.1
25,000 and above	419,208			0.0*
Total	57,425,700			
Benefits to Maryland Residents				
below $3,000	None	3,665,768	None	6.0
3,000–3,999		910,682		2.1
4,000–5,999		944,601		0.7
6,000–7,499		571,101		0.3
7,500–9,999		608,400		0.1
10,000–14,999		516,674		0.0*
15,000–24,999		621,055		0.0*
25,000 and above		195,302		0.0*
Total		8,033,583		

Benefits to Virginia Residents	None	None		
below $3,000			2,095,320	4.9
3,000–3,999			565,866	1.7
4,000–5,999			609,935	0.5
6,000–7,499			332,537	0.2
7,500–9,999			349,475	0.1
10,000–14,999			295,056	0.0*
15,000–24,999			452,168	0.0*
25,000 and above			151,741	0.0*
Total			4,852,098	

*Less than 0.05 percent.

Table 5-11
Distribution of Welfare Service Benefits by Income Class and by Jurisdiction: Welfare Basis

Income Class	From Use-of-Income Metropolitan-Wide Benefits	From Source-of-Income Local Benefits	Total Source Plus Use-of-Income Benefits	Total Benefits as a Percentage of Money Income
Benefits to D.C. Residents				
below $3,000	—	10,935,755	10,935,755	10.6
3,000–3,999	—	2,304,483	2,304,483	3.5
4,000–5,999	737,507	2,407,149	3,144,656	1.4
6,000–7,499	1,358,213	1,026,659	2,384,872	1.0
7,500–9,999	2,275,491	780,994	3,056,485	0.8
10,000–14,999	3,699,583	408,830	4,108,413	0.6
15,000–24,999	4,053,455	335,498	4,388,953	0.6
25,000 and above	3,885,067	133,832	4,018,899	0.6
Total	16,009,316	18,333,200	34,342,516	
Benefits to Maryland Residents				
below $3,000	—	1,729,658	1,729,658	2.8
3,000–3,999	—	431,092	431,092	1.0
4,000–5,999	460,120	449,408	909,528	0.7
6,000–7,499	1,019,944	272,381	1,292,325	0.7
7,500–9,999	2,427,509	289,775	2,717,284	0.6
10,000–14,999	6,756,336	244,103	7,000,439	0.6
15,000–24,999	11,400,269	286,540	11,686,809	0.6
25,000 and above	9,826,483	86,344	9,912,827	0.6
Total	31,890,661	3,789,301	35,679,962	

Benefits to
Virginia Residents

below $3,000	—	857,927	857,927	2.0
3,000–3,999	—	231,684	231,684	0.7
4,000–5,999	400,639	247,670	648,309	0.6
6,000–7,499	837,560	135,113	972,673	0.7
7,500–9,999	1,777,191	142,068	1,919,259	0.6
10,000–14,999	4,310,943	119,117	4,430,060	0.6
15,000–24,999	8,304,804	181,778	8,486,582	0.6
25,000 and above	6,780,267	61,190	6,841,457	0.6
Total	22,411,404	1,976,547	24,387,951	

Table 5-12

Distribution of Benefits from "All Other" Expenditures by Category and by Jurisdiction: Cost-of-Service Basis

Expenditure Category	From D.C. Expenditures	From Maryland Expenditures	From Virginia Expenditures
Benefits to D.C. Residents			
Library	5,108,500	–	–
Recreation and Parks	14,575,815	482,035	98,218
Transportation	10,781,745	2,871,280	595,293
Corrections	14,939,752	190,622	44,905
Courts	15,502,700	–	–
Refuse	18,939,200	–	–
General Government	32,368,393	417,878	145,317
Total	112,216,105	3,961,815	883,733
Benefits to Maryland Residents			
Library	304,100	5,428,449	–
Recreation and Parks	1,363,219	9,181,762	126,591
Transportation	5,677,221	24,710,313	2,705,387
Corrections	1,726,714	6,680,410	143,071
Courts	–	4,106,789	–
Refuse	–	3,118,993	–
General Government	1,253,299	31,290,301	490,927
Total	10,324,553	84,517,017	3,465,976
Benefits to Virginia Residents			
Library	130,000	–	4,431,866
Recreation and Parks	1,670,422	436,391	4,810,978
Transportation	2,124,382	4,567,225	11,510,892
Corrections	826,619	125,883	3,119,705
Courts	–	–	2,386,691
Refuse	–	–	3,860,231
General Government	646,074	495,078	23,470,820
Total	5,397,497	5,624,577	53,591,183

Recreation and Parks

Even though the option value from maintaining open space in the form of public parks may be significant in some instances and thus constitute public nonredistributive benefits, we assume that such is not the case generally for state and local parks in the Washington area.[14] However, since an express goal of most recreation and park programs is to provide services to low-income families,

Table 5–13

Distribution of Benefits from "All Other" Expenditures by Category and by Jurisdiction: Welfare Basis

Expenditure Category	From D.C. Expenditures	From Maryland Expenditures	From Virginia Expenditures
Benefits to D.C. Residents			
Library	4,295,592	214,761	176,479
Recreation and Parks	14,553,869	567,188	157,412
Transportation	11,121,758	2,322,186	502,334
Corrections	13,777,711	154,117	24,961
Courts	15,502,700	–	–
Refuse	18,939,200	–	–
General Government	24,082,326	1,419,946	952,146
Total	102,273,156	4,678,198	1,813,332
Benefits to Maryland Residents			
Library	842,624	4,882,194	445,131
Recreation and Parks	2,612,292	9,558,538	310,119
Transportation	5,675,314	25,507,995	2,823,368
Corrections	2,466,997	6,823,104	147,090
Courts	–	4,106,789	–
Refuse	–	3,118,913	–
General Government	6,168,672	28,617,075	2,503,083
Total	17,765,899	82,614,608	6,228,791
Benefits to Virginia Residents			
Library	510,701	362,624	3,840,833
Recreation and Parks	2,514,565	690,095	4,952,514
Transportation	2,092,863	4,649,556	11,930,321
Corrections	1,161,490	122,467	3,171,130
Courts	–	–	2,386,691
Refuse	–	–	3,860,231
General Government	3,981,819	2,229,274	20,716,798
Total	10,261,438	8,054,016	50,858,518

we allow for the generation of public redistributive benefits from these outlays. We assume that 60 percent of the use-of-income benefits are private benefits appropriated by direct users of the facilities and 40 percent are public redistributive benefits received by the nonpoor of the metropolitan area. Source-of-income transfers, equal in value to the public redistributive benefits, are allocated to those with less than $5,000 income who use the facilities (see Appendix B.11).

Table 5-14
Distribution of Benefits From "All Other" Expenditures by Income Class and by Jurisdiction: Cost-of-Service Basis

Income Class	From D.C. Expenditures	From Maryland Expenditures	From Virginia Expenditures	Total	Total Benefits as a Percentage of Money Income
Benefits to D.C. Residents					
below $3,000	21,637,165	404,455	91,760	22,133,380	21.4
3,000–3,999	6,386,207	151,176	34,859	6,572,242	10.0
4,000–5,999	15,152,164	457,251	101,801	15,711,216	7.0
6,000–7,499	12,300,817	439,626	96,702	12,837,145	5.5
7,500–9,999	19,602,693	737,758	159,598	20,500,049	5.2
10,000–14,999	18,101,445	761,806	170,257	19,033,508	3.0
15,000–24,999	12,800,228	667,243	147,537	13,615,008	1.9
25,000 and above	6,235,386	342,500	81,219	6,659,105	1.0
Total	112,216,105	3,961,815	883,733	117,061,653	
Benefits to Maryland Residents					
below $3,000	584,930	4,511,989	139,575	5,236,494	8.6
3,000–3,999	214,635	1,642,898	56,763	1,914,296	4.5
4,000–5,999	581,975	4,317,275	165,079	5,064,329	3.8
6,000–7,499	676,963	5,227,416	198,907	6,103,286	3.5
7,500–9,999	1,674,829	12,921,466	438,119	15,034,414	3.6
10,000–14,999	2,411,170	20,090,405	851,000	23,352,575	2.0
15,000–24,999	2,939,578	24,918,517	1,140,451	28,998,546	1.5
25,000 and above	1,240,473	10,887,051	476,082	12,603,606	0.7
Total	10,324,553	84,517,017	3,465,976	98,307,546	

Benefits to
Virginia Residents

below $3,000	336,806	203,150	3,012,801	3,552,757	8.3
3,000–3,999	150,402	99,540	1,245,737	1,495,679	4.4
4,000–5,999	416,917	316,464	3,213,845	3,947,226	3.5
6,000–7,499	453,824	372,078	3,612,174	4,438,076	3.1
7,500–9,999	1,201,036	798,085	7,777,925	9,777,046	3.2
10,000–14,999	1,049,102	1,216,941	11,963,663	14,229,706	1.9
15,000–24,999	1,233,011	1,840,092	16,094,832	19,167,935	1.3
25,000 and above	556,399	778,227	6,670,206	8,004,832	0.7
Total	5,397,497	5,624,577	53,591,183	64,613,257	

Table 5-15
Distribution of Benefits from "All Other" Expenditures by Income Class and by Jurisdiction: Welfare Basis

Income Class	From D.C. Expenditures	From Maryland Expenditures	From Virginia Expenditures	Total	Total Benefits as a Percentage of Money Income
Benefits to D.C. Residents					
below $3,000	6,368,960	98,431	28,382	6,495,773	6.3
3,000–3,999	2,038,682	56,201	15,267	2,110,150	3.2
4,000–5,999	7,054,691	241,998	84,993	7,381,682	3.3
6,000–7,499	8,024,237	319,719	124,453	8,468,409	3.6
7,500–9,999	17,124,204	668,481	241,866	18,034,551	4.6
10,000–14,999	19,700,488	946,608	396,823	21,043,919	3.3
15,000–24,999	20,842,180	1,160,591	465,495	22,468,266	3.2
25,000 and above	21,119,713	1,186,169	456,053	22,761,935	3.4
Total	102,273,155	4,678,198	1,813,332	108,764,685	
Benefits to Maryland Residents					
below $3,000	128,848	694,396	24,992	848,236	1.4
3,000–3,999	81,603	427,098	21,399	530,100	1.2
4,000–5,999	349,458	1,525,333	85,834	1,960,625	1.5
6,000–7,499	588,864	2,524,773	159,537	3,273,174	1.9
7,500–9,999	1,805,789	8,657,115	447,880	10,910,784	2.6
10,000–14,999	3,560,055	15,185,961	1,218,198	19,964,214	1.7
15,000–24,999	6,048,512	27,062,880	2,302,003	35,413,395	1.8
25,000 and above	5,202,770	26,537,132	1,968,948	33,708,850	2.0
Total	17,765,899	82,614,688	6,228,791	106,609,378	

Benefits to Virginia Residents					
below $3,000	104,354	33,600	482,611	620,565	1.4
3,000–3,999	67,592	33,505	355,178	456,275	1.3
4,000–5,999	267,330	149,658	1,228,305	1,645,293	1.4
6,000–7,499	452,168	240,409	1,815,313	2,507,890	1.7
7,500–9,999	1,429,740	671,198	5,281,455	7,382,393	2.4
10,000–14,999	1,939,038	1,386,248	9,324,655	12,649,941	1.7
15,000–24,999	3,300,233	3,025,555	17,683,861	24,009,649	1.7
25,000 and above	2,700,983	2,513,843	14,687,140	19,901,966	1.7
Total	10,261,438	8,054,016	50,858,518	69,173,972	

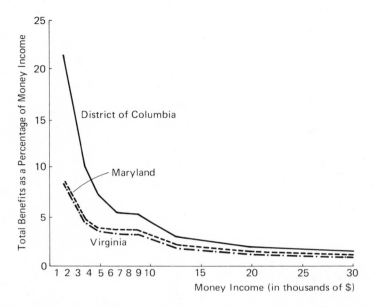

Figure 5-11. Total Benefits from "All Other" Expenditures as a Percentage of Money Income by Income Class and by Jurisdiction: Cost-of-Service Basis.

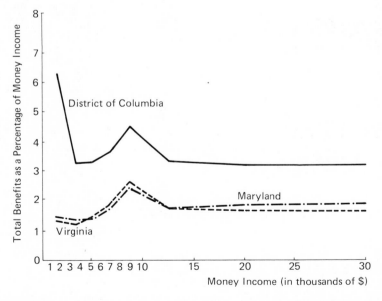

Figure 5-12. Total Benefits from "All Other" Expenditures as a Percentage of Money Income by Income Class and by Jurisdiction: Welfare Basis.

Transportation

Benefits from expenditures for road maintenance, police traffic control, and other minor transportation-related programs are assumed to be private and are allocated to commercial and noncommercial road users in proportion to vehicle miles traveled within the various jurisdictions. Benefits attributed to commercial users are treated as a subsidy to business and are assumed distributed between jurisdictions and income classes in the same proportions as business cost taxes.[i] While benefits attributed to noncommercial users are adjusted to the welfare basis by allowance for the declining marginal utility of income, benefits for commercial users are considered to be intermediate products and so always evaluated at cost (see Appendix B.12).

Corrections

While the direct users of these facilities are identifiable, it is difficult to determine who are the beneficiaries with an effective demand for these services. It has been contended that the correctional system is counterproductive since the jails may actually be "schools of crime" and thus serve to increase crime rates. However, it will be assumed here that incarceration does serve as a deterrent and also, for at least some period of time, does prevent offenders from committing additional crimes. On these premises, benefits from corrections expenditures are allocated in the same way as police expenditures, that is, according to hours spent in the jurisdiction by residents and nonresidents.

Courts

Traditionally benefits from the judicial system have been considered a pure public good—the promotion and protection of a social system ruled by law. However, there are difficulties with this assumption. The current overcrowding of court dockets indicates at least some rivalry in the consumption of this good. But if we were to treat the courts as yielding private benefits, we would be faced with the difficult task of identifying the income and residency characteristics of the beneficiaries. While it would be reasonable, for example, to assume that the beneficiaries of the family court are District of Columbia residents, the small and major claims courts handle cases involving residents of other areas. It would be reasonable to allocate benefits from the criminal courts in the same manner as benefits from police and correction services and presumably court services associated with traffic-related matters should be considered benefits to road users.

---

[i]See Chapter 6 for a discussion of business cost taxes.

In the face of the computational difficulties in making these various estimates we are assuming that court expenditures generate public nonredistributive
benefits equally to all families and unrelated individuals within the jurisdiction
making the expenditure.[j]

Refuse Collection

Public refuse collection services are treated as pure private goods and the
benefits are allocated to the users of the service. Consequently, no interjurisdictional benefit flows result from these expenditures (see Appendix B.13).

General Government

General government expenditures are assumed to provide needed support for
all the functions of government. Consequently we have assumed that benefits
from these expenditures are distributed in the same proportion as are the other
benefits from state and local expenditures in the Washington metropolitan area.

Distribution of Benefits from "All Other" Government Expenditures

The distribution of the benefits of "all other" government services by
jurisdiction is shown in tables 5-12 and 5-13. In table 5-12 the benefits are
measured on the cost-of-service basis and in table 5-13 on the welfare basis. As
can be noted from a comparison of these two tables the interjurisdictional
benefit flows are notably larger under the welfare measure than the cost-of-
service measure. Further, the welfare measure indicates a larger net flow of
benefits from the District to the suburban area, due principally to the benefits
from transportation, corrections, and recreation and park expenditures.

The benefit incidence by income class of "all other" government expenditures is shown in table 5-14 and 5-15 and figures 5-11 and 5-12 on a cost-of-
service and a welfare basis, respectively. As is generally the case with other
expenditure categories, the benefit level is uniformly higher across all income
classes in the District than in the suburban areas under both estimating procedures. The incidence pattern of the cost-of-service estimates, however, is
progressive across all income classes, whereas for the welfare estimates the pattern is more or less proportional.

---

[j]This procedure underestimates the benefits to suburbanites from the District of
Columbia since court expenditures are substantially higher in the District and because a
much larger proportion of total benefits from criminal-court and traffic-court related expenditures accrue to suburbanites from city expenditures than accrue to city residents from
suburban expenditures.

Summary of Benefits from State and Local
Expenditures in the Washington
Metropolitan Area

The benefits from all state and local government expenditures in the
Washington metropolitan area estimated under both the cost-of-service and
welfare measures and distributed by income class and jurisdiction are shown in
tables 5-16 and 5-17 and figures 5-13 and 5-14. Three observations are called for
concerning these estimates. First, the cost-of-service estimates indicate a strikingly
progressive, or pro-poor incidence, with total benefits from state and local
expenditures estimated to range from 35 percent of money income in Virginia
to 117 percent in the District of Columbia for those with income below $3,000,
as can be seen in table 5-16. This result suggests a massive redistribution through
state and local fiscs. It is consistent with many previous benefit incidence
studies that have (1) assigned benefits of welfare programs entirely to the direct
recipients, (2) assumed that there are no external benefits from such outlays as
education and parks and recreation, and (3) implicitly assumed that the marginal
utility of income is constant over all income classes.

Second, if, on the other hand, benefits are estimated in the spirit of the
analysis developed in Chapter 3, and it is assumed that externalities are generated
by some government expenditures and that citizens do derive public nonredistributive and redistributive benefits as well as private benefits from various state
and local programs and that the marginal utility of income does decline, then a
notably different incidence pattern emerges, as can be seen in table 5-17 and
figure 5-14. The benefit incidence pattern for these welfare estimates is also
progressive over the lowest income classes in all three areas, if source-of-income
transfers are considered. Over all other income classes the incidence pattern is
more or less proportional whether source-of-income transfers are included or not.
In other words, according to the welfare estimates, some redistribution does
occur, especially in favor of the very poorest, but the impact of state and local
expenditures on the nonpoor population does not in itself significantly alter
income distribution as measured by the Gini coefficient. This outcome, in contrast with the cost-of-service estimates, is what we would expect to find in the
light of the dictum that redistribution cannot be effectively carried out by local
agencies.

Third, the cost-of-service and the welfare estimates of benefit incidence
establish sensitivity limits both for the assumption concerning the marginal
utility of income as well as the assumptions underlying the classification of
benefits as private or public. Marginal utility is assumed to be constant over all
income classes for the cost-of-service estimates. This assumption can be considered the limiting case which implies the most progressive, that is, pro-poor,
benefit incidence. The assumption underlying the welfare estimates,
$MU_Y = (K/Y)$, results in a less progressive outcome than under the $MU_Y = K$
assumption, but not as regressive as would result from, say, assuming that
$MU_Y = (K/Y^2)$.

Table 5-16
Distribution of Total Benefits by Income Class and by Jurisdiction: Cost-of-Service Basis

Income Class	From D.C. Expenditures	From Maryland Expenditures	From Virginia Expenditures	Total	Total Benefits as a Percentage of Money Income
Benefits to D.C. Residents					
below $3,000	120,242,096	462,982	161,958	120,867,036	117.0
3,000–3,999	33,236,223	177,899	65,134	33,479,256	51.1
4,000–5,999	70,621,054	554,427	168,698	71,344,179	32.0
6,000–7,499	52,080,228	564,883	157,459	52,802,570	22.6
7,500–9,999	71,303,661	1,001,646	239,045	72,544,352	18.5
10,000–14,999	70,792,630	1,099,826	288,134	72,180,590	11.3
15,000–24,999	41,182,708	1,115,583	244,946	42,543,237	6.1
25,000 and above	17,589,519	671,579	146,479	18,407,577	2.7
Total	477,048,119	5,648,825	1,471,853	484,168,797	
Benefits to Maryland Residents					
below $3,000	1,365,922	21,208,977	247,310	22,822,209	37.4
3,000–3,999	449,515	7,268,025	114,288	7,831,828	18.4
4,000–5,999	1,116,166	17,848,321	285,989	19,250,476	14.4
6,000–7,499	1,220,955	23,425,969	320,375	24,967,299	14.2
7,500–9,999	2,712,500	53,326,268	622,034	56,660,802	13.5
10,000–14,999	4,220,587	106,325,493	1,200,628	111,746,708	9.6
15,000–24,999	5,095,202	134,290,460	1,506,633	140,892,295	7.2
25,000 and above	2,290,388	59,281,363	675,139	62,246,890	3.7
Total	18,471,235	422,974,876	4,972,396	446,418,507	

Benefits to Virginia Residents					
below $3,000	681,814	225,003	14,101,452	15,008,269	35.1
3,000–3,999	273,564	110,061	5,547,384	5,931,009	17.4
4,000–5,999	712,071	355,858	13,192,870	14,260,799	12.5
6,000–7,499	742,445	429,315	15,211,165	16,382,925	11.4
7,500–9,999	1,691,953	931,030	29,283,720	31,906,703	10.4
10,000–14,999	1,865,806	1,415,950	57,787,752	61,069,508	8.2
15,000–24,999	2,390,035	2,189,955	74,788,038	79,368,028	5.5
25,000 and above	1,164,204	1,035,240	27,813,611	30,013,055	2.6
Total	9,521,892	6,692,412	237,725,992	253,940,296	

Table 5-17
Distribution of Total Benefits by Income Class and by Jurisdiction: Welfare Basis

Income Class	From D.C. Expenditures	From Maryland Expenditures	From Virginia Expenditures	Total Benefits Excluding Source-of-Income Benefits	Total Benefits as a Percentage of Money Income	Total Benefits Including Source-of-Income Benefits	Total Benefits as a Percentage of Money Income
Benefits to D.C. Residents							
below $3,000	55,683,729	116,008	47,410	11,189,147	10.8	55,847,147	54.1
3,000–3,999	16,904,112	65,256	28,222	5,620,051	8.6	16,997,590	25.9
4,000–5,999	38,361,614	700,250	354,998	27,206,210	12.2	39,416,862	17.4
6,000–7,499	33,937,720	1,198,965	625,604	34,785,630	14.9	35,812,289	15.3
7,500–9,999	61,010,406	2,310,163	1,151,232	63,690,807	16.2	64,471,801	16.4
10,000–14,999	79,681,317	4,173,761	2,207,292	85,653,540	13.4	86,062,370	13.5
15,000–24,999	73,244,342	5,161,860	2,600,083	80,670,787	11.6	81,006,285	11.6
25,000 and above	66,893,944	5,538,554	2,651,091	74,949,757	11.2	75,083,589	11.2
Total	425,767,184	19,264,817	9,665,932	383,765,929		454,697,933	
Benefits to Maryland Residents							
below $3,000	269,231	9,561,299	46,487	1,459,561	2.4	9,877,017	16.2
3,000–3,999	175,270	3,351,826	53,711	1,002,220	2.4	3,580,807	8.4
4,000–5,999	1,435,420	7,134,408	303,845	6,166,380	4.6	8,873,673	6.6
6,000–7,499	2,803,336	9,745,710	655,295	12,931,960	7.4	13,204,341	7.5
7,500–9,999	7,250,927	28,258,644	1,716,459	36,936,255	8.8	37,226,030	8.9
10,000–14,999	18,799,538	73,541,443	5,182,621	97,279,499	8.3	97,523,602	8.4
15,000–24,999	32,331,844	138,857,668	9,308,062	180,211,034	9.2	180,497,574	9.2
25,000 and above	27,949,956	131,139,952	8,110,099	167,209,007	9.9	167,209,007	9.9
Total	91,015,522	401,590,950	25,385,579	506,898,873		517,992,051	

Benefits to
Virginia Residents

below $3,000	171,384	41,167	5,305,595	1,234,227	2.9	5,518,146	12.5
3,000–3,999	117,062	37,567	2,421,276	1,000,874	2.9	2,575,905	7.6
4,000–5,999	1,091,074	397,554	5,464,698	5,245,699	4.6	6,953,326	6.1
6,000–7,499	2,076,679	791,871	6,848,087	9,581,524	6.6	9,716,637	6.7
7,500–9,999	5,017,010	2,040,286	16,455,075	23,370,303	7.6	23,512,371	7.7
10,000–14,999	11,070,603	5,383,322	41,536,227	57,871,035	7.8	57,990,152	7.8
15,000–24,999	21,520,416	11,577,775	79,087,492	112,003,905	7.8	112,185,683	7.8
25,000 and above	17,743,711	9,903,546	60,757,508	88,343,575	7.6	88,404,765	7.6
Total	58,807,939	30,173,088	217,875,958	298,651,142		306,856,985	

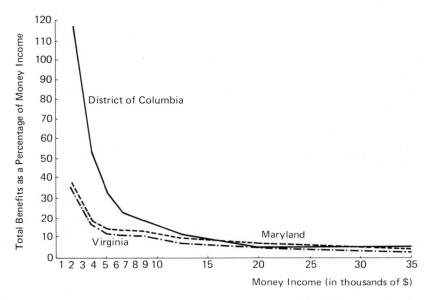

Figure 5-13. Total Benefits as a Percentage of Money Income by Income Class and by Jurisdiction: Cost-of-Service Basis.

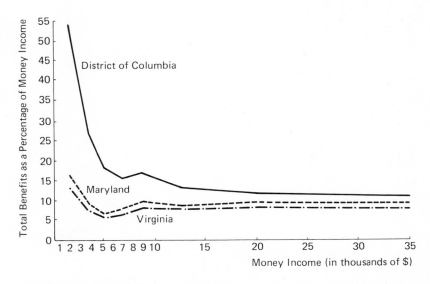

Figure 5-14. Total Benefits as a Percentage of Money Income by Income Class and by Jurisdiction: Welfare Basis.

The assumption that such services as education, welfare, public health, and recreation generate benefit externalities in the form of public nonredistributive and redistributive benefits carries the implication that the benefit area is more extensive and the benefits received by higher-income citizens more significant than under the assumption that the only beneficiaries are direct program recipients. Thus the cost-of-service estimates again serve as the limiting case which defines the most localized and pro-poor benefit incidence pattern. For example, according to the cost-of-service estimates, $27,993,127 in benefits is received by suburban Maryland and Virginia residents from District of Columbia expenditures, as can be derived from table 5-16; whereas the welfare estimates indicate that the benefits received by the suburban residents from District outlays is $149,825,461, as seen in table 5-17. There is, of course, a similar increase in the estimated value of the benefit flow into the District from the suburban jurisdictions under the assumptions underlying the welfare estimates.

The benefit estimates of the welfare approach indicate a notably less pro-poor impact of state and local expenditures than do the cost-of-service estimates. This effect follows from both assuming that the marginal utility of income declines proportionately with income and that some expenditures generate public benefits. Therefore simply contrasting the incidence patterns in tables 5-16 and 5-17 will not reveal the relative importance of these two assumptions in reducing the progressivity of benefit incidence relative to the cost-of-service estimates. It is clear, however, from a review of the incidence estimates for the various expenditure categories, that both assumptions are important.

6

Estimates of Incidence of State and Local Revenues in the Washington Metropolitan Area

Introduction

In this chapter tax incidence is estimated for all taxes imposed by state and local governments in the Washington metropolitan area. Three tasks are involved in this incidence analysis.[1] The first and most important is the identification of groups of individuals on whom the tax burdens rest. Thus it may be argued that a state excise tax on cigarette sales, for instance, falls not on the retail stores that must remit the tax collection to the revenue department, but rather on their customers, to whom the tax is shifted forward. Second, the burden of the taxes must be distributed across income classes. The cigarette excise tax, for example, may well be distributed by a series indicating the percentage distribution of tobacco purchases by income class. The distribution of the burden by income class also includes the question of the federal deductibility of various state and local taxes. If a dollar of state or local tax is allowed as an offset in estimating federal income tax, the state tax cannot be said to impose an additional burden of one dollar, but rather a burden of something less than a dollar. The burden is actually the one dollar multiplied by one minus the federal marginal tax rate.[2] In this chapter estimates of both gross tax burdens and burdens net of offset will be presented.[a] Third, some measure of the relative burden of taxes on each income class must be calculated. This measure will be computed by dividing the taxes attributed to each class by an income measure to arrive at an effective tax rate as well as to determine the degree of progressivity or regressivity of the tax.

In addition to the theoretical and empirical problems found in all tax incidence studies, some additional questions are encountered in our analysis of the Washington area because of its dual purpose. Here tax flows as well as tax incidence is measured by income class. In other words, using the example of the cigarette excise tax, we seek to measure not simply the distribution of the District of Columbia tax paid by residents of the District, but also the payment of the tax by residents of suburban Maryland and suburban Virginia. Similarly, we seek to estimate the total of all the state and local cigarette taxes collected by suburban Maryland and Virginia jurisdictions paid by residents of the District of Columbia and suburban Maryland and Virginia.

The net effect of these efforts is an estimate of the taxes paid by members

---

[a]For a more detailed discussion of the offsets see Appendix C.1.

of the various income classes in the District of Columbia and suburban Maryland and Virginia. Thus, both the total incidence of the state and local tax structure on area residents and the incidence of other jurisdictions' taxes on residents of a particular jurisdiction will be examined. For each tax we must measure the amount paid by residents of various jurisdictions in the metropolitan area. Data on working, tourist, and driving patterns will be used to measure interjurisdictional tax flows. For instance, if the cigarette tax is paid by the purchasers, data on tourist, working, and shopping patterns must be employed to estimate cigarette purchases by Maryland and Virginia residents in the District of Columbia.

Nineteen different taxes must be allocated in this manner. A detailed discussion of the methods used to allocate each tax by income class and by residency of the payer appears in Appendix C. The methodology employed for each tax is briefly discussed in the chapter itself. The methodology employed for the property tax, the sales tax, the income tax, and business cost taxes is presented at some length because of their importance for state-local revenues.

The Property Tax[b]

The incidence of the property tax has been treated in many ways in studies dealing with state and local tax incidence. Most often the tax on land is assumed to be levied on a quantity that cannot be altered. As a result, that tax must be borne by owners. The tax imposed on improvements is treated in a variety of ways. It may be assumed to be fully passed forward to those who purchase the goods or services produced by the improvement; or, if alternative sources of supply of goods and services are available, it is assumed that the tax might be absorbed by profits or passed backward to immobile factors, labor and land.

In this study it is assumed that the tax levied on land is absorbed by its owners. The tax levied on improvements is assumed to be borne three-fourths by the consumers of the products produced in the buildings, and one-fourth by the immobile factor, land. The argument that land is in almost completely inelastic supply and that a tax on it will decrease the demand for it and hence its capitalized value seems fairly convincing to us.[c] The assumptions concerning the distribution of the tax on improvements require further evaluation.

---

[b]Like the other taxes subsequently examined, the total tax that we allocate is not the total collected in fiscal year 1970, but rather the total amount collected to finance current expenditures. The portion used to finance debt service is therefore excluded.

[c]Like other studies we beg the question of whether any of those who bear this tax are still even alive since the original tax was passed many years ago. If the fiction is adopted that the legislature chooses each year to impose a non-zero level of tax, then one can argue that the tax is paid by current owners. If that tax were not imposed, the value of the current owner's land would be higher by the exact amount of the tax; assuming, of course, that this year's decision does not have any effect on the probability of the property tax being imposed in subsequent years.

Mieszkowski has argued that local property taxes on improvements may have some aspects of both profits and excise taxes.[3] Assuming the extreme case of capital (i.e., improvements) in completely inelastic supply, he argues that if each jurisdiction in the economy levies a tax on improvements of t percent, the return on capital falls from r to $r(1 - t)$. Similarly, if each jurisdiction levies different tax rates with the weighted average of t, the return on capital also falls to $r(1 - t)$. In this instance, however, an excise tax phenomenon would be found in all jurisdictions levying rates below or above t. In those jurisdictions with rates below t, the prices of final goods and services produced within the jurisdictions would fall and the price of land would rise. Assuming a Cobb-Douglas production function, Mieszkowski estimates that of the difference between a jurisdiction's actual tax yield and the yield which would have resulted from a tax levied at t percent, around 75 percent would be reflected in lower product prices and 25 percent in higher returns to land.[4]

The question that we are attempting to answer in this study is what is the effect of one of the jurisdictions levying its actual rate of property tax rather than levying no property tax. If the tax rate were zero, then land prices in the jurisdiction would be higher and the prices of products and services produced in the jurisdiction would be lower than elsewhere in the relevant market for the services of capital or improvements. The levying of the tax at a positive rate results in an increase in prices and a reduction in land values relative to the non-tax situation. The total of these charges or losses in well-being will be exactly equal to the property tax collected on improvements. It is for this reason that we attribute 75 percent of the tax on improvements to the users of services and 25 percent to landowners.

An alternative view, however, is that property tax payments, even those on land values, are fully shifted forward to tenants and other users of property. Since the demand for housing services in the Washington area is strong and growing rapidly, landowners may appear to be able to pass forward any increase in property taxes. While we feel that land prices would increase even more rapidly without the property tax than they do in its presence, we do present an alternative estimate of the incidence of the property tax computed on the assumption of complete forward shifting.

Given assumptions about the incidence of the property tax, the income class and the place of residence of those who bear the tax remain to be identified. The portion of the tax borne by users of the property is divided into six parts, that borne by: (a) homeowners, (b) apartment dwellers, (c) users of office buildings, (d) customers of commercial establishments, (e) customers of industrial establishments, and (f) patrons of motels and hotels.

The taxes borne by homeowners and renters are distributed between income classes by estimated series on house values and rent payments respectively (see Appendix C.2). The portion borne by the users of office building properties involves the possibility of payment by nonresidents. The utilization of office building space is estimated from a survey of office buildings in the District

of Columbia. From this survey estimates are derived of the dollar value of floor space occupied by: (a) firms or organizations serving the District of Columbia, its market or its residents; (b) the metropolitan area; and (c) the nation as whole. The ultimate users of group (a) are assumed distributed between jurisdictions in the same way as are the burdens of the taxing jurisdiction's sales taxes. Group (b) users are assumed to be distributed in the same way as the distribution of all the jurisdictions' sales taxes. The users of group (c) are assumed to be distributed between areas of the country in the same proportions as personal income (see Appendix C.3).

The tax falling on the users of services provided by commercial establishments is distributed between jurisdictions and by income class in the same way as the taxing jurisdiction's sales tax. The users of industrial property are assumed to have the same geographic location and income characteristics as the customers of firms subject to the corporate income tax. Finally, all hotel and motel users are assumed to come from outside the metropolitan area and so none of the tax shifted forward to them is borne by any of the citizens in the study area (see Appendix C.4). When we consider that part of the property tax borne by owners, only two basic ownership categories are considered. These are the owners of single-family homes and the owners of what we call income-producing property. With the exception of homes owned by nonoccupants (see Appendix C.5),[d] owners of single-family homes reside within the taxing jurisdiction. Hence the tax can be distributed among income classes by owner-occupied house values.

The income and residency characteristics of the owners of income-producing property are estimated by sampling the tax roles in each of the jurisdictions. The dollar volume of property values are classified into eight categories: (a) national corporations, (b) local corporations with mailing addresses in the metropolitan area, (c) noncommercial organizations serving interests of the particular jurisdiction, (d) noncommercial organizations serving interests of the metropolitan area, (e) noncommercial organizations serving national interests, (f) single individuals or partnerships with mailing addresses within the metropolitan area, (g) single individuals with national mailing addresses, and (h) corporations serving the regional area, such as the Chesapeake and Potomac Telephone Company, for which we suspected that local ownership is likely to be more substantial than for national corporations. Assumptions are made concerning the geographic distribution of the ownership of these different types of property. The result is a percentage distribution of the ownership of each jurisdiction's income-producing property according to whether the owner lives in the District of Columbia, suburban Maryland, suburban Virginia, or the rest of the world (see Appendix C.6).

---

[d]Nonowner occupied single-family homes represent a significant fraction of total single family homes in the Washington metropolitan area. Residency and income class characteristics of the owners are discussed in Appendix C.

These taxes are distributed by income class in different ways. Taxes paid on properties falling into categories (a), (b) and (h) are distributed by a series on dividend income by money income class. Categories (c) and (d) taxes are distributed in the same way as total income by income class. Category (f) taxes are assumed distributed like total income, but only among those with income in excess of $15,000.

Property tax incidence reflecting the assumption that owners bear part of the tax and consequently there is only partial forward shifting is displayed in table 6-1 with both the distribution of the property tax before and after the federal offset. The distribution of the property tax burden is more regressive when the alternative full forward shifting assumptions are used. Although the numbers are not shown, a visual summary of the results is shown in figure 6-2.

The figures in table 6-1 indicate that the property tax has a structure which is regressive up to the $10,000 to $14,999 level, slightly progressive between that bracket and the next highest bracket, and finally regressive between the $15,000 to $25,000 bracket and the $25,000 and over bracket. The presence of the federal offset has its strongest effect in the $15,000 and above brackets where it tends to make the structure more regressive. Figure 6-1 depicts the overall structure, both before and after offsets as basically an L-shaped curve. When it is assumed that the property tax is fully passed forward, then it becomes regressive across all income classes, as seen in figure 6-2. In figure 6-2 the lower curve refers to the tax burden after offset and falls below the gross burden curves by greater absolute amounts as income increases.

The Individual Income Tax

The second most important tax in the Washington metropolitan area is the individual income tax.[e] When this tax is considered in a national perspective, there is little doubt that the tax is paid by persons on whom it is levied. When employed at the subnational level there is some possibility that those subject to the tax will have to be paid a higher return to compensate them for working in the taxing jurisdiction. If only some forms of labor and land are immobile they may be forced to bear the entire brunt of the tax. This possibility is likely to be stronger in a city which levies the tax on commuters and is surrounded by tax-free suburbs that can supply ample job opportunities. However, this is not the situation in the Washington area. People working in the city may escape the city tax rates, which are higher for some income classes, simply by not living in the city. There is no need for employers to compensate these employees for coming

---

[e]In fact for the total of state plus local taxes raised to finance the current expenditures considered in the study, the individual income tax is quantitatively more significant in suburban Maryland than the real property tax.

Table 6-1
Distribution of Property Taxes by Income Class and by Jurisdiction: Partial Forward Shifting

Income Class	D.C. Taxes Before Offset	D.C. Taxes After Offset	Md. Taxes Before Offset	Md. Taxes After Offset	Va. Taxes Before Offset	Va. Taxes After Offset	Total Taxes Before Offset	Total Taxes After Offset	Total Taxes as a Percentage of Money Income Before Offset	Total Taxes as a Percentage of Money Income After Offset
A. Taxes Paid by D.C. Residents										
below $3,000	6,426,443	6,319,995	353,898	259,775	240,050	167,838	7,020,391	6,747,608	6.8	6.5
3,000–3,999	2,165,796	2,115,319	98,638	79,426	58,910	43,840	2,323,344	2,238,585	3.5	3.4
4,000–5,999	5,530,202	5,327,771	299,964	238,505	174,774	126,274	6,004,940	5,692,550	2.7	2.5
6,000–7,499	5,020,764	4,801,850	257,407	214,597	143,776	109,274	5,421,947	5,125,721	2.3	2.2
7,500–9,999	7,545,720	7,093,615	406,601	332,928	221,102	161,858	8,173,423	7,588,401	2.1	1.9
10,000–14,999	11,651,786	10,603,058	560,763	469,858	294,441	219,764	12,506,990	11,292,680	2.0	1.8
15,000–24,999	13,620,667	11,167,617	1,533,350	1,131,036	921,847	648,321	16,075,864	12,946,828	2.3	1.9
25,000 and above	12,631,242	8,517,618	1,621,911	1,126,117	1,043,351	687,665	15,296,504	10,331,400	2.3	1.5
Total	64,592,620	55,946,697	5,132,532	3,852,242	3,098,251	2,164,834	72,823,613	61,963,773		
B. Taxes Paid by Md. Residents										
below $3,000	331,000	240,969	5,030,693	4,930,600	182,202	119,832	5,543,895	5,291,401	9.1	8.7
3,000–3,999	93,565	73,939	1,787,394	1,734,752	45,845	31,936	1,926,804	1,840,627	4.5	4.3
4,000–5,999	273,752	212,129	4,636,822	4,438,045	132,725	89,923	5,043,299	4,740,097	3.8	3.5
6,000–7,499	286,523	233,643	5,399,758	5,111,565	130,659	93,181	5,816,940	5,438,389	3.3	3.1
7,500–9,999	645,410	511,567	9,889,256	9,164,687	292,358	200,716	10,827,024	9,876,970	2.6	2.4
10,000–14,999	1,504,226	1,213,215	28,082,940	25,078,943	647,327	453,913	30,234,493	26,746,071	2.6	2.3
15,000–24,999	5,678,572	4,155,287	48,844,795	39,198,248	2,739,171	1,893,567	57,262,536	45,247,102	2.9	2.3
25,000 and above	5,684,076	3,807,056	29,104,841	19,418,021	2,914,346	1,880,242	37,703,263	25,105,319	2.2	1.5
Total	14,497,124	10,447,805	132,776,499	109,074,861	7,084,633	4,763,310	154,358,254	124,285,976		
C. Taxes Paid by Va. Residents										
below $3,000	212,468	156,564	151,762	101,802	2,998,127	2,949,382	3,362,357	3,207,748	7.9	7.5
3,000–3,999	72,620	57,441	48,624	34,902	1,117,344	1,088,367	1,238,588	1,180,710	3.6	3.5
4,000–5,999	225,354	174,203	151,286	106,723	2,941,311	2,830,475	3,317,951	3,111,401	2.9	2.7
6,000–7,499	227,735	185,600	145,813	108,758	3,354,621	3,197,782	3,728,169	3,492,140	2.6	2.4
7,500–9,999	456,371	361,021	295,826	214,322	5,852,718	5,469,507	6,604,915	6,045,032	2.2	2.0
10,000–14,999	928,056	746,872	579,410	431,995	15,339,351	13,796,532	16,846,817	14,975,399	2.2	2.0
15,000–24,999	4,086,152	2,982,268	2,985,527	2,102,054	25,515,172	20,531,722	32,586,851	25,616,044	2.3	1.8
25,000 and above	3,989,252	2,675,930	2,950,441	1,948,979	15,005,164	9,914,099	31,944,857	14,539,008	1.9	1.2
Total	10,198,008	7,340,081	7,308,689	5,049,689	72,123,808	59,777,866	89,630,505	72,167,482		

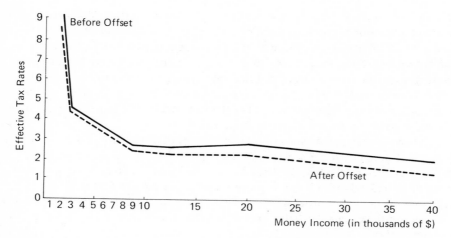

Figure 6-1. Incidence of Property Taxes Paid by Maryland Residents: Partial Forward Shifting.

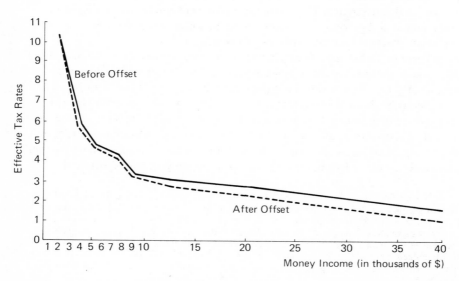

Figure 6-2. Incidence of Property Taxes Paid by Maryland Residents: Full Forward Shifting.

into the city to work since there is no income tax on nonresidents. Moreover, a substantial fraction of the work force does not have the alternative of working in the suburbs. They are employed by the government in jobs that are located in the federal city. Thus, the assumption that the individual income tax is paid by those who file the returns seems hard to dispute. Moreover, because there is no commuter income tax, all of the tax can be assumed to be borne by residents.[f] Table 6-2 contains a distribution of all of the state and local income taxes levied on area residents by income class (see Appendix C.7).

As one can see the income tax adds an element of progressivity to the state-local tax structure. But the degree of progressivity differs between jurisdictions and it is lessened by the federal offset. In fact, the Virginia income tax even without the federal offset becomes proportional above the $15,000 level, and in each case the tax net of offset becomes regressive above the $15,000 level. The incidence of the income tax before and after offset is shown in figures 6-3 and 6-4, respectively.

The Sales Tax

The tax levied on retail sales yields more revenues than all others except the property and income taxes. Each of the jurisdictions in the area levies such a tax on basically the same base. In Maryland, however, food purchased for consumption off the premises is exempt. A 4 percent tax rate is levied on all taxable sales in Maryland and Virginia. The District of Columbia taxes food to be eaten off the premises at 2 percent; food eaten on the premises, motel and hotel bills, and liquor at 5 percent;[g] and all other items at 4 percent.

There is controversy concerning whether or not a sales tax levied in a closed economy is shifted forward to consumers, or shifted backward to owners of factors of production employed in producing the commodities.[5] In general, however, it has been assumed that a national sales tax falls on consumers.[6] For this study, however, we are concerned with the analysis of a set of local sales taxes as opposed to a national tax. State economies, to say nothing of cities or metropolitan areas, are far from closed and thus there is the question of whether the incidence of a sales tax differs in an open economy which exports and

---

[f]Technically this is not precisely true. Income from property owned in one jurisdiction by residents of another is taxable in the jurisdiction where the property is located. But no way was found to get at this potential flow. The quantitative significance of this flow is likely to be small. For instance, the entire State of Maryland collects less than one-half percent of its income taxes from nonresidents. A similar figure is likely to apply to income taxes collected in the Maryland suburbs. Of this one-half percent certainly far less than 100 percent of the nonresidents paying these taxes were located in either D.C. or suburban Virginia.

[g]The higher rate applied to these items was in effect only during part of fiscal year 1970.

Table 6-2

Distribution of Individual Income Taxes by Income Class

Income Classes	Total Taxes		Taxes as a Percentage of Money Income	
	Before Offset	After Offset	Before Offset	After Offset
District of Columbia				
below $3,000	86,179	85,619	0.1	0.1
3,000–3,999	360,981	347,119	0.5	0.5
4,000–5,999	2,581,912	2,410,989	1.2	1.1
6,000–7,499	4,068,721	3,709,046	1.7	1.6
7,500–9,999	8,199,551	7,250,043	2.1	1.8
10,000–14,999	17,325,626	14,804,747	2.7	2.3
15,000–24,999	24,289,016	18,646,678	3.5	2.7
25,000 and above	25,241,255	15,336,587	3.8	2.8
Total	82,153,241	62,590,828		
Maryland				
below $3,000	127,733	126,903	0.2	0.2
3,000–3,999	367,131	353,034	0.9	0.8
4,000–5,999	2,346,798	2,191,440	1.7	1.6
6,000–7,499	4,695,245	4,280,186	2.7	2.4
7,500–9,999	12,404,181	10,967,777	3.0	2.6
10,000–14,999	38,573,114	32,960,726	3.3	2.8
15,000–24,999	73,288,258	56,263,396	3.7	2.9
25,000 and above	74,219,685	45,095,881	4.4	2.7
Total	206,022,145	152,239,343		
Virginia				
below $3,000	30,206	30,010	0.1	0.1
3,000–3,999	107,508	103,379	0.3	0.3
4,000–5,999	1,132,977	1,057,973	1.0	0.9
6,000–7,499	2,504,517	2,283,118	1.7	1.6
7,500–9,999	5,777,343	5,108,327	1.9	1.7
10,000–14,999	15,820,826	13,518,896	2.1	1.8
15,000–24,999	30,729,784	23,591,256	2.1	1.6
25,000 and above	25,096,325	15,248,527	2.1	1.3
Total	81,199,486	60,941,486		

imports a substantial portion of its goods or services from what it would be in a national economy.

In such a setting it is reasonable to assume that imports are in perfectly elastic supply. Any one city may be taken to be so small that it faces a given price for its imports and can buy all it wants at that price. If the city imposes a sales tax on goods which are imported, such as color television sets, then the net price given to the seller must remain the same. The price paid by city consumers rises by the full amount of the tax. The same conclusion will apply to any

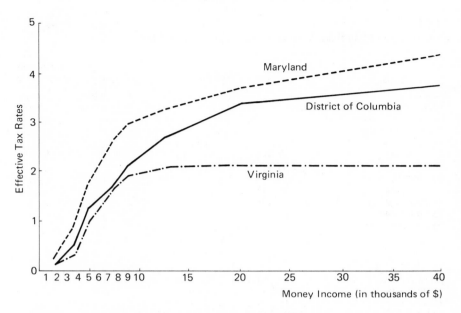

Figure 6-3. Effective Tax Rates of Individual Income Tax Before Offset.

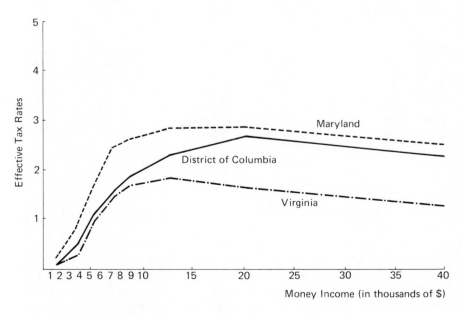

Figure 6-4. Effective Tax Rates of Individual Income Tax After Offset.

import-competing commodities because out-of-city suppliers will reduce their shipments until prices rise by the amount of the tax.

A complication is introduced by the fact that there may be some "non-traded" goods subject to the sales tax.[7] These are goods which are neither imported nor import-competing. Dry cleaning services and barbering are examples. Since they are insulated from markets outside the city or state they must be analyzed differently. Here prices may increase by less than the tax if there are increasing costs of production. If prices do behave in this fashion factor earnings of those employed in the industry must fall or some factors become unemployed. Those factors that are mobile will move and the burden falling on factors must be borne by immobile factor owners, presumably land and, perhaps, some labor. The volume of sales taxes collected from the sales of such nontraded goods is a small portion of the total. Moreover, since some of the tax would be passed forward in any case and since all would be passed forward, if they are produced at a constant cost, the assumption of full forward shifting of the sales tax seems warranted.[h]

What is most important for our study, therefore, is to determine the jurisdictional and income characteristics of the purchasers of the goods subject to the sales tax. In each jurisdiction we take total sales tax payments net of sales to businesses.[8] An estimate is made for sales tax payments made by tourists and visitors to the jurisdiction. On the basis of commutation patterns, differential price patterns for cigarettes and liquor, and family consumption data, we estimate sales tax payments made by commuters. Estimates of sales payments by shoppers from outside the jurisdiction are inferred from a survey of major shopping centers. These three estimates of tax payments made by nonresidents are subtracted from the total of sales taxes paid by individuals to derive an estimate of the jurisdiction's sales taxes paid by its own residents (see Appendix C.8). These taxes are distributed by income class by using a revised Bureau of Labor Statistics series on taxable consumption items by income class (see

---

[h]Since the tax rates are basically the same in the jurisdictions under study and where different apply to goods unlikely to involve significant amounts of cross-jurisdictional hauling, we have ignored the question of differential sales tax rates in a local market area. If tax rates differ, then the common base level of taxation may be analyzed just like the national sales tax.

   If one interprets this base level as being the tax rate of the lowest rate jurisdiction, then the remainder of the tax can be considered like one imposed in isolation by a particular city or state. If the tax rate base is treated as the weighted average rate, then a peculiar phenomenon may occur. Those cities who have an above average rate will have to compensate importers for the extra rate in the form of higher consumer prices. Those with below average rates may be able to get importers to bring commodities into their communities at gross prices below the average. Consumers there may pay lower prices because of the jurisdiction's lower sales tax rate. So if the national average is 4 percent and if a city imposes a 3 percent rate, one may conceive of the 4 percent as being shifted forward to consumers in the form of higher prices and the 1 percent differential as being in turn shifted forward in the form of lower prices. You can see, however, that on net even in such cities the full amount of the sales tax is shifted forward to local consumers.

Appendix C.9). The tax on sales to business is distributed in the same way as business cost taxes. Table 6-3 shows the distribution of the sales tax paid by income class both before and after offset.

The incidence of the sales tax falling on residents of various jurisdictions before and after offset is regressive as depicted in figures 6-5 and 6-6. The federal offset increases this regressivity. Despite the fact that the District of Columbia exports a greater percentage of its sales tax than suburban Maryland and Virginia, the overall burden on the District of Columbia residents is generally higher than that on Virginia residents which, in turn, is higher than the Maryland burden. The lower effective tax rates in Maryland is largely explained by its exemption of food from the sales tax base.

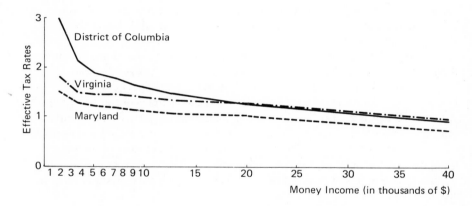

Figure 6-5. Effective Sales Tax Rates Before Offset.

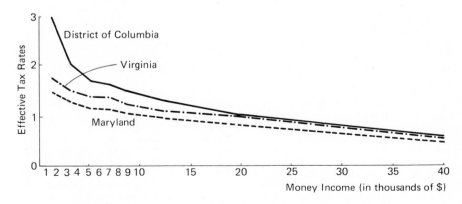

Figure 6-6. Effective Sales Tax Rates After Offset.

Table 6-3
Distribution of the Sales Tax by Income Class

Income Class	D.C. Taxes Before Offset	D.C. Taxes After Offset	Md. Taxes Before Offset	Md. Taxes After Offset	Va. Taxes Before Offset	Va. Taxes After Offset	Total Taxes Before Offset	Total Taxes After Offset	Total Taxes as a Percentage of Money Income Before Offset	Total Taxes as a Percentage of Money Income After Offset
A. Sales Tax Paid by D.C. Residents										
below $3,000	2,758,941	2,742,748	261,130	259,571	82,253	81,814	3,102,324	3,084,133	3.0	3.0
3,000–3,999	1,221,475	1,179,100	115,620	111,540	36,408	35,260	1,373,503	1,325,900	2.1	2.0
4,000–5,999	3,712,586	3,491,070	351,275	329,948	110,880	104,879	4,174,741	3,925,897	1.9	1.8
6,000–7,499	3,672,936	3,380,279	347,525	319,350	109,691	101,763	4,130,152	3,801,392	1.8	1.6
7,500–9,999	5,808,811	5,202,843	549,568	491,230	173,561	157,145	6,531,940	5,851,218	1.7	1.5
10,000–14,999	8,515,198	7,401,603	805,325	698,116	254,914	224,745	9,575,437	8,324,464	1.5	1.3
15,000–24,999	8,225,953	6,514,179	777,553	612,756	246,953	200,579	9,250,459	7,327,514	1.3	1.0
25,000 and above	5,734,906	3,737,378	541,304	348,996	173,484	119,368	6,449,694	4,205,742	1.0	0.6
Total	39,650,806	33,649,200	3,749,300	3,171,507	1,188,144	1,025,553	44,588,250	37,846,260		
B. Sales Tax Paid by Md. Residents										
below $3,000	126,138	125,672	775,625	771,025	33,077	32,926	934,840	929,623	1.5	1.5
3,000–3,999	70,471	68,751	474,301	457,321	19,152	18,596	563,924	544,668	1.3	1.3
4,000–5,999	211,413	202,514	1,422,903	1,335,084	57,457	54,580	1,691,773	1,592,178	1.3	1.2
6,000–7,499	265,727	250,676	1,799,763	1,651,221	72,404	67,537	2,137,894	1,969,434	1.2	1.1
7,500–9,999	605,686	560,546	4,117,146	3,671,653	165,280	150,683	4,888,112	4,382,882	1.2	1.0
10,000–14,999	1,569,731	1,421,746	10,729,154	9,262,652	429,316	381,463	12,728,201	11,065,861	1.1	0.9
15,000–24,999	2,486,601	2,105,658	17,243,533	13,483,914	684,145	560,961	20,414,279	16,150,533	1.0	0.8
25,000 and above	1,543,424	1,146,080	10,657,630	6,735,271	423,901	295,414	12,624,955	8,176,765	0.7	0.5
Total	6,879,191	5,881,643	47,220,055	37,368,141	1,884,732	1,562,160	55,983,978	44,811,944		
C. Sales Tax Paid by Va. Residents										
below $3,000	64,976	64,764	40,910	40,689	666,316	662,340	772,202	767,793	1.8	1.8
3,000–3,999	41,466	40,586	16,411	15,933	462,264	445,713	520,141	502,232	1.5	1.5
4,000–5,999	132,449	127,576	52,539	49,894	1,482,569	1,390,990	1,667,557	1,568,460	1.5	1.4
6,000–7,499	164,627	156,286	66,244	61,718	1,891,806	1,735,043	2,122,677	1,953,047	1.5	1.4
7,500–9,999	334,331	311,997	134,938	122,819	3,863,169	3,443,433	4,332,438	3,878,249	1.4	1.3
10,000–14,999	766,428	700,865	312,119	276,543	9,000,966	7,768,800	10,079,513	8,746,208	1.4	1.1
15,000–24,999	1,371,083	1,180,893	562,478	460,142	16,316,693	12,742,678	18,250,254	14,383,713	1.3	1.0
25,000 and above	853,246	657,569	346,492	240,312	9,969,408	6,291,997	11,169,146	7,189,878	1.0	0.6
Total	3,728,606	3,240,536	1,532,131	1,268,050	43,653,191	34,480,994	48,913,928	38,989,580		

Business Cost Taxes

A variety of taxes paid by business firms are classified as business cost taxes. For instance, part of the motor fuel tax is paid for by businesses. The taxes that we have included in this category are detailed in table 6-4. Once these taxes raise the costs of the firms using the taxable inputs, the question becomes whether the firms pass the tax forward in the form of higher prices, absorb the tax in decreased profits or pass the tax backward to factors of production. A distinction must be made between goods and services produced for the local market (and usually facing competition from goods produced elsewhere) and those produced for export.

If the business cost tax rate facing those firms producing for the local market is comparable to that facing their competitors, then the local firms will be much more likely to be able to pass the tax forward. If higher business cost taxes put these firms at a disadvantage, then the tax will be more difficult to shift forward and much of the burden may rest on local immobile factors of production. The data required to analyze the extent of shifting, however, are generally unavailable. Hence, we assume the business tax structure in the metropolitan area is not far out of line with the structure facing competing firms that produce outside the area. By assumption, therefore, this portion of the business cost tax is fully shifted forward.

A relevant consideration for those firms producing for export markets is whether or not their taxes fall short of or exceed those of their competitors. If the latter is the case, once again local, immobile factors may have to absorb the tax. The export sector, however, is not significant in the Washington metro-

Table 6-4
Types of Business Cost Taxes by Jurisdiction

Type	District of Columbia	Maryland	Virginia
		Jurisdiction	
Personal Property	$15,239,442	$ 8,601,027	$ 3,721,245
Public Utility	3,276,858	6,160,147	4,617,063
Business Licenses and Fees	2,996,381	3,622,434	8,805,680
Insurance Tax	1,036,183	940,404	636,647
Bank Tax	1,292,625	946,828	163,051
Fuel Tax	3,180,261	4,947,560	2,716,124
Motor Vehicle Excise	929,672	1,473,981	403,223
Registration of Motor Vehicles	1,705,652	1,794,696	1,252,886
Total	$29,657,074	$28,487,077	$22,315,919

politan area. The area does not have large manufacturing, mining or agricultural sectors producing for a national or even regional market. This consideration and the absence of better knowledge about taxes facing the competitors of the few exporters in the area leads us to our assumption that this part of the tax is also fully passed forward.[9]

Of course in the Washington area, there may be little exporting of goods and services to national markets and yet considerable exporting of goods and services across jurisdictional boundaries. The differential rates of business taxes between jurisdictions therefore might be an important consideration in determining whether all of those business cost taxes can be passed forward. If firms in one area face considerably lower tax rates, then firms or rather immobile factors elsewhere might be forced to absorb the differential.

We could find no clear evidence, however, that such differentials existed. The Washington Metropolitan Board of Trade [10] indicates that tax rates on manufacturing and wholesale corporations of specific asset sizes were as much as 100 percent higher in the District of Columbia than in some of the suburbs. This would tend to indicate that suburban firms might be at a considerable competitive advantage. On the other hand, when we calculated our own measure of total business taxes paid as a percentage of payrolls in the various jurisdiction, we found the exact opposite. By this measure, firms based in the city of Washington were advantageously located as far as tax considerations. While we do not deny the possible usefulness of discovering a "correct" measure of relative business tax burdens, the lack of such a measure at present forces us to assume that such tax differentials are not significant in the Washington metropolitan area. Thus business cost taxes exported over jurisdictional boundaries are also assumed fully shifted forward.

The geographical locations of the customers of the firms paying the business cost taxes are derived from our analysis of the geographic locations of customers of firms paying corporate and unincorporated income taxes. The taxes are distributed between income classes in proportion to total consumption.

The distribution of these tax burdens by income class and by jurisdiction is presented in table 6-5. There are no alternative estimates here for before and after tax offsets. If the tax is shifted forward 100 percent, then federal tax liabilities of the firms would be the same as if no such taxes were imposed at all. Indirect business taxes such as these are not deductible against the individual income tax. The incidence of these taxes are thoroughly regressive as figure 6-7 depicts.

All Other Taxes

In this section the incidence of all other taxes and fees levied by state and local governments in the Washington metropolitan area are estimated. A brief

Table 6-5
Distribution of the Business Cost Taxes by Income Class

Income Class	D.C. Taxes	Md. Taxes	Va. Taxes	Total Taxes	Taxes as a Percentage of Money Income
Business Cost Taxes Paid by D.C. Residents					
below $3,000	723,129	143,613	85,285	952,027	0.9
3,000–3,999	319,318	63,443	37,659	420,420	0.6
4,000–5,999	991,969	197,005	116,991	1,305,965	0.6
6,000–7,499	980,997	194,825	115,697	1,291,519	0.5
7,500–9,999	1,559,280	309,673	183,898	2,052,851	0.5
10,000–14,999	2,332,885	463,301	275,136	3,071,322	0.5
15,000–24,999	2,320,814	460,906	273,712	3,055,432	0.4
25,000 and above	1,744,725	346,494	205,770	2,296,989	0.3
Total	10,973,117	2,179,260	1,294,148	14,446,525	
Business Cost Taxes Paid by Md. Residents					
below $3,000	147,434	460,743	57,234	665,411	1.1
3,000–3,999	69,495	217,179	26,979	313,653	0.7
4,000–5,999	208,486	651,535	80,936	940,957	0.7
6,000–7,499	258,497	807,822	100,350	1,166,669	0.7
7,500–9,999	584,541	1,826,734	226,922	2,638,197	0.6
10,000–14,999	1,496,425	4,676,439	580,921	6,753,785	0.6
15,000–24,999	2,292,699	7,164,856	890,040	10,347,595	0.5
25,000 and above	1,437,321	4,491,735	557,978	6,487,034	0.4
Total	6,494,898	20,297,043	2,521,360	29,313,301	

Business Cost Taxes Paid by Va. Residents					
below $3,000	87,815	46,961	316,286	451,062	1.1
3,000–3,999	50,180	26,834	180,735	257,749	0.8
4,000–5,999	159,320	85,200	573,832	818,352	0.7
6,000–7,499	190,265	101,748	685,285	977,298	0.7
7,500–9,999	383,039	204,839	1,379,608	1,967,486	0.6
10,000–14,999	855,147	457,310	3,080,019	4,392,476	0.6
15,000–24,999	1,495,759	799,903	5,387,398	7,683,060	0.5
25,000 and above	960,106	513,439	3,458,055	4,931,600	0.4
Total	4,181,631	2,236,234	15,061,218	21,479,083	

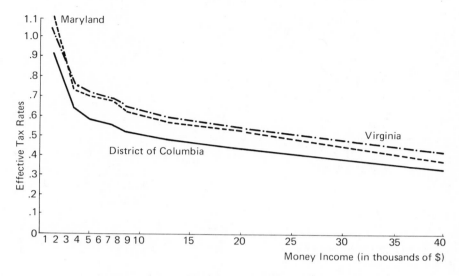

Figure 6-7. Business Cost Effective Tax Rates.

statement of the assumptions employed in estimating the incidence for each tax is followed by a discussion of the estimated incidence by jurisdiction and income class.

The Corporate and Unincorporated Income Taxes

The District of Columbia, as well as Maryland and Virginia imposes a tax on net corporate income (see Appendix C.10). Even at the national level there is considerable debate over the incidence of this tax.[11] Therefore we have employed two alternative assumptions. In the one case we assume that the tax is borne entirely by consumers of the goods and services produced by these firms. In the other case, we assume that only one-half of the tax is borne by customers; the rest is absorbed by profits. The District of Columbia also imposed a similar tax on unincorporated business income. It is treated in the same way.

The residency of the consumers of the goods and services produced by corporations in the various jurisdictions is estimated by breaking down the tax payments into industrial categories and in turn determining the portion of the sales of firms in the various categories taking place within the jurisdictions under study. Our estimates of the residency of the owners of the corporations utilize data concerning ownership of income-producing property owned by corporations (see Appendix C.11).

The customers of the firms paying the unincorporated income tax are assumed to be distributed between residents of the jurisdictions in the same proportions as the retail sales tax. Owners of unincorporated businesses in the District of Columbia are assumed to reside in the various jurisdictions in the same proportion as members of the District of Columbia labor force (see Appendix C.12).

Motor Fuel Excise Taxes

Excise taxes on goods largely produced outside the jurisdiction but purchased within the jurisdiction can be assumed with some certainty to be fully passed forward since the goods are in perfectly elastic supply to any one jurisdiction. Thus producers need not and will not absorb the taxes. The jurisdictional characteristics of the purchasers of motor fuel are estimated utilizing data on vehicle miles traveled and purchasing patterns. The tax is then allocated to income classes by a series reflecting gasoline purchases by income class (see Appendix C.13).

Alcoholic Beverage Excise Taxes and Fees

These are assumed fully shifted forward. The important question to be resolved here is the extent of purchases by nonresidents. These purchases are likely to be substantial because of lower price levels in Washington. We first estimate the purchases of tourists in the jurisdictions under study on the basis of national consumption patterns of alcohol. The remaining sales in any jurisdiction are made either to residents or to those from other jurisdictions in the area. Suburban purchases in the District of Columbia can be deduced from estimates of total consumption in the area and total sales in the various jurisdictions provided we assume the per capita physical consumption of alcohol by residents is the same in each jurisdiction in the area. Minor corrections are made for miniscule purchases of alcoholic beverages by District of Columbia residents in the suburbs. Once the tax is distributed between jurisdictions, it is then allocated to income classes by a series on alcoholic beverage expenditures (see Appendix C.14).

Public Utility Taxes

Each of the jurisdictions levies a tax on the gross receipts of public utilities. Because of the regulated nature of the industry and the policy of allowing the companies a "fair return" it can be assumed that these taxes are passed forward to consumers. After sales to businesses and governments are subtracted, the rest of the tax is distributed solely among the taxing jurisdiction's residents. Separate

expenditure series are used to distribute the taxes levied on telephone and tele-graph as opposed to gas and electric companies (see Appendix C.15).

Death and Gift Taxes

The question of whether death and gift taxes are paid by the donor or donee is similar to the question of whether the golden egg or the goose that laid it came first. We have chosen the goose. Donors are assumed to pay the tax. Although some property subject to a state's death or gift taxes may be owned by donors who lived outside the state, we have assumed this to be minimal. Thus death and gift taxes, net of federal offset, are assumed paid by residents of the taxing jurisdiction. The tax is distributed among income classes by a series on net wealth by income class. This procedure differs somewhat from the usual assumption that all is borne by the highest income class. Exemption levels are so low for the states under consideration, however, that we feel that some of the tax could be paid for by those with lower money income (see Appendix C.16).

Tobacco Excise Taxes

These taxes are assumed to be passed forward. Because of price differentials between the District, suburban Maryland, and suburban Virginia and the pur-chase of cigarettes by people at their place of work, substantial interjurisdictional purchases are likely to occur. Estimates of these flows are arrived at by deductive reasoning. Given total cigarette sales, sales to tourists are estimated using average cigarette consumption statistics for the United States as a whole. The remainder must be sold either to residents of the jurisdiction or other residents of the area. Once estimates of purchases by own residents are made, the remainder is pre-sumed purchased by residents of other Washington area jurisdictions (see Appendix C.17).

Motor Vehicle Traffic Fines, Parking
Fines and Fees

These were allocated between jurisdictions either by direct data on the residency of those paying the fines or by vehicle miles traveled in the jurisdiction by residents of the various jurisdictions (see Appendix C.18).

Motor Vehicle Excise Tax

Each jurisdiction levies an ad valorem tax on the purchase of automobiles. An individual residing in one jurisdiction and buying a car in another is subject

to the tax in his home jurisdiction. Thus once a deduction is made for excise tax payments by businesses, the rest is passed forward to residents of the jurisdiction levying the tax and assumed distributed in the same way as automobile purchases (see Appendix C.19).

Insurance Companies Tax

Each of the states levies a tax on the premiums received net of dividends on all risks within their jurisdictions. This is basically an ad valorem excise tax on the purchase of insurance by economic units within the taxing jurisdiction. As such it is likely to be fully shifted forward to the insurees.

In each jurisdiction a distinction is made between taxes on commercial, ordinary life, group life, automobile and homeownership policies. The tax on commercial premiums is treated like a business cost tax. The tax on ordinary life is assumed paid for solely by residents; that on group life by workers; that on automobiles and homes is assumed paid for solely by residents. Appropriate series are used to distribute the burdens by income class (see Appendix C.20).

Bank Tax

Each of the states also imposes a tax on commercial banks and both D.C. and Maryland also tax savings and loan associations. In Virginia the tax is on the value of bank stock. In the District of Columbia and Maryland the tax is on gross and net earnings respectively. We have assumed that these taxes are fully passed forward to bank customers, that is, borrowers.

Estimates of the different types of loans issued by the types of banks weighted by their share of the tax are calculated. Four categories were employed: (a) mortgage loans, (b) security loans, (c) personal loans, and (d) business loans.

The tax passed forward on business loans is treated as a buisness cost tax. Estimates are made of mortgage, security and personal loans by nonresidents. The taxes are distributed among income classes by appropriate series (see Appendix C.21).

Motor Registration and License Fees

Commercial vehicle registration fees are separated from the total of registration fees and treated as a business cost tax. The remainder is distributed by a series on number of automobiles owned by income class. All licenses are assumed to be personal fees as opposed to fees required in order to conduct a business. They are distributed among income class by a distribution of the incidence of automobile ownership by income class (see Appendix C.22).

Personal Fees

Included in this category are a variety of fees attributed to individuals rather than businesses. Such things as marriage licenses, birth certificates, and dog licenses are included. These are distributed among income class by a series on total consumption expenditures by income class.

Property Related Taxes

These include a variety of taxes and fees such as real estate transfer taxes, deed and property recordation fees and sidewalk assessments. They are distributed by income class and between jurisdictions in the same way as the real property tax.

Personal Property

Personal property taxes are basically confined to the taxation of business property in the District and Maryland. In Virginia a large portion of the tax is on individual property, with automobiles and boats being the main items taxed. Taxes levied on business property have been treated as business cost taxes. The remainder of the tax is distributed between income classes by a series on automobile purchases (see Appendix C.23).

Taxes on Horse Racing

Maryland collects considerable monies from its tax on parimutuel betting. A license plate survey of a local track enabled us to estimate the residency of those attending the track. We assume that betting volume is equal per person attending. The tax is distributed by income class in proportion to total consumption expenditures (see Appendix C.24).

Railroad Taxes

Both Maryland and Virginia levy taxes on railroad companies. Since this is a regulated industry we assume that the tax is fully shifted forward. Jurisdictional characteristics of the ultimate consumers are unknown. We assume that 25 percent of the tax is shifted out of the area, and that the services provided in any one jurisdiction serve the entire metropolitan market and thus are divided between jurisdictions in proportion to their share of the area's total personal consumption. The tax is distributed by income class according to total consumption.

Capitation Tax

Virginia levies these taxes equally on each resident individual at least twenty-one years of age. We distribute them by a series which approximates the distribution of individuals twenty-one years of age or over by income class (see Appendix C.25).

The Distribution of All Other Taxes

The distribution of all state and local taxes in the Washington metropolitan area with the exception of the real property tax, the individual income tax, the sales tax, and business cost taxes are shown in tables 6-6 and 6-7. Estimates are presented for both gross tax burdens and burdens after offset. The figures in table 6-6 assume that only part of the corporate and unincorporated income taxes are shifted forward. Figures 6-8 and 6-9 present a graphical depiction of the incidence of these taxes gross and net of offset respectively and assume that the tax is partially borne by owners. The incidence assuming full forward shifting produces only slightly different results.

The incidence of "all other" taxes falling on residents of the District of Columbia is quite irregular. It is regressive between the lowest and next to lowest classes, stays roughly proportional between $3,000 and $10,000, becomes regressive between $10,000 and $25,000, and is slightly progressive between the highest and next to highest income bracket. The federal offset leaves this pattern intact with the exception that it eliminates the slight progressivity at the upper end of the income distribution.

The taxes falling on residents of Maryland and Virginia display basically the same pattern with but one exception. Even before the federal offset there is no progressivity between the highest and next to highest income brackets. The yield of "all other" taxes for 1970 is shown in table 6-7.

Total Taxes

The most relevant consideration as far as tax incidence and tax flows are concerned is the total incidence of all taxes. The incidence of all state and local taxes on residents of various jurisdictions under the partial forward shifting assumption is shown in table 6-8 and figures 6-10 and 6-11. The incidence of all taxes under the alternative full-forward-shifting assumptions is shown in table 6-9 and figures 6-12 and 6-13.

If we consider the incidence of the area's state and local tax structure on residents before offset, then the assumption that part of the property and business income taxes are paid by owners results in a tax structure which is thoroughly regressive only for residents of suburban Virginia. For District of Columbia residents the structure is regressive up to the $4,000-$6,000 income

Table 6-6
Distribution of the Burden of "All Other" Taxes: Partial Forward Shifting

Income Class	D.C. Taxes Before Offset	D.C. Taxes After Offset	Md. Taxes Before Offset	Md. Taxes After Offset	Va. Taxes Before Offset	Va. Taxes After Offset	Total Taxes Before Offset	Total Taxes After Offset	Total Taxes as % of Money Income Before Offset	Total Taxes as % of Money Income After Offset
A. Total Taxes Paid by D.C. Residents										
below $3,000	2,841,257	2,812,589	150,640	132,813	68,728	57,120	3,060,625	3,002,522	3.0	2.9
3,000–3,999	1,505,063	1,484,877	88,845	80,523	36,770	31,542	1,630,678	1,596,942	2.5	2.4
4,000–5,999	5,122,165	5,036,697	305,259	274,738	121,127	103,957	5,548,551	5,415,392	2.5	2.4
6,000–7,499	5,359,399	5,249,579	331,551	296,753	127,883	109,979	5,818,833	5,656,311	2.5	2.4
7,500–9,999	8,348,598	8,124,497	547,303	483,396	208,313	178,239	9,104,214	8,786,132	2.3	2.2
10,000–14,999	11,783,412	11,393,950	815,522	711,350	313,281	266,421	12,912,215	12,371,721	2.0	1.9
15,000–24,999	11,204,381	10,676,515	794,740	662,866	316,681	264,876	12,315,802	11,604,257	1.8	1.7
25,000 and above	12,929,583	10,258,239	494,865	393,332	217,344	177,952	13,641,792	10,829,523	2.0	1.6
Total	59,093,858	55,036,943	3,528,725	3,035,771	1,410,127	1,190,086	64,032,710	59,262,800		
B. Total Taxes Paid by Md. Residents										
below $3,000	359,872	339,376	1,649,929	1,632,978	56,515	46,361	2,066,316	2,018,715	3.4	3.3
3,000–3,999	275,423	264,030	882,238	870,423	35,651	30,689	1,193,312	1,165,142	2.8	2.7
4,000–5,999	962,271	920,057	2,831,325	2,779,009	118,688	102,581	3,912,284	3,801,647	2.9	2.8
6,000–7,499	1,066,212	1,001,007	3,693,167	3,605,742	159,304	137,717	4,918,683	4,752,666	2.8	2.7
7,500–9,999	1,884,845	1,755,324	8,047,239	7,799,072	361,132	308,423	10,293,216	9,862,819	2.5	2.4
10,000–14,999	3,474,428	3,177,797	19,313,821	18,553,824	899,978	746,160	23,688,227	22,477,781	2.0	1.9
15,000–24,999	4,240,843	3,778,214	27,765,358	26,149,043	1,296,602	1,053,528	33,302,803	30,980,785	1.7	1.6
25,000 and above	2,694,759	2,354,527	14,853,486	13,216,360	714,470	560,100	18,262,715	16,130,987	1.1	0.9
Total	14,958,653	13,598,532	79,036,563	74,606,451	3,642,340	2,985,559	97,637,556	91,190,542		
C. Total Taxes Paid by Va. Residents										
below $3,000	234,575	221,511	55,291	45,832	959,563	945,072	1,249,429	1,212,415	2.9	2.8
3,000–3,999	177,580	170,005	40,178	34,745	632,748	620,392	850,506	825,142	2.5	2.4
4,000–5,999	611,819	586,457	139,944	120,658	2,191,270	2,136,438	2,943,033	2,843,553	2.6	2.5
6,000–7,499	665,036	633,506	185,903	159,999	2,896,214	2,799,385	3,747,153	3,592,890	2.6	2.5
7,500–9,999	1,152,976	1,085,895	388,571	330,993	5,701,143	5,460,118	7,242,690	6,877,006	2.4	2.2
10,000–14,999	2,131,348	1,973,791	859,741	721,864	12,787,788	12,063,723	15,778,877	14,759,378	2.1	2.0
15,000–24,999	2,912,775	2,603,274	1,424,946	1,132,586	20,424,906	18,775,020	24,762,627	22,510,880	1.7	1.6
25,000 and above	1,865,320	1,643,694	790,536	589,141	15,116,815	12,306,006	17,772,671	14,538,841	1.5	1.2
Total	9,751,429	8,918,133	3,885,110	3,135,818	60,710,447	55,106,154	74,346,986	67,160,105		

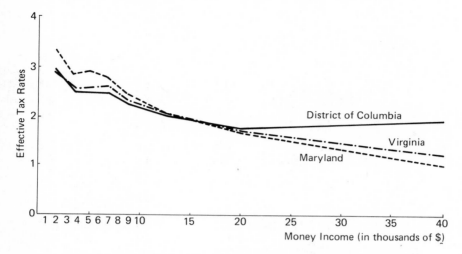

Figure 6-8. Effective Tax Rates of Other Taxes Before Offset.

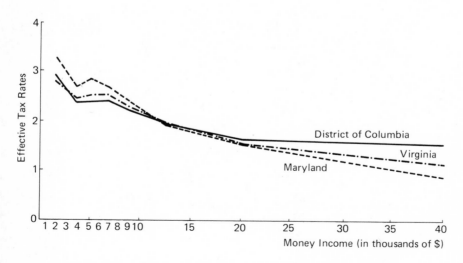

Figure 6-9. Effective Tax Rates of Other Taxes After Offset.

Table 6-7
Yield of "All Other" Taxes, 1970

	D.C. Taxes		Maryland Taxes		Virginia Taxes	
	Before Offset	After Offset	Before Offset	After Offset	Before Offset	After Offset
Taxes Paid by Residents of D.C.						
Tobacco Tax	$ 4,007,338	$ 4,007,338	$ 83,306	$ 83,306	$ 73,876	$ 73,876
Alcohol Excise	6,989,729	6,989,729	19,714	19,714	38,659	38,659
Insurance	2,982,053	2,982,053	118,240	118,240	107,083	107,083
Motor Fuel	6,957,430	5,846,326	1,407,400	1,177,721	280,264	234,506
Horse Racing	—		561,655	561,655	—	—
Railroad			27,545	27,545	110,952	110,952
Bank	2,350,459	2,350,459	71,764	71,764	7,975	7,975
Motor Fines	2,788,047	2,788,047	139,370	139,370	65,331	65,331
Corporate Income A	3,877,988	3,500,514	936,136	714,420	701,469	534,453
B	6,238,892	6,238,892	886,866	886,866	660,643	660,643
Unincorporated Income A	1,258,353	1,141,572	—	—	—	—
B	1,326,540	1,326,540				
Property Related A	762,277	660,243	162,595	122,036	24,520	17,132
B	1,040,229	1,040,229	98,570	98,570	6,418	6,418
Public Utility	4,919,028	4,919,028	—	—	—	—
Personal Fees	559,862	559,862	—	—	—	—
Estate & Gift Taxes	6,712,917	4,363,395	—	—	—	—
Motor Vehicle Ex.	4,880,779	4,880,779	—	—	—	—
Motor Vehicle Registrations & Licenses	10,047,598	10,047,598				
Total Taxes A	59,093,858	55,036,943	3,527,725	3,035,771	1,410,129	1,189,986
B	61,800,901	58,340,275	3,414,430	3,184,751	1,351,201	1,305,443
Taxes Paid by Residents of Md.						
Tobacco Tax	786,284	786,284	7,419,516	7,419,516	155,739	155,739
Alcohol Excise	3,789,995	3,789,995	4,816,939	4,816,939	184,255	184,255
Insurance	888,953	888,953	5,116,960	5,116,960	188,320	188,320
Motor Fuel	2,294,422	1,919,987	12,720,103	10,182,968	1,019,573	816,159
Horse Racing	—		46,416	46,416	—	
Railroad			2,206,502	2,206,502	186,967	186,967
Bank	1,073,370	1,073,370	2,097,571	2,097,571	12,349	12,349
Motor Fines	1,517,026	1,517,026	1,260,633	1,260,633	239,796	239,796
Corporate Income A	3,931,848	3,090,256	3,803,668	3,267,115	1,588,821	1,164,662
B	4,260,400	4,260,400	5,222,653	5,222,653	1,365,824	1,365,824

Unincorporated Income A	505,820	409,475	—	—	55,421	37,262
Unincorporated Income B	218,198	218,198	—	—	9,297	9,297
Property Related A	170,933	123,186	4,447,903	3,651,048	—	—
Property Related B	61,285	61,285	4,998,932	4,998,932	—	—
Public Utility	—	—	14,224,883	14,224,883	—	—
Personal Fees	—	—	1,258,725	1,258,725	—	—
Estate & Gift Taxes	—	—	1,600,097	1,040,528	—	—
Motor Vehicle Ex.	—	—	7,859,277	7,859,277	—	—
Motor Vehicle Registrations & Licenses	—	—	10,157,370	10,157,370	—	—
Total Taxes A	14,958,651	13,598,532	79,036,563	74,606,451	3,631,241	2,985,559
Total Taxes B	14,889,933	14,515,498	81,006,577	77,909,873	3,362,120	3,158,706

Taxes Paid by Residents of Va.

Tobacco Tax	455,502	455,502	15,146	15,146	1,737,091	1,737,091
Alcohol Excise	3,055,389	3,055,389	34,586	34,586	7,152,842	7,152,842
Insurance	520,084	520,084	79,308	79,308	5,415,949	5,415,949
Motor Fuel	734,809	586,674	1,514,292	1,209,304	7,126,674	5,692,638
Horse Racing	—	—	320,946	320,946	—	—
Railroad	—	—	33,384	33,384	—	—
Bank	855,205	855,205	28,301	28,301	134,475	134,475
Motor Fines	1,083,590	1,083,590	149,956	149,956	541,297	541,297
Corporate Income A	2,639,186	2,051,290	1,478,110	1,105,626	1,658,053	1,658,053
Corporate Income B	2,770,248	2,770,248	1,300,736	1,300,736	2,360,050	2,086,593
Unincorporated Income A	287,624	223,905	—	—	3,503,635	3,503,635
Unincorporated Income B	104,140	104,140	—	—	—	—
Property Related A	120,193	86,510	231,082	159,620	667,830	553,511
Property Related B	40,458	40,458	63,721	63,721	779,360	779,360
Public Utility	—	—	—	—	9,179,708	9,179,708
Personal Fees	—	—	—	—	741,083	741,083
Estate & Gift Taxes	—	—	—	—	5,537,645	3,599,459
Motor Vehicle Ex.	—	—	—	—	2,147,737	2,147,737
Motor Vehicle Registrations & Licenses	—	—	—	—	7,291,284	7,291,284
Personal Property	—	—	—	—	8,884,342	7,063,448
Capitation	—	—	—	—	134,387	110,986
Total Taxes A	9,751,582	8,918,149	3,885,111	3,136,177	60,710,447	55,106,154
Total Taxes B	9,619,425	9,471,290	3,540,376	3,235,388	61,965,562	56,749,045

Table 6-8
Distribution of the Burden of Total Taxes: Partial Forward Shifting

Income Class	D.C. Taxes		Md. Taxes		Va. Taxes		Total Taxes		Total Taxes as a Percentage of Money Income	
	Before Offset	After Offset	Before Offset	After Offset	Before Offset	After Offset	Before Offset	After Offset	Before Offset	After Offset
A. Total Taxes Paid by D.C. Residents										
below $3,000	12,835,949	12,684,079	909,281	795,772	476,316	392,057	14,221,546	13,871,908	13.8	13.4
3,000–3,999	5,572,633	5,445,733	366,546	334,932	169,747	148,301	6,108,925	5,928,966	9.3	9.0
4,000–5,999	17,938,835	17,258,497	1,153,503	1,040,196	523,772	452,101	19,616,110	18,750,794	8.8	8.4
6,000–7,499	19,102,817	18,121,751	1,131,308	1,025,525	497,047	436,713	20,731,172	19,583,989	8.9	8.4
7,500–9,999	31,461,960	29,330,278	1,813,145	1,617,227	786,874	681,040	34,061,979	31,528,545	8.7	8.0
10,000–14,999	51,608,907	46,536,243	2,644,911	2,342,625	1,137,772	986,066	55,391,590	49,864,934	8.7	7.8
15,000–24,999	59,660,831	49,325,657	3,566,549	2,867,564	1,759,193	1,387,488	64,986,573	53,580,709	9.3	7.7
25,000 and above	58,281,711	39,594,547	3,004,574	2,214,939	1,639,949	1,190,755	62,926,234	43,000,241	9.4	6.4
Total	256,463,643	218,196,785	14,589,817	12,238,780	6,990,670	5,674,521	278,044,129	236,110,086		
B. Total Taxes Paid by Md. Residents										
below $3,000	964,444	853,451	8,044,723	7,922,249	329,028	256,353	9,338,195	9,032,053	15.3	14.8
3,000–3,999	508,954	476,215	3,728,243	3,632,709	127,627	108,200	4,364,824	4,217,124	10.2	9.9
4,000–5,999	1,655,922	1,543,186	11,889,383	11,395,113	389,806	328,020	13,935,111	13,266,319	10.4	9.9
6,000–7,499	1,876,959	1,752,023	16,395,755	15,456,536	462,717	398,785	18,735,431	17,607,344	10.7	10.0
7,500–9,999	3,720,482	3,411,978	36,284,556	33,429,923	1,045,692	886,744	41,050,730	37,728,645	9.8	9.0
10,000–14,999	8,044,810	7,309,183	101,375,468	90,532,584	2,557,542	2,162,457	111,977,820	100,004,224	9.6	8.6
15,000–24,999	14,698,715	12,331,858	174,306,800	142,259,457	5,610,858	4,398,096	194,616,373	158,989,411	9.9	8.1
25,000 and above	11,359,580	8,744,984	133,273,377	88,957,268	4,610,694	3,293,733	149,243,651	100,995,985	8.8	6.0
Total	42,829,866	36,422,878	485,352,305	393,585,839	15,133,964	11,832,388	543,262,135	441,841,105		
C. Total Taxes Paid by Va. Residents										
below $3,000	599,834	530,654	294,924	235,284	4,970,498	4,903,090	5,865,256	5,669,028	13.7	13.2
3,000–3,999	341,846	318,212	132,047	112,414	2,500,599	2,438,586	2,974,492	2,869,212	8.7	8.4
4,000–5,999	1,128,942	1,047,556	428,969	362,475	8,321,959	7,989,708	9,879,870	9,399,739	8.7	8.2
6,000–7,499	1,247,663	1,165,657	499,708	432,583	11,332,443	10,700,613	13,079,814	12,298,853	9.9	8.5
7,500–9,999	2,326,717	2,142,134	1,024,174	872,973	22,573,981	20,860,993	25,924,872	23,876,100	8.5	7.8
10,000–14,999	4,680,979	4,276,675	2,208,580	1,887,712	56,028,950	50,227,970	62,918,509	56,392,357	8.5	7.6
15,000–24,999	9,856,753	8,262,210	5,772,854	4,494,685	98,373,953	81,028,074	114,012,560	93,784,969	8.0	6.6
25,000 and above	7,667,924	5,937,299	4,600,908	3,291,870	68,645,767	47,218,684	80,914,599	56,447,853	6.9	4.8
Total	27,850,658	23,680,397	14,962,164	11,689,996	272,748,150	225,367,718	315,569,972	260,738,111		

Table 6-9
Distribution of Total Taxes: Full Forward Shifting

Income Class	D.C. Taxes Before Offset	D.C. Taxes After Offset	Md. Taxes Before Offset	Md. Taxes After Offset	Va. Taxes Before Offset	Va. Taxes After Offset	Total Taxes Before Offset	Total Taxes After Offset	Total Taxes as a Percentage of Money Income Before Offset	After Offset
A. Total Taxes Paid by D.C. Residents										
below $3,000	16,482,932	16,449,658	747,029	745,305	287,459	286,987	17,517,420	17,481,950	17.0	16.9
3,000–3,999	6,959,900	6,867,604	354,376	349,053	133,820	132,424	7,448,096	7,349,081	11.4	11.2
4,000–5,999	21,584,489	21,027,172	1,122,365	1,092,560	420,449	412,760	23,127,303	22,532,492	10.4	10.1
6,000–7,499	22,388,725	21,521,386	1,140,986	1,099,250	424,161	413,532	23,953,872	23,034,168	10.3	9.9
7,500–9,999	36,254,005	34,221,219	1,831,171	1,742,845	678,594	656,206	38,763,770	36,620,270	9.9	9.3
10,000–14,999	57,396,657	52,641,521	2,720,965	2,559,695	1,012,287	971,353	61,129,909	56,172,569	9.6	8.8
15,000–24,999	62,747,607	53,237,274	2,635,611	2,398,887	1,000,451	939,754	66,383,669	56,575,915	9.5	8.1
25,000 and above	58,761,385	41,248,630	1,820,592	1,578,028	716,443	652,299	61,298,420	43,478,957	9.2	6.5
Total	282,575,700	247,214,464	12,373,095	11,565,623	4,673,664	4,465,315	299,622,459	263,245,402		
B. Total Taxes Paid by Md. Residents										
below $3,000	749,983	749,249	9,330,972	9,220,287	168,102	167,911	10,249,057	10,137,447	16.8	16.6
3,000–3,999	471,592	467,846	4,367,118	4,297,573	92,123	91,254	4,930,833	4,856,673	11.6	11.4
4,000–5,999	1,551,824	1,529,105	13,682,937	13,270,858	288,147	283,110	15,522,908	15,083,073	11.6	11.3
6,000–7,499	1,801,806	1,764,646	18,389,765	17,535,462	370,842	361,559	20,562,413	19,661,667	11.7	11.2
7,500–9,999	3,550,785	3,456,756	39,685,122	37,034,322	841,055	812,644	44,076,962	41,303,722	10.5	9.9
10,000–14,999	7,754,583	7,518,463	108,065,309	97,739,580	2,123,572	2,033,143	117,943,464	107,291,186	10.1	9.3
15,000–24,999	10,829,888	10,331,685	178,386,977	148,224,368	3,203,299	2,992,482	192,420,164	161,548,535	9.8	8.2
25,000 and above	6,739,740	6,260,468	132,800,916	90,548,805	1,894,871	1,713,973	141,435,527	98,523,246	8.3	5.9
Total	33,450,201	32,078,218	504,709,116	417,871,255	8,982,011	8,456,076	547,141,328	458,405,549		
C. Total Taxes Paid by Va. Residents										
below $3,000	456,238	455,996	177,275	176,994	6,014,643	5,997,803	6,648,156	6,630,793	15.5	15.5
3,000–3,999	309,917	308,778	104,040	103,027	3,015,686	2,970,836	3,429,643	3,382,641	10.1	9.9
4,000–5,999	1,033,148	1,026,490	343,876	337,552	9,771,625	9,494,969	11,148,649	10,859,011	9.8	9.5
6,000–7,499	1,175,387	1,163,441	434,057	422,102	12,908,488	12,333,429	14,517,932	13,918,972	10.1	9.7
7,500–9,999	2,181,897	2,149,440	889,627	856,641	25,143,587	23,549,343	28,215,111	26,555,424	9.2	8.7
10,000–14,999	4,446,486	4,353,250	1,991,800	1,899,181	60,687,297	55,138,191	67,125,583	61,390,622	9.0	8.3
15,000–24,999	6,957,869	6,703,881	3,359,282	3,125,771	101,528,481	85,137,008	111,845,632	94,966,660	7.8	6.6
25,000 and above	4,391,498	4,154,975	1,984,900	1,794,521	68,529,748	48,739,738	74,906,146	54,689,234	6.4	4.7
Total	20,952,440	20,316,251	9,284,857	8,715,789	287,599,555	243,361,317	317,836,852	272,393,357		

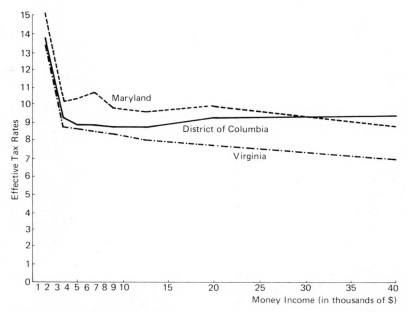

Figure 6–10. Effective Tax Rates for Total Taxes: Partial Shifting Before Offset.

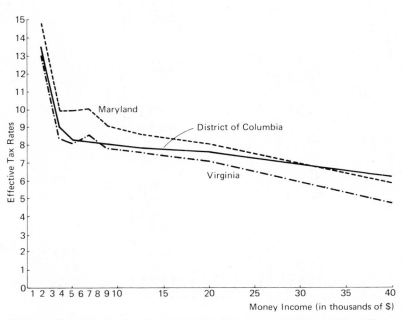

Figure 6–11. Effective Tax Rates for Total Taxes: Partial Shifting After Offset.

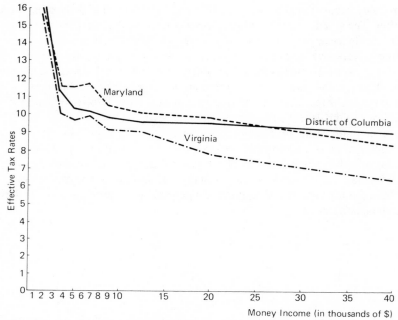

Figure 6-12. Effective Tax Rates for Total Taxes: Full Forward Shifting Before Offset.

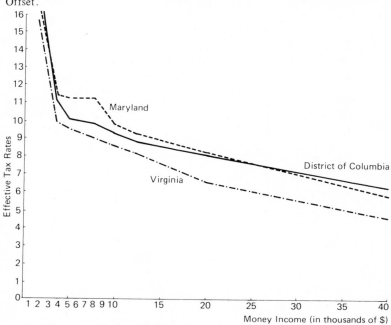

Figure 6-13. Effective Tax Rates for Total Taxes: Full Forward Shifting After Offset.

class, roughly proportional between $6,000 and $15,000 and slightly progressive thereafter. The situation for Maryland residents is irregular. In general the Maryland tax incidence appears to be slightly regressive. Actually, however, the incidence is regressive between the two lowest income brackets, and slightly regressive between the two highest, but generally proportional across the middle-income classes. Under the assumption that all of the property and business income taxes are shifted forward, the structure in each area, despite some minor aberrations, can be described as thoroughly regressive.

The presence of the federal offset guarantees that the overall incidence under both sets of assumptions is regressive in each jurisdiction. The tax incidence for suburban Virginia residents, who are subject to only a mildly progressive income tax, is the most regressive. Finally, the absolute levels of taxation differ between jurisdictions, with taxes as a percentage of money income highest in Maryland and lowest in Virginia.

7

Interjurisdictional Fiscal Flows in Metropolitan Washington

Introduction

The net benefit flow from the District of Columbia into the suburban areas and the net tax flow from the suburbs into the District do not in themselves provide a complete picture of metropolitan fiscal interaction. Only the difference between these flows shows the fiscal relation between the areas. In this chapter, we present estimates of these net fiscal flows between the jurisdictions. First estimates are aggregated by jurisdiction, following the example of other "fiscal exploitation" studies. In addition, however, we also present net fiscal flows by income class. These estimates are particularly relevant for public policy considerations. If it is found, for example, that suburbs obtain more benefits from a city than they return in the form of taxes, some corrective action is implied. Two possible alternatives, for example, would be (a) the imposition of a progressive income tax by a higher level of government with the proceeds used to finance compensating grants to the city, or (b) the imposition of a tax on every individual or automobile entering the city. The choice between such policy instruments depends on whether upper-income suburbanites derive the largest net fiscal residuals in their relationship with the city, while lower-income suburbanites derive small or possibly even negative residuals, or whether the net gains to suburbanites are more or less equally distributed across commuters.

There have been two approaches to the measurement of "fiscal exploitation," as discussed in Chapter 2. One approach is to determine whether the total net taxes contributed to the city by suburbanites exceed the total net cost of physical services provided by the city to the suburbs.[1] Such cost-of-service estimates of fiscal flows for the Washington area are presented below. This approach is a useful measure if one's purpose is, for instance, to measure whether an expanded level of city services together with increased tax rates are likely to pay for themselves as far as nonresident contributions are concerned, or if one conceives of "fairness" being achieved if people pay the cost of physical services received.

We also present fiscal flow estimates based on "welfare" measure. Benefits in this instance are determined by what an individual would be willing to pay for particular public services whether they are physically received by himself or by others. Since these welfare estimates are based on subjective evaluations of benefits, allowance is made for the offset against the federal income tax. In other words, the second set of fiscal flows presented measures the net welfare

gain from the metropolitan fiscal process derived by the suburban residents. These net gains are also presented both in the aggregate and by income class.

Net Fiscal Flows in the Aggregate

A summary of the net fiscal flows between jurisdictions is shown in table 7-1. Benefits measured on a cost-of-service basis are compared with taxes which are not corrected for the federal offset. The welfare estimate of benefits, however, are compared with tax payments net of the offset. In both cases two alternative sets of assumptions about the incidence of taxes are employed. Net fiscal flows labeled "A" are based on the assumption that part of the property-related and business income taxes are borne by owners. The fiscal flows referred to as "B" are based on the assumption that all of these taxes are shifted forward.

According to the cost-of-service estimates there is a net fiscal flow from the suburbs into the city. Under the assumption of partial forward shifting, it is estimated that the net fiscal flow from suburban Maryland to the District is $15,417,639, or nearly $40.00 per household. The net flow from suburban Virginia to the District is $12,809,949, or $46.36 per household. Under the assumption of complete forward shifting these estimates are reduced by 40 percent, to $21.37 per family for Maryland and by 36 percent to $29.78 in Virginia. In other words, these estimates indicate that if all state and local expenditures in the Washington metropolitan area were, for example, increased proportionately and if the revenues were derived from a proportionate increase in all taxes, the extra revenues derived from suburbanites would more than pay for the extra costs of services provided to them.

Therefore, if one is ready to accept the proposition that suburbanites receive no welfare gain from the redistributive expenditures of the city government, and if one defines exploitation as a failure to pay for the costs of services provided an individual, one must conclude there is no "exploitation" of the District by the suburbs. In fact, both District and suburban residents more than pay for the cost of services provided to them by other jurisdictions in the metropolitan area. The net flow into the District is caused by the fact that the excess of suburban residents' tax payments over the cost of services provided to them by the District is greater than the excess of tax payments by District residents over the cost of the services that the suburban jurisdictions provided to District residents. As a result, given this definition of exploitation, the District "exploits" the suburbs. It exploits Maryland by somewhere between $21.37 and $39.93 per household unit per year and Virginia by somewhere between $29.78 and $44.36 per household unit per year.

While such measures may be useful for some purposes, it is our contention that this usefulness is extremely limited since they account neither for the city's support of a greater concentration of poor people, nor for the greater willingness

Table 7-1
Fiscal Flows Between Jurisdictions

		Cost-of-Service Basis				Welfare Basis			
		Maryland		Virginia		Maryland		Virginia	
		Total	Per Household Unit	Total	Per Household Unit	Total	Per Household Unit	Total	Per Household Unit
Benefit Flows									
Benefits Received from D.C.		$18,471,235	$47.83	$9,521,892	$34.46	$91,015,522	$235.66	$58,807,939	$212.81
Benefits Given to D.C.		5,648,825	14.63	1,471,853	5.33	19,264,817	49.88	9,665,932	34.98
Net Benefit Flows from D.C.		+12,822,410	+33.20	+8,050,039	+29.13	+71,750,705	+185.78	+49,142,007	+177.83
Tax Flows									
Taxes Paid to D.C.	A	42,829,867	110.90	27,850,658	100.78	36,422,878	94.31	23,680,397	85.69
	B	33,450,201	86.61	20,952,440	75.82	32,078,218	83.06	20,316,235	73.52
Taxes Received from D.C. Residents	A	14,589,818	37.78	6,990,670	25.30	12,238,780	31.69	5,674,521	20.53
	B	12,373,095	32.04	4,673,664	16.91	11,565,623	29.95	4,465,334	16.16
Net Tax Flows to D.C.	A	28,240,049	73.12	20,859,988	75.49	24,184,098	62.62	18,005,876	65.16
	B	21,077,106	54.57	16,278,776	58.91	20,512,585	53.11	15,850,901	57.36
Net Fiscal Flows from D.C. (Net Benefits Less Net Taxes)	A	-15,417,639	-39.93	-12,809,949	-46.36	+47,566,607	+123.16	+31,136,131	+112.67
	B	-8,254,696	-21.37	-8,228,737	-29.78	+51,238,120	+132.67	+33,291,106	+120.47

of higher-income individuals to support both redistributive and other public
services. The welfare calculations, however, do reflect these considerations.
Flows estimated on a welfare basis measure the amount people in other jurisdictions would be willing to pay for services provided them by other jurisdictions
as well as the true costs imposed upon them by the tax structure of the other
metropolitan jurisdictions. On such a welfare basis it appears that the suburban
areas enjoy substantial net gains, as can be seen in table 7-1. In the aggregate, we
estimate net flows from the District of Columbia into Maryland of between
$47,566,607 and $51,238,120 and into Virginia of between $31,136,131 and
$33,291,106. On a per household unit basis, the net fiscal flows into Maryland
are between $132.67 and $123.16, whereas the flows into Virginia are between
$120.47 and $112.67.

Even though there is a substantial net flow of taxes into the District of
Columbia from the suburbs, this is swamped by the much larger net flow of
benefits from the District into the suburbs. The net result is a considerable gain
to suburban household units. Thus if one defines "exploitation" as a situation
wherein one does not pay, at the margin, what one would be willing to pay for
services received, then there exists considerable "fiscal exploitation" of the city
by the suburbs in the Washington metropolitan area.

The breakdown of the flows by tax and expenditure categories are presented in tables 7-2 through 7-5. For instance, table 7-2 shows gross tax flows
from suburban Maryland residents into the District amounting to either
$42,829,867 or $33,450,201 depending on incidence assumptions. The individual taxes that make up these gross tax flows are presented in the first two
columns in table 7-2. We will confine our remarks here only to those net tax
flows after offset that are based on the assumption that some of the taxes are
borne by owners and on the assumption that the net benefits flows are calculated
on a welfare basis.

The net tax flow after federal offset into the District from Maryland totals
$24,184,098, as can be derived from table 7-3. Of this total 27.3 percent is
constituted by the net property tax flow, 11.2 percent by the net sales tax flow,
17.8 percent by the net business cost tax flow, 15.6 percent by the net alcohol
beverage excise tax flow, and 28.1 percent net flow from other taxes. The total
net tax flow after federal offset to the District from Virginia is $18,005,876, as
can be derived from table 7-3. Of this total 28.7 percent is derived from net
property tax flow, 12.3 percent from the net sales tax flow, 16.0 percent net
business cost tax flow, 16.8 percent net alcohol beverage excise tax flow, and
26.1 percent net flow from other taxes. It should be noted that a considerable
fraction of the suburban tax flow into the District is due to the high liquor sales
there, a fact which may not be replicated in other metropolitan areas.

Net benefit flows on a welfare basis from the District into Maryland are
$71,750,705 and $49,142,007 into Virginia, as can be derived from table 7-5.
Of these total net flows into Maryland, 33.8 percent are from social services,

Table 7-2
Tax Flows Between Jurisdictions Before Federal Tax Offset

Tax		D.C. Taxes Paid by Residents of:		Maryland Taxes Paid by Residents of D.C.	Virginia Taxes Paid by Residents of D.C.
		Maryland	Virginia		
Property Tax					
	A	$14,497,124	$10,198,008	$ 5,132,532	$3,098,251
	B	5,186,179	3,422,778	3,030,105	840,171
Sales Tax		6,879,191	3,728,606	3,749,300	1,188,144
Business Cost Taxes		6,494,898	4,181,631	2,179,260	1,294,148
Corporate Income Tax					
	A	3,931,848	2,639,186	936,136	701,469
	B	4,260,400	2,770,248	886,866	660,643
Motor Fuel Excise Tax		2,294,422	734,809	1,407,400	280,264
Alcohol Beverage Excise Tax		3,789,995	3,055,389	19,714	38,659
Tobacco Excise		786,284	455,502	83,306	73,876
Insurance Tax		888,953	520,084	118,240	107,083
Bank Tax		1,073,370	855,205	71,764	7,975
Motor Fines		1,517,026	1,083,590	139,370	65,331
Property Related					
	A	170,933	120,372	162,595	24,518
	B	61,285	40,458	98,570	6,418
Unincorporated Income Tax					
	A	505,820	287,624	–	–
	B	218,198	104,140	–	–
Railroad Tax		–	–	27,545	110,952
Tax on Horse Racing		–	–	561,655	–
Total					
	A	42,829,867	27,859,658	14,589,818	6,990,670
	B	33,450,201	20,952,440	12,373,095	4,673,664

Table 7-3
Tax Flows Between Jurisdictions After Federal Tax Offset

Tax		D.C. Taxes Paid by Residents of:		Maryland Taxes Paid by Residents of D.C.	Virginia Taxes Paid by Residents of D.C.
		Maryland	Virginia		
Property Tax					
	A	$10,447,805	$ 7,340,081	$ 3,852,242	$2,164,834
	B	5,186,179	3,422,778	3,030,105	840,171
Sales Tax		5,881,643	3,240,536	3,171,507	1,025,553
Business Cost Taxes		6,494,898	4,181,631	2,179,260	1,294,148
Corporate Income Tax					
	A	3,090,256	2,051,290	714,420	534,453
	B	4,260,400	2,770,248	886,866	660,643
Motor Fuel Excise Tax		1,919,987	586,674	1,177,721	234,525
Alcohol Beverage Excise Tax		3,789,995	3,055,389	19,714	38,659
Tobacco Excise		786,284	455,502	83,306	73,876
Insurance Tax		888,953	520,084	118,240	107,083
Bank Tax		1,073,370	855,205	71,764	7,975
Motor Fines		1,517,026	1,083,590	139,370	65,331
Property Related					
	A	123,186	86,510	122,036	17,132
	B	61,285	40,458	98,570	6,418
Unincorporated Income Tax					
	A	409,475	223,905	–	–
	B	218,198	104,140	–	–
Railroad Tax		–	–	27,545	110,952
Tax on Horse Racing		–	–	561,655	–
Total					
	A	36,422,878	23,680,397	12,387,780	5,674,521
	B	32,078,218	20,316,235	11,565,623	4,465,334

Table 7-4

Benefit Flows Between Jurisdictions on a Cost-of-Service Basis

Expenditure Category	Benefits Received from D.C. Expenditures by Residents of:		Benefits Received by D.C. Residents from Maryland Expenditures	Benefits Received by D.C. Residents from Virginia Expenditures
	Maryland	Virginia		
Higher Education	$ 283,734	$ 66,649	$ 975,712	$ 248,519
Police	6,112,265	2,926,085	541,989	172,726
Library	304,100	130,000		
Recreation and Parks	1,363,219	1,670,422	482,035	98,218
Corrections	1,726,714	826,619	190,622	44,905
Transportation	5,677,221	2,124,382	2,871,280	595,293
Fire	1,750,683	1,131,661	169,309	166,875
General Government	1,253,299	646,074	417,878	145,317
Total	18,471,235	9,521,892	5,648,825	1,471,853

Table 7-5

Benefit Flows Between Jurisdictions on a Welfare Basis

Expenditure Category	Benefits Received from D.C. Expenditures by Residents of:		Benefits Received by D.C. Residents from Maryland Expenditures	Benefits Received by D. C. Residents from Virginia Expenditures
	Maryland	Virginia		
Elementary and Secondary Education	$18,688,926	$12,512,955	$ 9,727,135	$5,515,693
Higher Education	767,181	381,776	1,091,019	416,092
Health	17,335,083	12,182,442	1,361,712	583,306
Police	8,732,736	4,111,474	438,196	96,010
Library	842,624	510,701	214,761	176,479
Recreation and Parks	2,612,292	2,514,565	567,188	157,412
Corrections	2,466,997	1,161,490	154,117	24,961
Transportation	5,675,314	2,092,863	2,322,186	502,334
Fire	1,679,468	1,053,698	139,353	136,702
Social Services	26,046,229	18,304,156	1,829,204	1,104,797
General Government	6,168,672	3,981,819	1,419,946	952,146
Total	91,015,522	58,807,939	19,264,817	9,665,932

22.3 percent from health services, 12.5 percent from elementary and secondary education, 11.6 percent from police services, 6.6 percent from general government, and 13.2 percent from all other services. Of the net flows into Virginia, 35.0 percent are from social services, 23.6 percent from health services, 14.2 percent from elementary and secondary education, 8.2 percent from police, 6.2 percent from general government, and 12.8 percent from all other services.

One can readily see that the bulk of these net expenditure flows are generated by poverty-related expenditures. If the poor were equally distributed between jurisdictions and if each jurisdiction spent the same amount per capita on services given the poor, the net benefit flows would be reduced to little more than one-quarter of their current levels and the net fiscal flows would be negligible.

Net Fiscal Flows By Income Class

The estimates of the aggregate net flows are consonant with earlier studies. When benefits have been measured on a cost-of-service basis and poverty-related expenditures assumed to be beneficial solely to residents, it has been found that suburbs more than compensated for the services they receive.[a] In the one instance that accounted for differences in willingness-to-pay and poverty-related expenditures, it was found that suburbs "exploited" the central city.[2] However, we are in a position to move beyond these previous findings because benefits received from and taxes paid to other jurisdictions have been estimated by income class. Thus, we can get at least some idea of whether a net fiscal flow into the suburbs is made up of flows of approximately equal size for all income classes or of flows concentrated in particular income classes.

Table 7-6 presents the breakdown of net fiscal flows between the District and the suburban areas by income class with benefits measured on a cost-of-service basis and taxes assumed to be partially borne by owners of property and estimated before the federal offset. The fiscal residuals are negative for all income classes except the very lowest in the suburbs. Even though the negative interjurisdictional fiscal residuals grow in absolute size as income increases, they are of substantial size only for the two highest income classes. For the income classes below $15,000, they never amount to as much as $50 per year. But for income classes above $15,000, the residuals are quite large. Household units with incomes above $25,000 in suburban Maryland are estimated to pay $243.40 and those in suburban Virginia pay $235.20 more in taxes to the District than it costs the District to supply them with services. District residents contribute an excess of $152.99 and $97.94 to suburban Maryland and suburban Virginia, respectively.

---

[a]See discussion in Chapter 2.

Table 7-6

Net Fiscal Flows by Income Class: Benefits Estimated on Cost-of-Service Basis— Taxes Before Offset

Residents of the District of Columbia Income Classes	Benefits Received From Maryland Less Taxes Paid to Maryland		Benefits Received From Virginia Less Taxes Paid to Virginia	
	Total	Per House-hold Unit	Total	Per House-hold Unit
below $3,000	-$ 446,299	-$ 5.63	-$ 314,358	-$ 3.97
3,000-3,999	-188,647	-9.64	-104,613	-5.35
4,000-5,999	-599,425	-13.48	-355,074	-7.98
6,000-7,499	-566,425	-16.38	-339,588	-9.82
7,500-9,999	-811,499	-18.11	-547,829	-12.22
10,000-14,999	-1,545,085	-30.27	-849,638	-16.64
15,000-24,999	-2,450,966	-70.27	-1,514,247	-43.41
25,000 and above	-2,332,995	-152.99	-1,493,470	-97.94
Total	-8,940,992		-5,518,817	

Residents of Maryland Income Classes	Benefits Received From the District of Columbia Less Taxes Paid to the District of Columbia	
	Total	Per House-hold Unit
below $3,000	+$ 401,478	+$ 8.89
3,000-3,999	-59,439	-4.89
4,000-5,999	-539,756	-20.33
6,000-7,499	-656,004	-25.26
7,500-9,999	-1,007,982	-21.08
10,000-14,999	-3,824,223	-41.02
15,000-24,999	-9,603,513	-97.90
25,000 and above	-9,069,192	-243.40
Total	-24,358,631	

Residents of Virginia Income Classes		
below $3,000	+$ 81,980	+$ 2.81
3,000-3,999	-68,282	-7.01
4,000-5,999	-416,871	-18.51
6,000-7,499	-505,218	-23.69
7,500-9,999	-634,764	-18.13
10,000-14,999	-2,815,173	-47.33
15,000-24,999	-7,466,718	-104.49
25,000 and above	-6,503,720	-235.20
Total	-18,328,766	

These estimates imply that it is advantageous for a jurisdiction to have wealthy nonresidents who work, shop, and own property therein. Thus an increase in a bordering jurisdiction's wealthy population, as long as it is not created by outmigration, is likely to lead to greater increases in tax revenues than in expenditure requirements.

The interjurisdictional fiscal flows presented in table 7-7, however, present a different picture. These calculations also assume that taxes are partially borne by owners of property and are net of the federal offset. The benefit estimates take account of effective demand rising with income and use-of-income benefits from redistributional public goods.[b] The aggregate interjurisdictional flows shown in table 7-7 are positive. In other words, benefits received exceed taxes paid for all jurisdictions. The excess of benefits received over taxes paid is greater, however, for suburban residents than for District residents. For particular income classes, these flows are generally negative below the $6,000 income level and become positive above that level. Their absolute sizes are fairly inconsequential up to $10,000. However, we estimate that the excess of benefits received over taxes paid to the District are $515.42 and $426.96 for Maryland and Virginia household units, respectively, with incomes in excess of $25,000. District residents in this income class, on the other hand, receive net gains from Maryland of $217.96 and from Virginia of $95.77.

It is important to keep in mind the correct interpretation of these results. Our estimates *do not* indicate that the District treasury loses, for example, $515.42 to the average suburban Maryland household with income in excess of $25,000. Rather, they indicate that such a Maryland household derives a net gain from the services provided by the District amounting to $515.42 It values the benefits received from District of Columbia services at $515.42 more than the taxes actually paid to the District.[c]

Summary

Two conclusions emerge from the discussion of this chapter. First, suburbanites pay the costs for the services directly provided to them. However, second, if the estimation of benefits allows for the positive income elasticity of marginal evaluations of public services and for the existence of use-of-income benefits from redistributional transactions between the District of Columbia and its

---

[b]The size of these fiscal flows is hardly affected at all by source-of-income benefits. Such benefits are almost entirely retained by residents of the jurisdiction making the expenditure.

[c]Of course, this does not mean that a suburbanite would voluntarily agree to pay this amount. The contention is that if he were assured that others with the same income throughout the suburban area would pay this amount, then he would agree to make the payment rather than see the District of Columbia's expenditure programs, including poverty-related expenditures, cut back.

Table 7-7

Net Fiscal Flows by Income Class: Benefits Estimated on Welfare Basis—Taxes Net of Offset

Residents of the District of Columbia Income Classes	Benefits Received From Maryland Less Taxes Paid to Maryland		Benefits Received From Virginia Less Taxes Paid to Virginia	
	Total	Per House-hold Unit	Total	Per House-hold Unit
below $3,000	-$ 679,764	-$ 8.57	-$ 344,647	-$ 4.35
3,000–3,999	-269,676	-13.78	-120,079	-6.14
4,000–5,999	-339,946	-7.64	-97,103	-2.18
6,000–7,499	+173,440	+5.01	+188,891	+5.46
7,500–9,999	+692,936	+15.46	+470,192	+10.49
10,000–14,999	+1,831,136	+35.87	+1,221,226	+23.92
15,000–24,999	+2,294,296	+65.78	+1,212,595	+34.77
25,000 and above	+3,323,615	+217.96	+1,460,336	+95.77
Total	+7,026,037		+3,991,411	

Residents of Maryland Income Classes	Benefits Received From the District of Columbia Less Taxes Paid to the District of Columbia	
	Total	Per House-hold Unit
below $3,000	-$ 584,220	-$ 12.94
3,000–3,999	-300,945	-24.78
4,000–5,999	-107,766	-4.06
6,000–7,499	+1,051,313	+40.48
7,500–9,999	+3,838,949	+80.28
10,000–14,999	+11,490,355	+123.26
15,000–24,999	+19,999,986	+203.88
25,000 and above	+19,204,972	+515.42
Total	+54,592,644	

Residents of Virginia Income Classes		
below $3,000	-$ 359,270	-$ 12.33
3,000–3,999	-201,150	-20.66
4,000–5,999	+43,518	+1.93
6,000–7,499	+911,022	+42.71
7,500–9,999	+2,874,876	+82.12
10,000–14,999	+6,793,928	+114.22
15,000–24,999	+13,258,206	+185.53
25,000 and above	+11,806,412	+426.96
Total	+35,127,542	

suburbs, then residents of the suburbs are seen to enjoy net benefits. Such net benefits would be eliminated if the costs of financing redistributional expenditures were to be distributed equally over the entire metropolitan area.

An objection to this measurement of redistributional benefits can be offered on the grounds that the nonpoor in neighboring jurisdictions do not value redistributional programs on behalf of poor residents of other jurisdictions as highly as those for the poor in their own jurisdictions.[d] Even if we assume such evaluations are considerably less, however, there would still be substantial benefit flows from the District to the suburbs. Assume, for instance, that the benefits to nonresidents from a jurisdiction's welfare and health expenditures are only half as great as the benefits yielded to the jurisdiction's own nonpoor. Under this assumption the fiscal flows estimated on a welfare basis[e] would still be $26,017,499 or $67.37 per household unit in Maryland, and $15,728,333 or $56.92 per household unit in Virginia. Thus, given the form of the utility function as assumed, any specification of the geographical pattern of utility interdependence that admits any substantial degree of interdependence between individuals in the same metropolitan area will result in significant net fiscal flows from the District to the suburbs.

---

[d]Two considerations that might suggest this have been discussed in Chapter 3. In the first place, charity may begin at home. Secondly, if redistributional transfers are given for nonbenevolent purposes as a type of bribe for the guarantee of one's own safety, then, for the average nonpoor resident, expenditures made in his own jurisdiction are likely to be more productive.

There is another consideration that may work in the same direction. It is possible that there exist systematic differences in the demand for redistribution between the suburbs and the city. Those who remain in the city, with the knowledge that they will be surrounded by poor people, may be a self-selecting group of altruists. Those who migrate to the suburbs may simply not care as much about the plight of the poor. Data presented in Chapter 9, however, do not confirm this fundamental difference between demands for redistribution on the part of the city and suburban residents.

[e]Assuming some taxes are borne by property and capital owners.

8

Fiscal Incidence of State and Local Public
Sectors in Metropolitan Washington

Introduction

The overall incidence of the government fiscal process measures the difference between benefits from public services less taxes paid by income class.
Previous studies that have sought to allocate both benefits and tax burdens of
fiscal actions have usually either been restricted to federal finances, specific
state finances, or to the finances of all state and local governments within a state.
While such studies permit an estimation of the impact of budgetary action by
income class, they do not provide incidence estimates by geographical units.
From them we do not have estimates of the effects of the fiscal process on
individuals within the same income class but living in different jurisdictions within one metropolitan area. However, there is evidence that differential fiscal
incidence can influence incentives within a metropolitan area. Thus if people are
alike in other respects but are affected differently by the fiscal process, both
efficiency and income distributional goals of society may be violated. This
chapter reviews the economic literature concerned with geographically discriminatory fiscal incidence. Estimates will be presented of the fiscal incidence by
household units for the three areas of the Washington metropolitan area.

The Concept of Fiscal Residuals

The term fiscal residual was first applied by Buchanan to describe the net
incidence of the budget on individuals.[1] He pointed out that the principle of
horizontal equity, or equal treatment of equals, should be applied to the net
impact of expenditures and taxes rather than solely to tax incidence. Equals are
treated equally if the excess of their benefits from public expenditures over their
taxes paid, or their net fiscal residuals, are equalized.[a] In a federal system, however, such fiscal residuals are likely to differ because jurisdictions have different
income distributions and tax bases, employ different tax systems, and spend
their resources in various ways. For example, a wealthier jurisdiction can provide the same services to its citizens at a lower overall tax rate than can a poor

---

[a]Buchanan actually measured a net fiscal residuum as the difference between taxes
paid and benefits received. Since a residuum implies something of value which is left over,
we choose to measure it as benefits less taxes. We also adopt residual, the anglicized form of
residuum.

jurisdiction. Thus equals, who happen to live in different jurisdictions, will be treated unequally.

Assume the income distributions of two states, A and B, are as depicted in table 8-1. Assume that each levies a proportional income tax of 10 percent and uses the proceeds to provide services whose total benefits are equal to cost, and which are equally provided to each individual. In this example the fiscal residual facing individuals with equal incomes will be larger in the wealthier state. Buchanan was primarily concerned with this anomaly because of its violation of justice; he also noted that it could create an artificial incentive to move to the wealthier location. These distributional and allocative inequalities arising from differing fiscal residuals are best dealt with, in Buchanan's opinion, by a set of geographically discriminatory taxes imposed by higher levels of government. If this were impossible, Buchanan favors a set of equalizing grants from higher level governments.

Scott challenged Buchanan's contention that grants to correct these disparities in fiscal residuals would lead to greater efficiency.[2] The grants given to the poorer areas would indeed provide an incentive for people to stay in these areas, but in general these are areas where growth is not as rapid and increases in marginal labor productivity are not as large. Buchanan rejoined that the type of grant employed is an important consideration.[3] Grants to increase unemployment compensation in the low-income area might have the detrimental effects cited by Scott, but grants for job-retraining programs, for example, would not. In the final analysis, however, Buchanan admitted that Scott's point was well taken, but maintained that Scott ignored the conceivably substantial costs involved with migration. Later Musgrave pointed out that if public services are

Table 8-1
Hypothetical State Income Distributions and Fiscal Residuals

	Number of House- holds	Income Per Unit	Total Taxes	Taxes Per Unit	Benefits Per Unit	Net Fiscal Residual
Community A						
Rich	3	$20,000	$ 6,000	$2,000	$1,200	$-800
Middle	5	10,000	5,000	1,000	1,200	+200
Poor	2	5,000	1,000	500	1,200	+700
Total			$12,000			
Community B						
Rich	2	20,000	4,000	2,000	1,050	-950
Middle	5	10,000	5,000	1,000	1,050	+50
Poor	3	5,000	1,500	500	1,050	+550
Total			$10,500			

provided efficiently and people still sustain these migration costs in order to garner the greater fiscal residuals, there is nothing inefficient about their movement.[4]

The effect of differing fiscal residuals on people's incentives to migrate has also been addressed by Buchanan and Wagner.[5] They contend that these differing fiscal residuals can result in excessive migration to wealthier areas.[b] People will move there so long as their average fiscal residual can be increased thereby. In the course of such migration, however, external costs are imposed on people already residing in the wealthier communities since as population densities increase, the average costs of congestion rise. The marginal costs of congestion are thus higher than the average cost. Since these externalities do not influence the private decisions, excess immigration to the richer areas would occur. In other words, intercommunity differences in fiscal residuals due to differences in income levels can lead to inefficient as well as inequitable consequences.[6] Through use of the zoning process it is possible for current residents to prevent the dissipation of their own fiscal surpluses through immigration. Immigrants can be required to contribute as much or more to the fiscal base than they cost current residents.[7]

Greene has argued that differing income distributions between jurisdictions and differing degrees of tax progressivity between levels of government in a federal hierarchy may lead to a transfer of functions from lower to higher levels of government. Since substantial minorities of the population of the larger jurisdiction may face lower tax prices for the same level of service at the higher level of government, they may join in coalition with those who would like to see provision of the service extended to favor a transfer of the function to a higher level of government even though the service could be performed more efficiently at the lower level of government.[8]

The literature reviewed up to this point concerns merely the potential importance of fiscal residuals in motivating economic behavior. It does not try to measure such residuals nor to test whether or not differing residuals do motivate behavior and affect location patterns.[c] Haskell and Leshinski have attempted the first task and Bradford and Kelejian the second.[9, 10] Haskell and Leshinski attempt to measure fiscal residuals for 280 communities in the New York metropolitan area. They assume that a family unit has $12,500 in income and two children in public school, that the suburban family lives in a $25,000 home, and that the city family pays the average amount of rent paid by families with that income. They also distinguish between suburban families whose household heads work in New York City, and are therefore subject to the New York City commuter income tax, and those whose household heads work in the

---

[b]At least when the goods provided by local governments are not purely public.

[c]Though Greene does present some estimates for differences in tax prices per dollar of expenditures for different individuals at the state and federal levels in the United States.

suburbs. The estimated fiscal residuals range from a high of $3,991 to a low of $253 for noncommuters and from $3,959 to $-37 for commuters, with the means $918 for noncommuters and $764 for commuters. They estimate that the fiscal residual for a family residing in New York City is $836, thereby implying that those with jobs in the city on the average would be better off living in the city than in the average suburb.[d]

The Haskell-Leshinski study may be criticized on several counts. Their representative family approach conceals useful information about the fiscal incentives given to different income classes. Taxes paid by businesses but passed on to the consumer are not allowed for in their analysis and their assumption that the average family with two children would also have two children in *public* school, whether they lived in the city or the suburb, is open to question.

While the existence of variation in fiscal residuals may violate principles of horizontal equity, their mere existence does not necessarily indicate that they affect household location patterns. This depends on whether people respond to these residuals. For example, we may ask, can the flight to the suburbs observed across the nation be explained, at least in part, by differentials in these residuals? Bradford and Kelejian present evidence that suggest that the answer to this question is yes. In their cross-sectional analysis of data concerning eighty-seven large cities in 1960 in the United States they find that the portion of upper-income individuals in the entire urbanized area who live within the city is negatively related with median family income, the portion of the city's population that was poor ten years ago as well as several other variables. This variable, however, is positively related to the size of the upper-income classes' net fiscal residuals in previous years.[11] In turn, the relative concentration of the urban area's poor people within city borders is dependent positively on such factors as the relative concentration of older housing in the central city, but also depends strongly on their net fiscal advantage from living in the central city rather than the suburbs. Thus the evidence that Bradford and Kelejian present lend some credibility to the thesis that the fiscal residuals measured in the next section affect location patterns within the metropolitan area.

Fiscal Residuals in the Metropolitan Area

The first set of estimates of fiscal residuals that we present are based on cost-of-service estimates of benefits and on taxes before offsets. While table 7-6 showed only a household's taxes paid to and benefits received from metropolitan jurisdictions other than his own, table 8-2 and figure 8-1 incorporate taxes

---

[d]The residuals that they calculate for some of the older cities of northeast New Jersey such as Patterson, Newark and Jersey City as well as Yonkers, New York, show them yielding severe fiscal disadvantages to the "representative" family.

Table 8-2
Net Fiscal Incidence by Income Class: Benefits Estimated on a Cost-of-Service
Basis—Taxes Before Offset

Income Classes	Total Benefits Less Total Taxes	Net Fiscal Residual per Household Unit	Net Fiscal Residuals as a Percentage of Money Income
Residents of the District of Columbia			
below $3,000	+$106,637,569	+$1345.04	+103.2
3,000–3,999	+27,368,372	+1398.56	+40.0
4,000–5,999	+51,722,245	+1162.90	+25.8
6,000–7,499	+32,066,591	+927.13	+13.7
7,500–9,999	+38,474,961	+858.34	+9.8
10,000–14,999	+16,779,109	+328.62	+2.6
15,000–24,999	−22,473,992	−644.34	−3.2
25,000 and above	−44,553,200	−2921.71	−6.7
Total	+$206,021,655		
Residents of Suburban Maryland			
below $3,000	+$ 13,479,698	+$ 296.14	+21.9
3,000–3,999	+3,465,918	+285.33	+8.2
4,000–5,999	+5,312,245	+200.19	+4.0
6,000–7,499	+6,228,808	+239.82	+3.6
7,500–9,999	+15,603,204	+326.29	+3.7
10,000–14,999	−246,264	−2.64	−.0
15,000–24,999	−53,788,581	−548.33	−2.7
25,000 and above	−87,065,616	−2336.64	−5.1
Total	−$ 97,010,588		
Residents of Suburban Virginia			
below $3,000	+$ 9,148,653	+$ 313.90	+21.4
3,000–3,999	+2,958,354	+303.92	+8.7
4,000–5,999	+4,386,676	+194.73	+3.9
6,000–7,499	+3,308,737	+155.13	+3.1
7,500–9,999	+5,993,224	+171.19	+2.0
10,000–14,999	−1,826,380	−30.70	−.2
15,000–24,999	−34,534,506	−483.27	−2.4
25,000 and above	−50,793,269	−1349.27	−3.2
Total	−$ 61,358,511		

before offset paid to and cost-of-service benefits received from one's own jurisdiction as well. The total cost of service benefits received less the total taxes
paid before offsets constitute the fiscal residuals displayed in table 8-1. While we
feel that the validity of these estimates is somewhat limited, they are compatible
with the measures of fiscal residuals calculated by Haskell and Leshinski and
those utilized by Bradford and Kelejian.

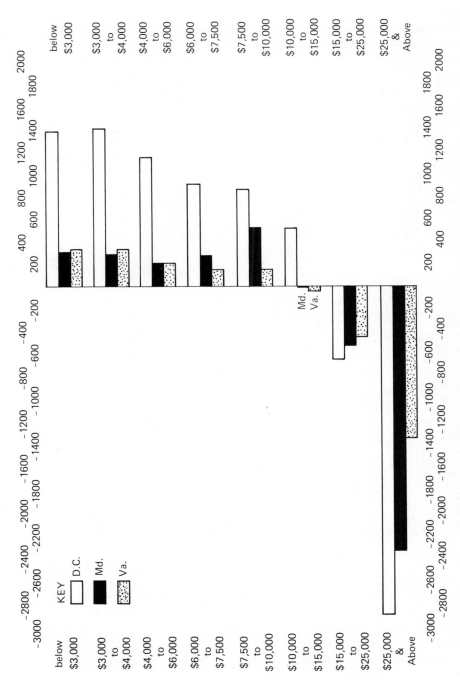

Figure 8-1. Fiscal Residuals by Income Class: Cost-of-Service Estimates

Three conclusions emerge from these cost-of-service estimates. First, except for the two highest income classes, the fiscal residual is uniformly higher for all income classes in the District of Columbia than in the suburban areas. This result is due to the District's ability to export tax liability and the federal payment to the city by the federal government. We have estimated that there is not an offsetting outflow of benefits from the District. Moreover, the suburbs in the Washington area on net support other jurisdictions in their own states. These suburban areas are the wealthiest parts of Maryland and Virginia and their tax liabilities are greater than state expenditures in their behalf. The second conclusion is that these fiscal residuals are most favorable to the lowest income classes. Finally, for those with incomes in excess of $15,000, the residuals are negative, even though less so in the suburbs.

Fiscal residuals based on a welfare measure of benefits, from which we will derive testable behavioral hypotheses, are shown in table 8-3 and figure 8-2. As with the other estimates, every income class below $15,000 enjoys a larger fiscal residual within the District of Columbia than in the suburban areas.[e] However, the District residuals are more advantageous for those above $15,000 as well and the residuals are largest for those in the highest income classes. In fact, the residual pattern is roughly J-shaped in relation to income. Fiscal residuals are most adverse for those in the $4,000 to $7,500 income range. Household units below this income level enjoy larger positive or smaller negative fiscal residuals. The most favorable residuals confront the highest income classes. If renters do not perceive they are paying any property tax, the greater concentration of rental housing among the lowest income classes would mean that the perceived fiscal residuals for these classes would be substantially less than shown here and a U-shaped relationship for perceived fiscal residuals would be implied. If the perceived size of these fiscal residuals does influence attitudes toward public expenditure programs, then the residuals measured here imply behavior that can be tested. In Chapter 9, we pursue this question of the compatibility of our fiscal residual measures with individual voting and attitude patterns.

It can be noted here, however, that a relative fiscal advantage from living in the District for different income classes can be inferred from an examination of table 8-4. Each income class within the District is seen to have a larger fiscal residual than its suburban counterpart. The differences in these residuals increases in absolute size up to the $10,000 level and decreases thereafter with exception only of the highest income class in suburban Virginia.

It is questionable, however, whether these differences in fiscal residuals can be interpreted as measures of the net fiscal incentives to locate in one area rather than another. In the first place the positive difference between residuals in the

---

[e]The residuals for suburban residents may be understated if they derive benefits from expenditures made elsewhere in the state which are not accounted for by our calculations, but insofar as District of Columbia residents are unlikely to receive benefits much different than these, this analysis of comparative sizes of fiscal residuals remains valid.

Table 8-3
Net Fiscal Incidence by Income Class: Benefits Estimated on a Welfare Basis—
Taxes Net of Offset

Income Classes	Total Benefits Less Total Taxes	Net Fiscal Residual per Household Unit	Net Fiscal Residuals as a Percentage of Money Income
Residents of the District of Columbia			
below $3,000	+$ 41,975,239	+$ 529.44	+40.6
3,000–3,999	+11,068,624	+565.62	+16.2
4,000–5,999	+20,666,068	+464.65	+10.3
6,000–7,499	+16,228,300	+469.20	+7.0
7,500–9,999	+32,943,256	+734.93	+8.4
10,000–14,999	+36,197,436	+709.10	+5.7
15,000–24,999	+27,425,576	+786.31	+3.9
25,000 and above	+32,083,348	+2103.96	+4.8
Total	+$218,587,847		
Residents of Suburban Maryland			
below $3,000	+$ 844,964	+$ 18.71	+1.4
3,000–3,999	−636,317	−52.38	−1.5
4,000–5,999	−4,392,646	−165.54	−3.3
6,000–7,499	−4,403,003	−169.52	−2.5
7,500–9,999	−502,615	−10.51	−.1
10,000–14,999	−2,480,622	−26.61	−.2
15,000–24,999	+21,508,163	+219.26	+1.1
25,000 and above	+66,213,022	+1777.01	+3.9
Total	+$ 76,150,946		
Residents of Suburban Virginia			
below $3,000	−$ 150,882	−$ 5.18	−.4
3,000–3,999	−293,307	−30.13	−.9
4,000–5,999	−2,446,413	−108.60	−2.1
6,000–7,499	−2,582,216	−121.07	−1.8
7,500–9,999	−363,729	+10.39	+.1
10,000–14,999	+1,597,795	+26.86	+.2
15,000–24,999	+18,400,714	+257.50	+1.3
25,000 and above	+31,956,912	+1155.68	+2.7
Total	+$ 48,118,875		

District of Columbia and suburban Maryland and between residuals in Maryland and Virginia may be overstated. Our calculations are based on the assumption that individuals in the same income brackets, but receiving different levels of service in different jurisdictions, place the same marginal evaluation on the last unit of service received. To the extent that the marginal utility of public goods

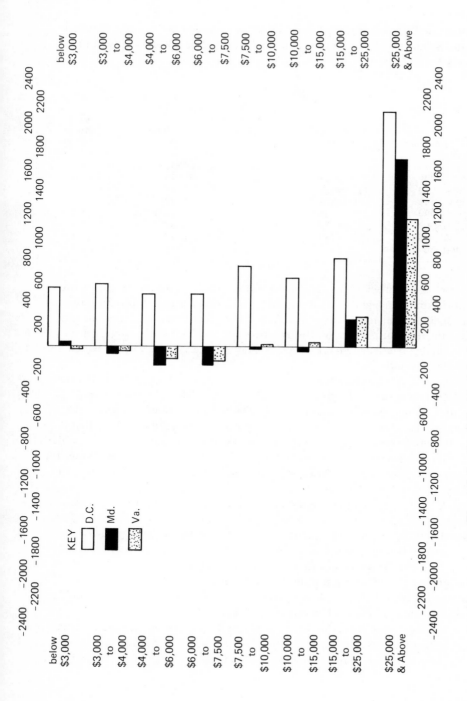

Figure 8–2. Fiscal Residuals by Income Class: Welfare Estimates.

Table 8–4

Difference Between the Fiscal Residual in the District and the Fiscal Residual in the Suburbs by Income Class: Benefits Estimated on a Welfare Basis and Taxes Net of Offset

	Maryland		Virginia	
Income Classes	Per Household Unit	As a Per- centage of Money Income	Per Household Unit	As a Per- centage of Money Income
below $3,000	+$510.73	+37.8	+$534.62	+36.4
3,000–3,999	+618.00	17.7	+595.75	17.0
4,000–5,999	+630.19	12.5	+573.25	11.3
6,000–7,499	+638.72	9.5	+590.27	8.7
7,500–9,999	+724.42	8.3	+724.54	8.3
10,000–14,999	+672.49	5.4	+682.24	5.5
15,000–24,999	+489.84	2.4	+528.81	2.6
25,000 and above	+$326.95	.8	+$948.28	2.3

declines as output increases this means that we would overstate marginal evaluations for those in higher output jurisdictions relative to those for lower output jurisdictions. Individuals with the same income would receive more goods and value them less at the margin. If this is true, the fiscal advantage of the District of Columbia relative to Maryland and of Maryland relative to Virginia would not be as large as indicated.

Secondly, a significant portion of the higher fiscal residuals in the District of Columbia is due to the greater expenditures on police protection in the District. If the greater expendtures in the District are required to provide the same or even a lower level of safety, then it may not be valid to believe that people, when considering where to locate in the metropolitan area, will consider this fact an advantage for the District. It may well be that these expenditures for police protection may be considered instead simply the cost of establishing an acceptable level of public safety.

A similar argument also applies to fire protection. Institutional arrangements in fire protection in the metropolitan area imply that real services in the suburbs are understated by expenditures. While fire protection is publicly financed in the District, a substantial fraction is provided by volunteers in suburban areas. If we assume that equally capable fire protection is provided in the different jurisdictions, it is only the differences in tax burdens needed to finance fire protection that affect people's location patterns. Benefits would be the same and only the tax liabilities would vary.

Finally, refuse collection is also provided by different institutional means across the metropolitan area. We attribute positive fiscal residuals from refuse collection to the upper-income classes where it is provided publicly. Since it is

Table 8-5

Net Fiscal Advantages by Income Class Net Fiscal Advantage of Living in the District Rather than in:

	Maryland		Virginia	
Income Classes	Per Household Unit	As a Per-centage of Money Income	Per Household Unit	As a Per-centage of Money Income
below $3,000	+$ 460.56	+34.1	+$ 493.21	+33.6
3,000–3,999	+1021.57	+29.2	+1006.85	+28.8
4,000–5,999	+485.10	+9.6	+444.91	+8.8
6,000–7,499	+452.93	+6.7	+421.15	+6.2
7,500–9,999	+505.22	+5.8	+531.57	+6.1
10,000–14,999	+415.76	+3.3	+392.05	+3.1
15,000–24,999	+95.73	+.5	+58.51	+.3
25,000 and above	−501.36	−1.1	−197.24	−.5

provided privately in many suburban communities, no such fiscal residuals arise but households enjoy the same service.

To take account of these difficulties a different set of net residuals, called fiscal advantages, is shown in table 8-5. These residuals are derived from the net fiscal residuals of table 8-4 by eliminating benefits from police and fire protection, correctional facilities, refuse collection and general government. Taxes paid to various jurisdictions are reduced by the ratio of that jurisdiction's refuse collection expenditures to its total taxes.[f]

These net fiscal advantages reflect the fiscal attractiveness of locating in the District rather than in the suburbs for all but the highest income classes. In absolute terms the fiscal advantage is significantly positive for all income classes below the $15,000 level. The advantage shrinks to less than $100 for the $15,000–$24,999 class and it becomes negative for the highest income classes. Accordingly, the very high-income classes should consider it fiscally disadvantageous to live in the District. However, fiscal residuals may also vary with the characteristics of a household unit. Thus, families with children, because of their greater probability of attending public schools in the suburbs, might have an incentive to locate in the suburbs, and families without children and single individuals might enjoy a net fiscal advantage in the District even if they are in the highest income class.

---

[f]To the extent that the professional fire protection in the District is of higher quality or to the extent that either the level of safety is greater in the District or people perceive greater benefits from seeing more frequent police patrols, these estimates may underestimate the fiscal advantage of living in the city for high income classes. But as explained above, if the marginal utility of public good provision declines as output increases there is an offsetting bias that tends to overestimate this advantage.

If we express these fiscal advantages as a percentage of money income, then the advantage offered by the District constantly declines across income classes. The advantage is over one-third of total money income for the lowest income classes, but shrinks to slightly more than 3 percent for the $10,000-14,999 class and to one-half percent or less for the $15,000-24,999 class. If the suburban life style represents the American dream, the fiscal cost of this dream decreases both absolutely and relative to income throughout the income distribution in the Washington metropolitan area.

Summary

We find from our fiscal incidence estimates that when benefits are measured on a welfare basis and taxes are considered net of offset, the relative fiscal position is lowest for those households in the Washington metropolitan area in the $5,000-7,500 income class. The relative fiscal position is more favorable both for those with incomes less than $5,000 and for those above $7,500. Second, the fiscal residual is found to be larger in the District than in the suburban areas. This finding is largely due to the significant contribution of the rest of the country, through the federal payment, in support of District services. The fiscal advantage from living in the District is greatest for those in the lowest income classes. This advantage decreases constantly as income increases, but remains positive up to the highest income classes. The very highest income classes, however, enjoy a positive fiscal advantage from living in the suburbs.

Discussion of the Results

Introduction

In this chapter estimates of both fiscal flows and incidence in the Washington metropolitan area are summarized. A number of pertinent theoretical and policy questions are then addressed in the light of these estimates. Specifically, the chapter includes: (1) an evaluation of the suburban-central city exploitation thesis in terms of the fiscal flows found in the Washington metropolitan area; (2) an indication of why fiscal residuals are generally positive across the whole area with a discussion of consequences this fact has concerning the optimal provision of public services; (3) a comparison of these fiscal incidence estimates with the incidence reported in other studies; (4) a comparison of the actual pattern of fiscal residuals that results from redistributive programs in the area with taxpayer sentiment toward these programs as reflected in attitude surveys and voting data; (5) an attempt to explain the "flight-to-suburb" phenomenon in terms of the fiscal residuals estimated for the Washington area; and (6) an · enumeration of the limitations of this study.

Suburban–Central City Exploitation in the Washington Area

The order of the magnitude of the interjurisdictional fiscal flows between the District of Columbia and suburban Maryland and Virginia which were estimated in Chapter 7 are consonant with the flows between central city and suburban area reported in other studies.[a] Thus if benefits are allocated to household units on the basis of "cost-of-service," and if tax incidence is estimated with no allowance for federal offset, then the District of Columbia enjoyed an estimated net fiscal gain of between $16.5 million and $28.2 million from suburban Maryland and Virginia in 1970, as can be derived from table 7-1. However, if benefits are measured in terms of effective demand and tax incidence is estimated net of federal offset, it is found that suburban Maryland enjoyed a welfare gain through its interaction with the District of Columbia ranging from $47.6 million to $51.2 million, while suburban Virginia gained from $31.1 to $33.3 million, as also shown in table 7-1. In terms of gains per

[a]For a discussion of other studies, see Chapter 2.

household unit, the net flow to suburban Maryland ranged from $123 to $133 and from $113 to $120 for suburban Virginia. The major components of the net benefit flow from the District to the suburban areas are the use-of-income redistributive and nonredistributive benefits generated by expenditures for elementary and secondary education, health services, and social services. As can be seen in table 7-5, benefits in these three categories constitute more than two-thirds of the total benefit flow, estimated on a welfare basis, from the District to suburban Maryland and Virginia. In fact, the practical import of the choice between the cost-of-service measure of benefits and the welfare measure of benefits is the different allocation of benefits from these three functional categories. In contrast with the notable benefit flow between the District and the suburban areas under the welfare measure of benefits, there is absolutely no benefit flow from these expenditures under the cost-of-service index, as can be noted in table 7-4. This index allocates benefits only to direct recipients, that is, only to those who are directly affected by programs in education, health services, and social services. Hence the schooling, health care, and public assistance provided to specific individuals in the District is assumed to be of value to these individuals and these alone. Further, the cost-of-service measure of benefits is based implicitly on the strong assumption that the marginal utility of income is constant across all income classes. Thus if per pupil public school expenditures is $1,200, each and every pupil, and only a pupil, is assumed to enjoy benefits equaling $1,200. The welfare measure, on the other hand, is based on public expenditure analysis in which benefits are defined in terms of the utility received by individuals. Thus the allocation of benefits recognizes the possibility that public outlays often generate utility for individuals other than direct program recipients and that this utility may vary with income.

The existence of notable interjurisdictional flows caused by expenditures in certain categories is consonant with another result which can be inferred from the estimates of fiscal flows, namely, that commuters pay the District for the benefits they receive *qua* commuters. Under certain assumptions concerning the benefits received by suburban Maryland and Virginia from District expenditures for protection services, recreation and parks, transportation, and for general government expenditures, the total value of benefits enjoyed by suburban commuters is $15.7 million.[b] Commuters *qua* commuters, on the other hand, contribute to the District through the property, sales, business cost, corporate income, and alcohol, tobacco, and motor fuel excise taxes. The sales, alcohol, tobacco, and motor fuel excise taxes, motor vehicle and parking fines and fees, and insurance taxes paid by commuters are estimated to be $15.5

---

[b]This estimate embodies the following assumptions: police, fire and correction benefits are in proportion to time spent in the jurisdiction; transportation benefits are in proportion to vehicle miles traveled; 5 percent of the suburban benefits from parks and zoos are assumed received by commuters; and 30 percent of the suburban benefits from library services are assumed received by commuters.

million.[c] And if allowance is also made for the business cost, business income, and bank and property taxes borne by commuters, their tax payments would exceed the benefits they obtain from District services.[d] These results are consistent with earlier studies which indicate that commuters in the San Francisco and Detroit metropolitan areas pay for the benefits they receive. However, a study for the New York City area came to the opposite conclusion.[e]

Any policy recommendation whereby suburban areas would compensate the District for the public sector welfare gain they receive from it should recognize the fact that commuters as such do currently fully compensate the District for the public sector benefits they enjoy. Thus, to impose a levy on commuters in the form, say, of a nonresident payroll tax, in order to offset the suburban welfare gain from the District would discriminate against the commuting sector of the suburban population. However, a nonresident income tax could be devised with a tax-credit provision which would not be subject to this criticism. Assume, for example, that a one percent nonresident income tax would generate a revenue flow from suburban communities to the District sufficient to offset fully the net benefit flow from the District currently enjoyed by all suburbanites. Thus a commuter with $20,000 of taxable income subject to the District tax would make a payment of $200 to the District. If in turn this payment were credited against his income tax liability in his resident suburban jurisdiction his total tax liability would be unchanged.[f] The suburban jurisdiction would then find that its total revenue was reduced by the value of the tax credit. In the face of this loss of revenue the jurisdiction could either raise its tax rate, which would fall on all suburban residents, or it could provide a lower level of services. With either of these outcomes the question of the discriminatory treatment of commuters would be resolved and full compensation would be paid to the District for the public sector benefits received by suburbanites.

The tax-credit scheme gives rise to a problem, however, if the suburban communities would respond to a reduction in their net revenue by increasing their income tax rates. The incidence of the interjurisdictional benefit flow from

---

[c]This estimate is based on the assumptions that of the total alcohol and tobacco excise taxes paid by suburbanites, the commuter fraction is proportional to their percentage of suburban hours spent in the District and their fraction of the motor fuel excise tax and motor vehicle and parking fines and fees is proportional to their share of vehicle miles traveled in the District.

[d]We do not perform these calculations because they would involve extremely arbitrary assumptions about what portions of these taxes are paid by commuters. But if they pay as little as 27.6 percent of the total amount of these taxes paid by suburbanites, then their tax contributions would be 150 percent of their benefits, and if they pay as little as 1 percent, their tax payments at least exceed the benefits they derive from the District of Columbia as commuters.

[e]See Chapter 2 for a critical discussion of these studies.

[f]Of course, if the commuter's tax liability in the District of Columbia exceeded that of his own jurisdiction, a negative tax credit could be employed and the commuter reimbursed.

the District to the suburban areas is a positive function of income, as is shown in table 7-7. Thus net benefits received by suburban Maryland residents from the District range from small negative values for households with income below $6,000 to $515 for households with income in excess of $25,000. The pattern for suburban Virginia residents is similar, where households with less than $4,000 income experience a slight welfare loss with the gain ranging up to $427 for those with income of $25,000 and over. Given these data, the vertical equity criterion requires that the incidence of the tax imposed on suburbanites to compensate for the net benefit flow they enjoy should replicate the pattern of benefits they enjoy. As can be seen in table 7-7, these benefits rise more than proportionately with income for both suburban Maryland and Virginia. The incidence of the Maryland and Virginia income taxes after offset (see table 6-3) is not sufficiently progressive so that merely a proportionate increase in tax rates would match the incidence of these benefits. The effective state income tax rates for those in the $25,000 and over income class, for example, would have to be raised notably relative to those with lower incomes to meet vertical equity criteria.

The cooperation of the various areas that would be required to implement such a tax-credit plan could be achieved simply through the political consolidation of the metropolitan area. However, consolidation of the federal district with suburban areas in two states stands even less chance of adoption than does consolidation in other metropolitan areas. A policy more likely to be adopted and one which would notably reduce the relative fiscal disparity resulting from public sector benefit flows is the federalization of the financing of the major social services. Benefits from social service expenditures by the District constituted in 1970 the largest single source of interjurisdictional benefit flow to suburban Maryland and Virginia, as seen in table 7-5. A partial step in this direction was indeed taken in 1974, when the federal government assumed full responsibility for three of the public assistance programs, payments to those sixty-five and older, the blind, and the disabled. The AFDC program, however, which is the largest of the public assistance programs, remains a joint financial responsibility of the District and the federal governments.

Fiscal Residuals and Optimal
Supply of Public Services

Even though the net public sector benefit flow from the District to suburban Maryland and Virginia indicates that the District provides uncompensated benefits to suburban communities through public sector interactions, still the fiscal residuals from all subfederal budgetary action are positive for households in all income classes in the District of Columbia, as shown in table 8-2. The principal reason why the District can be "exploited" by suburban areas and

District residents still enjoy positive fiscal residuals is that the federal payment to the District, which amounted in 1970 to $115 million or 22 percent of the District revenue, is greater than the benefits estimated to be received by those residing outside the Washington metropolitan area. In other words, the District is able to export to nonresidents tax liability which has greater dollar value than the benefits generated for nonresidents by its public expenditures.

Two major conclusions therefore emerge from this study of fiscal flows in the Washington metropolitan area: (1) the suburban areas enjoy a welfare gain in their public sector interactions with the District of Columbia, and (2) the fiscal residuals are more favorable for all income classes in the District than in suburban areas. The finding that the District of Columbia is "exploited" by its suburban area can be graphically presented, as shown in figure 9-1. Here it is assumed that (1) G_A equals total expenditures by all subfederal governments in the Washington metropolitan area; (2) the evaluation of benefits generated by G_A for individuals in the District of Columbia, the suburban areas, and the rest of the world is represented by the indifference curves U_{DC}, U_S, and U_W, respectively; and (3) the cost of metropolitan public services to these three groups, net of the federal offset, tax exporting, and the federal payment to the District, is implied in the slopes of Y_{DC}, Y_S, and Y_W. The community indifference curves for the District and the suburban areas, U_{DC} and U_S, cut their respective budget lines from above to reflect the fact that these areas both enjoy positive fiscal residuals at the actual level of public services, given the current citizen evaluation of these services as well as the current means of financing them. However, the suburban area enjoys a net welfare gain through its fiscal interactions with the District. The value of this gain, estimated at the level of actual expenditures, in 1970, is shown in table 7-1. If the suburban areas were to make a lump sum compensation to the District for this gain, the District's budget line would be displaced upward and the suburban budget line downward by an amount equal to the compensation, as is depicted by the respective shifts to Y'_{DC} and Y'_S. There would be a corresponding change in the level of welfare enjoyed by the two areas as represented by the shift from U_{DC} to U'_{DC} and U_S and U'_S.

The total use- and source-of-income benefits, net of taxes, received by the District of Columbia, suburban Maryland, and suburban Virginia from all subfederal public sectors in the Washington metropolitan area are $218.6 million, $76.1 million, and $48.1 million, respectively, as shown in table 8-2. Since the money and in-kind transfers which constitute the source-of-income benefits accrue entirely to individuals within the dispersing jurisdiction, they do not affect interjurisdictional flows. If only use-of-income benefits are considered, the positive fiscal residuals for the District, suburban Maryland, and suburban Virginia are reduced to $147.7 million, $65.1 million, and $38.0 million, respectively. Further, since we have assumed an optimal supply of public services in the metropolitan area any positive use-of-income fiscal residuals enjoyed by one group must be offset by negative residuals for other groups, it follows that the

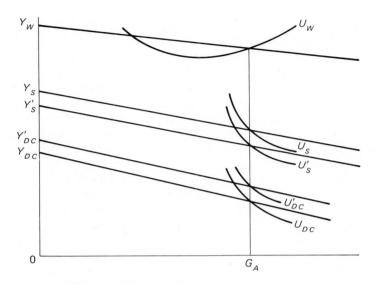

Figure 9-1. Exploitation and Fiscal Residuals.

negative residual received by the rest of the world must be the sum of the positive residuals enjoyed by metropolitan Washington residents, or $250.3 million, as shown in table 9-1.

Geometrically the positive fiscal residuals for the District and the suburban area can be seen in figure 9-1 as the product of the difference between the slopes of an area's budget line and community indifference curve times total output, G_A. The residuals for the District and suburbs are positive because the marginal rate of substitution between income and public output (the slope of the community indifference curve) is greater than the marginal cost to the community (the slope of the budget line). Conversely, the fiscal residual for the rest of the world is negative because its marginal rate of substitution is less than its tax-price at G_A level of output.

The conclusion that the aggregate fiscal residual for the rest of the world is negative and that the District's is larger than suburban residual, as shown in table 9-1, is primarily the result of the significance of three factors: tax-exporting, the federal offset, and the federal payment to the District. Because of tax-exporting and the federal offset both District and suburban residents are able to shift part of the cost of metropolitan public services to nonresidents, whereas District residents are the principal beneficiaries of the federal payment. Through these three mechanisms funds which more than compensate at the margin for the estimated benefits supplied by these governments to the rest of the world, are transferred to metropolitan Washington governments. Programs benefiting the rest of the world are, for example, services to tourists and services provided

Table 9-1

Use-of-Income Residuals from Metropolitan Washington Public Expenditures

Area	Use-of-Income Benefits (less)	Taxes Net of Offset (equal)	Net Use-of-Income Benefits
District of Columbia	$383.3 million	$236.1 million	+$147.2 million
Suburban Maryland	506.9	441.8	+65.1
Suburban Virginia	298.7	260.7	+38.0
Rest of World	24.4	275.2*	−250.3

Sources: See tables 1-1, 5-17, and 6-11.

*This figure is the net of $426.5 million contributed to the Washington metropolitan area by the rest of the world through tax-exporting and the Federal Payment to the District less $151.3 million transferred from suburban Maryland and Virginia to the rest of their respective states.

by the District in its capacity as seat of the federal government. In other words, the marginal rate of substitution between income and metropolitan Washington public services for the rest of the world is less than its marginal tax contribution to metropolitan Washington at output G_A, as shown graphically in figure 9-1 by U_W cutting Y_W from below. As a consequence, the rest of the world suffers a negative fiscal residual in this exchange, as estimated in table 9-1.

The question of the optimal provision of public services was discussed in Chapter 4 with the inference drawn that it is reasonable to assume that actual outlays tend to cluster around the social optimum. An implication of this assumption is that the positive fiscal residuals enjoyed by Washington metropolitan residents are equal to the negative fiscal residuals received by the rest of the world. From the fact that positive residuals have been estimated for metropolitan residents it follows that there is a disequilibrium undersupply of services from the viewpoint of metropolitan residents. Such an underprovision of services could be explained in terms of various influences. First of all, Congress may well act as a constraining influence on the expenditure decisions of the District government. Further, the taxing powers of the various jurisdictions in the metropolitan area are limited by statutory and constitutional provisions. For example, in 1970 Montgomery County was the only Maryland county at the upper limit of the income tax rate allowed by Maryland law. Finally, jurisdictions in the Washington metropolitan area have generally experienced rapid growth both in population and in average income level over the past decade with the consequence that actual expenditures may be lagging below desired levels. In the last analysis, however, the determination of whether any area's actual provision of public services is optimal remains an empirical question. It may seem reasonable to judge such is the case in the Washington metropolitan area but we must admit that such a judgment remains problematical.

Incidence of State and Local Fisc

A comparison of the impact of the state and local fisc estimated in this study with the incidence pattern that emerges from earlier studies may serve to highlight the practical import of the issues discussed in earlier chapters and examined in this study. Thus the incidence of the sum of use- and source-of-income benefits generated by state and local governments in the Washington metropolitan area in 1970 is presented in table 9-2 along with the benefit incidence of all state and local expenditures estimated for 1960 by Gillespie. A strong caveat must be entered concerning any conclusions to be drawn from a comparison of the results of two studies a decade apart and using different conceptual frameworks and definitions. More specifically, it must be noted that the definition of "income" used as the denominator for computing both benefit incidence percentages and the tax incidence percentage below is different in the two studies. In the Washington study estimates are presented as a percentage of money income as defined by the Census Bureau (see Appendix B), whereas Gillespie's estimates are presented in terms of a "broad" income concept which includes family money income, various in-kind imputations, as well as imputations for retained earnings, the unshifted portion of the corporate profits tax, part of the employer's social security payment, and capital gains.[1] The principal effect of these differences is that both benefits and taxes allocated to higher income families are larger as a percentage of "income" in the Washington study than in the Gillespie study. This statement must be understood in the aggregate, however, since different subgroups are included in different income classes under the two definitions of income used.

Second, even though both inflation and the growth in real income between 1960 and 1970 further weaken the meaning of a comparison of incidence by income class, some general inferences can be drawn which point up the practical consequences of the two methodologies employed. Thus the poor appear to fare much better under the Gillespie estimates than they do under the estimates for the Washington area, even with the source-of-income benefits included, as done in table 9-2. This consequence follows principally from Gillespie's use of the cost of a service as the measure of benefits received by an income class. With benefits measured by the welfare index used in the Washington study, the estimated benefit incidence is reduced for the poor and increased for high-income families relative to any cost-of-service imputation. Not only are benefits higher for the poor under the cost-of-service procedure but they decline consistently over all income classes. Estimates for the Washington area, on the other hand, are found generally to be proportional across income classes above the poverty line.

The incidence of state and local taxes borne by residents in the Washington metropolitan area in 1970 together with the incidence of all state and local taxes in the United States estimated by Gillespie for 1960 are shown in table 9-3. The incidence of all taxes levied by subfederal governments in the District

Table 9-2
Benefit Incidence for Washington Metropolitan Area, 1970, and for State and Local Governments in United States, 1960, by Income Class

| Income Class | Use- and Source-of-Income Benefits from State and Local Expenditures in Washington Metropolitan Area, as Percentage of Money Income, 1970 | | | Income Class | Benefits from all State and Local Expenditures as Percentage of "Broad" Income, 1960 |
| | Residents of: | | | | All Residents of United States |
	District of Columbia	Suburban Maryland	Suburban Virginia		
below $3,000	54.1	16.2	12.9	below $2,000	92.5
3,000–3,999	25.9	8.4	7.6	2,000–2,999	68.3
4,000–5,999	17.7	6.6	6.1	3,000–3,999	28.9
6,000–7,499	15.3	7.5	6.7	4,000–4,999	18.8
7,500–9,999	16.4	8.9	7.7	5,000–7,499	12.2
10,000–14,999	13.5	8.4	7.8	7,500–9,999	8.4
15,000–24,999	11.6	9.2	7.9	10,000 and over	5.4
25,000 and over	11.2	9.9	7.6		

Sources: Table 5–17; figures in the last column are from Gillespie, "Effects of Public Expenditure," table 17.

of Columbia, suburban Maryland, and suburban Virginia are shown as a percentage of money income before tax offset in comparison with the Gillespie
estimates, which are also before offset but shown as a percentage of the "broad"
income concept discussed above. The most notable difference between the two
estimates is that in the Washington area the incidence is much less regressive.
Since assumptions under which the tax burdens are distributed in the two
studies are similar,[2] this difference undoubtedly is attributed to the fact that
greater reliance is placed on the relatively progressive income tax in the
Washington area in 1970 than was true of all state and local governments in
1960. In 1960, for example, less than 7 percent of total state and local revenue
was raised through the individual income tax, whereas in 1970 the District
raised over 16 percent of its revenue through the individual income tax and state
and local governments in suburban Maryland and Virginia raised approximately
40 and 25 percent, respectively from this source.[3] Thus the estimated incidence of expenditure benefits for the Washington metropolitan area in 1970
under the procedures of this study prove to be more "pro-rich" than is the
incidence for all state and local expenditures in 1960 under the Gillespie
methodology. On the other hand, the tax burden is estimated to fall relatively
heavier on high income classes in the Washington area, due to greater reliance on
more progresssive taxes, than is seen to be the case for all state and local taxes in
the United States in 1960.

Fiscal Residuals and Attitude Toward
Government Expenditures

The pattern of fiscal residuals derived from welfare estimates of benefits, as
shown in table 8-2, purportedly represents the welfare gain or loss an income
class receives from the expenditure and tax activity of state and local governments evaluated at the margin. Therefore it should be possible to derive testable
hypotheses concerning attitudes of citizens toward government programs from
these residuals. For suburban Maryland and Virginia the pattern is generally
proportional with respect to income, with a slight tendency to be U-shaped. The
pattern in the District, on the other hand, is an inverted J-shape, with benefits as
a percentage of money income highest in the lowest income class. The pattern of
fiscal residuals that emerges from the cost-of-service estimate of benefits, as seen
in table 8-1, is notably different. In all three areas the incidence of fiscal
residuals is progressive, that is, the very lowest income class enjoys the largest
fiscal residual and the residuals decline monotonically over all income classes,
with the highest income class having the most negative residual of all.
    Since these fiscal residuals result from the average of all estimated benefits
and taxes of state and local programs, they need not replicate the pattern from
any one program. However, at least as a check on the general validity of the

Table 9-3

Tax Incidence for Washington Metropolitan Area, 1970, and for All State and Local Governments in United States, 1960, by Income Class

	Total Taxes Paid to Washington Metropolitan Area Governments as Percentage of Money Income, 1970					All State and Local Taxes as Percentage of "Broad" Income, 1960	
		Residents of:					
Income Class	District of Columbia	Suburban Maryland	Suburban Virginia		Income Class	All Residents of United States	
below $3,000	13.8	15.3	13.7		below $2,000	26.2	
3,000–3,999	9.3	10.3	8.7		2,000–2,999	25.1	
4,000–5,999	8.8	10.4	8.7		3,000–3,999	18.0	
6,000–7,499	8.9	10.7	9.1		4,000–4,999	17.4	
7,500–9,999	8.7	9.8	8.5		5,000–7,499	12.4	
10,000–14,999	8.7	9.6	8.5		7,500–9,999	7.1	
15,000–24,999	9.3	9.9	8.0		10,000 and over	5.3	
25,000 and over	9.4	8.8	7.0				

Sources: Table 6–11; figures in the last column are from Gillespie "Effects of Public Expenditures," table 3.

welfare estimates versus the cost-of-service estimates, it will be useful to determine which estimating procedure is the better predictor of citizen attitudes as revealed by voting and survey data.

There are no studies of voting and survey data which directly pertain to citizen attitudes toward government programs in the Washington metropolitan area. However, there are a number of studies concerning voting and survey outcomes which are pertinent.[4] Thus Banfield and Wilson, for example, concluded that their analysis of thirty-five referenda in a number of cities that the very lowest and the highest income voting areas typically provide the greatest support for any expenditure program.[5] This U-shaped pattern of support for such programs is compatible with the welfare-based estimates of fiscal residuals in the Washington area but the favorable attitudes of the high income areas is just the opposite to what we would expect from the cost-of-service residuals.

In their analysis of a national survey conducted in 1971–72 Watts and Free report that a U-shaped pattern of support is generally verified for redistributive programs such as educational services for low-income children, medicaid, welfare, support of senior citizens, and programs for black Americans.[6] These results are also generally consonant with the assumptions made in this study concerning the distribution of redistributive use-of-income benefits and the declining marginal utility of income and again are contrary to what we would expect from the cost-of-service estimates. Two cautionary observations should be made, however. First, the U-shaped pattern of support is not verified for all programs. Support for public parks and recreation outlays, for example, rises with income up to the $10,000 class and then declines over the next two classes ($10,000–14,999 and $15,000 and over).[7] Presumably this reflects the fact that higher-income classes substitute private for public recreational spending. Secondly, there is no guarantee that all programs will be supported by a majority of the population. Thus even though the redistributive programs mentioned above meet with the approval of a majority of Americans the space program is supported by percentages ranging only from 19 to 33 percent of Americans.[8]

Net Fiscal Advantages and Locational Decisions

Some important implications may be drawn from the net fiscal advantages enjoyed by residents of various income classes and areas are shown in Chapter 8. These estimates indicate that there exists a net fiscal advantage from living in the District of Columbia for every income class except the very highest. We might expect that it might be more advantageous to live in the suburbs of other metropolitan areas than in the Washington area for those with high incomes, since other areas do not receive the federal payments and may not be able to export sig-

nificant tax liability. In other words, it might be expected that there should be a smaller decline in the concentration of high-income classes in the central city in the Washington area than elsewhere. The data are difficult to interpret, however. On the one hand, there has been a decline in the concentration of high income families in the District. In 1960, 39.1 percent of families with incomes in excess of $25,000 in the Washington SMSA, lived in the District of Columbia. By 1970 this figure had fallen to only 17.2 percent. In contrast the same figures in the SMSAs of the other nine largest central cities were 41.7 percent and 37.5 percent respectively.[g] However, during the same decade the District's population as a percentage of its SMSA also declined, from 37 to 26 percent, whereas the percentage of the SMSA population living in the nine largest cities in the aggregate declined from 56 to 40 percent. Thus relatively fewer people, whether high or low income, reside in the District than in other large metropolitan areas. This disparity between the Washington and other metropolitan areas makes it difficult to assess the precise role of fiscal advantages in location decisions.

Thus a number of factors may be important in explaining the residential choices of high-income families. In the first place, the Washington SMSA's growth rate between 1960 and 1970 was approximately four times as great as that of the other nine SMSAs in the aggregate. In any rapidly growing area, housing sought by upper-income classes is generally concentrated in the newer, developing areas, which in the Washington area means suburban Maryland and Virginia. Secondly, there is a substantial incentive for the low-income individuals to live within the District of Columbia. And while the percentage of all *families* in the area who lived in the District fell from 47 percent to 25 percent, the percentage of those with incomes less than $3,000 who lived in the District fell only from 60 percent to 50 percent. Thus the concentration of the metropolitan area's poor in the central city increased considerably. If, however, apart from fiscal considerations, the upper-income classes prefer not to live close to the poor, especially if these poor are predominantly black while the upper-income classes are predominantly white, then there may be a more basic sociological explanation of migration to the suburbs in the Washington area. Such migration may simply have been more severe without the relatively favorable fiscal position enjoyed by the District.

A subsidiary reason for the relative erosion of higher-income families in the District may be a real, or at least a perceived, relative deterioration of the public school system occasioned by an increase in the relative concentration of poor families in the District. Given a real or perceived deterioration, which may involve racial overtones, the District may appear to be a less attractive place for families with school age children in comparison with other central cities. This is another reason to have expected greater flight to the suburbs than would be indicated by the relatively favorable fiscal residuals. Indeed it has been families,

[g]The nine cities were: New York, Los Angeles, Chicago, Philadelphia, Detroit, Cleveland, Houston, Milwaukee, and Baltimore.

rather than individuals, who have moved to the suburbs between 1960 and 1970. In that period the number of individuals in the District of Columbia remained constant while there was a 6 percent drop in the number of families.

Suburban living may be relatively less expensive in the Washington than in other metropolitan areas. One of the most important costs of suburban locations is the commutation time that they often entail. But the Washington area is one of the most compact of the ten largest SMSAs, with its outer reaches easily accessible from the central city in less than an hour. Relative to cities such as New York, Chicago, Los Angeles, and Philadelphia, this accessibility makes the suburban life-style considerably less expensive in Washington than elsewhere.

Finally, it may be questioned whether the upper-income classes do face a considerable fiscal advantage vis-à-vis equally situated households in other big cities. Cities with substantial industrial and commercial bases, such as New York, Chicago, Philadelphia, Detroit, Cleveland, and Baltimore, may in fact be able to export as much of their taxes as does the District. If this is the case, high-income people may receive a fiscal incentive from remaining in these cities as well, even though this incentive in itself has not been powerful enough to prevent many of them from moving to the suburbs.

Limitations of the Analysis

Even though the Washington area fiscal interactions have been comprehensively examined in this study, we are not in the least inclined to succumb to temptation, as did John Stuart Mill in another context, and claim that "all problems in metropolitan public finance have now been resolved." Some estimates in this study are indeed based on formulations that enjoy fairly broad acceptance. In other instances, however, strong assumptions have been employed. Although we have argued their plausibility, we have no illusions that this argumentation is beyond dispute. Some of the more crucial assumptions are arrayed here in the form of an epilogue, which can be construed as either an *apologia* or an admission of guilt.

In the first place, it has been assumed that the summed marginal benefits from public services equal the cost of providing these services. In other words, in the context of our analytical model we have assumed that from society's viewpoint there is an optimal level of provision of public services.[h] If, however, a superoptimal level of provision is chosen, because nonresidents of the area bear taxes which are disproportionate to the benefits they receive, then the total benefits in the Washington area are overstated. In this instance the summed

---

[h]Summed marginal benefits multiplied by output would equal total cost of service provision only if the marginal cost of service provision equals the average cost. If marginal costs are rising, the optimal level of provision implies summed marginal benefits in excess of average cost. The assumption of constant marginal cost of service provision is therefore another implicit and limiting assumption.

marginal benefits would fall short of the cost of providing the services. Moreover, the extent of overprovision might well differ between jurisdictions. Since the District of Columbia has the most external financing we might expect overprovision to be greatest there. However, the external constraints on the local political decision-making process are also most important in the case of the District.

Another problem involves the treatment of source-of-income benefits. One could argue that these benefits are not additive with use-of-income benefits, which measure willingness and ability to pay for public services and are analogous to values generated in market exchange. Source-of-income benefits are analogs to factor payments, and factor payments are not in themselves benefits, but rather are means to increase utility. Still, it is true that ultimately source-of-income benefits do enhance the well-being of recipients and so may well alter the distribution of welfare by income class. Yet the fact that including source-of-income benefits in some of our calculations violates the accounting identity between benefits and costs may disturb some. The problem of evaluating in-kind transfers is especially perplexing. The measurement of these benefits at their full dollar value admittedly must somewhat overstate the value placed on them by the recipients. Currently, however, there is no commonly accepted procedure for determining their value.[9]

The geographical extent of the benefit area of income redistributional programs is difficult to define with any precision. If, for example, within a metropolitan area, the nonpoor enjoy greater use-of-income benefits per dollar spent in behalf of poor people who live within their own jurisdiction rather than in behalf of those living elsewhere in the area, then the assumptions employed in this study somewhat overstate the magnitude of the fiscal flows between jurisdictions as well as benefits going to high-income suburban residents.[10]

We have also assumed that tastes are homogeneous throughout the metropolitan area. An assumption of the Tiebout analysis, however, is that people with similar tastes will tend to congregate in the same jurisdiction. If this is true then the nonpoor in the suburbs, especially in Virginia, may well be a self-selecting group of individuals who prefer lower levels of income redistributional activities. To the extent this is true, we have overstated the proportion of the use-of-income benefits from redistributional programs attributed to these people.

Again while this is possibly a characteristic of suburban residents in the Washington area, there is little evidence that this type of preference pattern exists at the national level. Thus Watts and Free found that on five explicitly income redistributional questions[i] the average percentage of those with $15,000

---

[i]They are welfare, medicaid, public housing, programs to improve the education of low-income children, and programs to make college education possible for low-income students.

or more income favoring expansion or maintenance of current service levels was 86.4 percent in the city but only slightly less, or 83.3 percent, in the suburbs.[11]

In addition to these major conceptual problems, there are a number of additional technical questions, some of major consequence, that had to be resolved in the course of generating the estimates. Thus in Chapter 5, use-of-income benefits from the various public services are divided between the private, public nonredistributive, and redistributive categories. While the rank order of these estimates may well be correct, the choice of precise percentages imparts an air of certainty to the results which we do not claim. Some assumptions, which may be contested, are also used to distribute benefits and tax by income class. It is also impossible to account for the services received from public sector capital goods. Quite apparently the benefit flows from these facilities do not occur entirely in the year of expenditure. Yet the utilization of debt service expenditures, for example, as a proxy for these capital services is not possible because of the widely different historical patterns of deficit financing in the Washington area. The allocation of the use-of-income benefits from public pension programs poses a similar problem. Current outlays for pension payments often are compensation for public services provided in previous years, with payment for present services to be made only sometime in the future.ʲ Finally, the services provided through the public sector vary across the Washington metropolitan area with the consequence that the estimated fiscal residuals for a given income class are not fully comparable between jurisdictions.

Limiting characteristics of all incidence study of course apply here also. Thus the estimates of interjurisdictional flows as well as net incidence by income class apply only to the average household unit. The characteristics of these household units vary considerably within income classes and between jurisdictions. For example, a family with $15,000 income and having four children in a public school enjoys a higher fiscal residual than a childless couple with the same income. A misanthrope receives a lower fiscal residual than the altruist with the same income due to their different evaluations of redistributive programs. Moreover, the estimated differences berween families may blur true differences in fiscal treatment of identical units. Thus the *average* household unit with $12,000 income may be slightly better off living in the city, when actually a childless couple with this income may be much better off living in the city while a large family may be considerably worse off.

It has been implicitly assumed that the outputs of government programs can be measured in relation to their inputs. In other words, higher public expenditures are assumed to generate higher service levels. But there may be variation in efficiencies in the production process, as well as in the production

ʲFor example, public pension plans in the District of Columbia are on a pay-as-you-go basis.

function itself, and in factor prices across a metropolitan area. Even though it seems reasonable to assume that factor prices should be similar across a metropolitan area, there is less guarantee that production relationships are.

The measurement of the fiscal impact of metropolitan governments on citizens reports only one chapter in the life of any metropolitan economy. While fiscal considerations undoubtedly create important incentives affecting individual choices and may result in the unequal treatment of equally situated individuals, still they do not capture the importance of many other variables, such as the locational, cultural, and environmental advantages of a place. Finally, while the methodologies employed in this study are indeed applicable to other areas, the precise results found in the Washington area can be extended to other areas only with great caution and by making allowance for specific institutional and economic conditions.

Appendixes

Appendix A
Documentation of the Revenue and Expenditure Data for the Washington Metropolitan Area

Prepared by Rodney Frame

I. Scope of the Study

The metropolitan Washington, D.C. area is defined as:

A. The District of Columbia

B. Suburban Virginia, which includes Arlington and Fairfax counties and the independent cities of Alexandria, Fairfax and Falls Church. The less urbanized counties of London and Prince William are not treated in our study although they are a part of the SMSA.

C. Suburban Maryland, which includes Montgomery and Prince Georges counties.

Within the confines of the suburban districts there are several unincorporated and incorporated cities and towns whose revenues and expenditures are also included in the study.[a] Also included in the tax and expenditure estimates are those made by such regional authorities as the Maryland National Capital Park and Planning Commission, the Washington Suburban Sanitary Commission, and the Northern Virginia Regional Park Authority.

Statewide revenue and expenditure figures must be examined in addition to local revenue and expenditure figures in order to maintain comparability with the District of Columbia, which functions both as a city and a state. In the suburbs it is necessary to allocate a share of the statewide revenue and expenditure figures to each of the localities involved. Procedures used in making these allocations are discussed in a later section.

Fiscal 1970, covering the period July 1969 through June 1970, is the period selected for study. The bulk of the revenue-expenditure data for this period come from the individual jurisdictions' annual financial reports.[1] Budget

---

[a]The revenues and expenditures for the following local governments are included in the totals of the county in which they are located:

a. Fairfax County: Herndon and Vienna

b. Montgomery County: Barnesville, Brookville, Chevy Chase Martin's Addition, Chevy Chase Section 3, Chevy Chase Section 4, Chevy Chase Section 5, Chevy Chase View, Chevy Chase Village, Drummond Citizen's Committee, Friendship Heights, Gaithersburg, Garrett Park, Glen Echo, Kensington, Laytonsville, North Chevy Chase, Oakmont, Poolesville, Rockville, Somerset, Takoma Park, and Washington Grove

c. Prince Georges County: Berwyn Heights, Bladensburg, Bowie, Brentwood, Capitol Heights, Cheverly, College Park, Colmar Manor, Cottage City, District Heights, Eagle Harbor, Edmonston, Fairmont Heights, Forest Heights, Glenarden, Greenbelt, Hyattsville, Landover Hills, Laurel, Morningside, Mt. Rainier, New Carrollton, North Brentwood, Riverdale, Seat Pleasant, Takoma Park, University Park, and Upper Marlboro.

plans which listed past actual expenditures were used in some cases. Separate documents were required for independent school districts and special districts which operate outside the regular county government. Numerous reports from separate state agencies were also used to obtain more detailed figures on expenditures than were available in the annual state reports.

II. Expenditure Classification

The following expenditure classifications are made:

1. General Government
2. Courts and Corrections
3. Education
4. Health and Hospitals
5. Social Services
6. Recreation and Cultural
7. Transportation
8. Public Safety
9. Public Works

1. In addition to the obvious legislative and administrative bodies, this category also includes regulatory agencies, planning and zoning commissions, state's or commonwealth's attorneys, and contributions to regional advisory boards such as the Washington Metropolitan Area Council of Governments. This category also includes certain small, miscellaneous expenditures not otherwise classified.

2. The "courts" classification is straightforward. "Corrections" includes state penitentiaries, juvenile detention centers, and local sheriff and jail expenditures.

3. "Education" is divided into primary, secondary, and higher.

4. "Health" and "Hospitals" includes Health Department expenditures, as well as mental health expenditures and expenditures on air pollution control. The local suburban hospitals in the area are largely either private or financed through user charges, thus their expenditures are not fully included in our totals. Local government contributions to various private health and mental health facilities are also included here.

5. "Social Service" expenditures are divided between direct public welfare payments to individuals and "all other" expenditures. Unfortunately, for certain types of expenditures no unambiguous line can be drawn between the "health" and "social services" categories.

6. "Recreation" expenditures include departmental expenditures plus the two regional authorities serving the area—the Maryland National Capital Park

and Planning Commission and the Northern Virginia Regional Park Authority. Certain of the Maryland National Capital Park and Planning Commission expenditures are included in the "General Government" category; for example, expenditures for planning and zoning purposes.

"Cultural" expenditures are mainly for libraries at the local level and for museums and historical commissions at the state level. Only the library expenditures are quantitatively significant.

7. The "Transportation" category includes street and sidewalk maintenance, street cleaning, snow removal, and street lighting. In addition, traffic-oriented expenditures of the local and state police departments are included in this category. At the state level, these traffic-oriented police expenditures comprise more than 80 percent of total police expenditures. Local and state contributions to regional transit authorities such as the Washington Metropolitan Area Transit Authority and the Northern Virginia Transit Commission are also included.

8. The "Public Safety" category is divided into "police and fire." Included in police are expenditures for civil defense and animal shelters.

9. Refuse and sanitation comprise the bulk of what is termed "public works." Refuse collection expenditures are stated net of charges and therefore are not large. Much of what is termed "Public Works" in local government financial statements has been placed in other categories for our purposes. For example, we have included building and ground maintenance expenditures under "General Government" and street cleaning expenditures under "Transportation."

III. Elimination of Federal and Capital Expenditures

Federally-financed expenditures and capital expenditures are not included in the study. Our study focuses on the differential state plus local burden borne and the differential benefits received by citizens in the various jurisdictions. The elimination of such revenues and expenditures allows us to concentrate on those fiscal flows which are the product of local (and state) decisionmakers. It is an analysis of these flows which will be a useful input to decisionmakers at the local level.

A number of factors influenced the decision to exclude capital expenditures from the study. While it would be possible to include capital expenditures which were made in fiscal year 1970, the procedure seemed undesirable because of the lumpy nature of such expenditures. This could lead to unusually high or low expenditures for a particular service, which would not accurately reflect the level of service provided in that year. A possible way to circumvent this difficulty would be to use an average of several years' capital expenditures. Data limitations prohibited us from implementing this procedure.

Another approach considered was to treat debt service in fiscal 1970 as an

expenditure for the current use of capital. Initially, this approach seemed desirable, but was rejected because of the very different historical debt issue behavior exhibited in the several jurisdictions. The state of Virginia, for example, has a history of pay-as-you-go finance for its capital expenditures and issued no general obligation bonds until quite recently. Thus, current debt service requirements would be unusually low when compared with those of other jurisdictions who had a long history of debt service financing of capital expenditures.

In light of these considerations, the decision is made to focus solely on current operating expenditures. This decision requires some adjustments in the primary data. On the expenditure side we do not include either debt service payments or capital expenditures.[b] Thus, on the revenue side, a downward adjustment is needed to insure that only revenue for current operating expenditures is included. This adjustment is easy to make in Montgomery County where all debt service is financed through earmarked taxes. However, this is not the case in the other jurisdictions. The procedure adopted for these jurisdictions is to compute total expenditures less debt service and currently-financed capital as a percentage of total expenditures in fiscal year 1970. This percentage is then applied to all locally-generated revenues. The resulting revenue figures are an estimate of revenues used to finance current expenditures. In making these deflations, expenditures are used net of the deductions described in the following section and inter-governmental transfers are considered as expenditures of the grantor.

IV. Other Expenditure Adjustments

A. "Market-Type" Transactions

In addition to adjusting the data for federal contributions and capital expenditure, adjustments are made to account for what we might term "market-type" transactions. Interest receipts, sales, dividends, tuitions, and service charges all fall into this category. The idea of a "burden" being imposed in the raising of such a revenue is without meaning in that there is no coercive force involved. The transactions essentially operate through the market. On these grounds, we choose not to include such revenues in our study. The procedure used is to eliminate these amounts from the revenue side of our estimates and to net out such revenues from the appropriate expenditure category.

---

[b]The elimination of capital expenditures is not as obvious as it might first appear. Local government budgets often list the purchase of tables, chairs, typewriters, and filing cabinets as "capital" expenditures. For our purposes, this seemed undesirable and we chose to include them. More "obvious" capital expenditures such as the construction of a new highway or the expansion of an office building are, of course, excluded.

B. Retirement Contributions

Government retirement contributions should be treated as current expenditures for whatever function the employee is currently performing. For most political jurisdictions this kind of breakdown is unavailable except for police and teacher retirement funds, which are generally operated separately. In general, therefore, we are forced to allocate the rest of retirement contributions to the various different service categories on the basis of their personnel costs. Moreover, in Washington, D.C., apparently retirement pensions are paid for on a pay-as-you-go basis. We are forced to use such payments as a proxy for current obligations incurred to support current employees in the future. It may be a rather poor proxy since the real value of retirement obligations is growing over time.

V. Treatment of State Taxes Raised and Expenditures Made in the Local Jurisdiction

The allocation of state finances to the different localities presents some technical problems. In what follows, we describe the procedure employed first in Maryland and then in Virginia. In each state we first consider the allocation of state revenues and then move on to the state expenditures.

A. Maryland

1. Revenues. In many cases the estimation of the taxes raised in the particular jurisdictions under study is quite straightforward. The state compiled tax collection data on a county basis. This is true for such taxes as the income tax, the sales tax, the state property tax, the public utility tax, the estate taxes, admission and amusement taxes, the recordation tax, the estate and inheritance taxes, and certain franchise taxes. In addition, distilled spirit tax revenues can be allocated to the localities based on local revenue distribution information supplied by the state Alcoholic Beverages Division.

For the other revenue categories, we rely on indirect allocations. For example, the various motor vehicle taxes are allocated to the localities according to either vehicle registration percentages or vehicle miles traveled on roads in the county. Since these taxes are almost entirely earmarked for the state highway commission, they are adjusted for capital expenditures independent of the other revenues. Information for this adjustment comes from the *Annual Report* of the State Highway Commission.

The remaining major revenue figures are allocated to the suburban localities as follows:

a. The corporation income tax is estimated by applying the ratio of estimated local corporate profits to state corporate profits;

b. The bonus tax (tax on authorized capital stock of corporations) is allocated using the same percentages as the corporation income tax;

c. The building, savings and loan association tax on gross receipts is allocated using the percentages derived from state data on the gross receipts tax on savings banks;

d. The tax on rolling stock owned by persons other than railroads is allocated using the same percentages as the corporation income tax;

e. The tax on the net earnings of financial institutions is allocated to the localities according to income;

f. The tax on gross receipts of railroads and public utilities is allocated according to rail and public utility operating property located in the localities;

g. The wine and beer excise tax is allocated to the localities using the same direct percentages computed for distilled spirits since information was unavailable on local sales of beer and wine;

h. The tobacco tax in Maryland is allocated based upon an adjusted BLS series on tobacco expenditures which was applied to the state and county income distributions to estimate the proportion of state sales in these counties. The estimates were then adjusted to reflect the impact of price differentials on consumption;

i. The tax on insurance companies is allocated to the localities according to income;

j. The boxing, wrestling, and sparring taxes are allocated to the localities on a per capita basis;

k. The horse racing taxes are set equal to the amount of revenue from tracks located in the localities;

l. The shellfish taxes are not allocated because the suburban counties are not shellfish producing areas;

m. The apple tax is allocated to the localities using agricultural employment figures from the *County Business Patterns;*

n. The boat titling tax is allocated according to income; and

o. The various business licenses and permits are allocated using data from *County Business Patterns.* Separate license revenue allocations can be made according to legal employment, bank employment, medical employment, construction employment, etc., where appropriate. Motor vehicle licenses and alcoholic beverage licenses are allocated in the same way as motor fuel and alcoholic beverage taxes.

2. Expenditures. Less direct information is available on the geographical incidence of expenditure benefits than of taxes and thus more reliance is placed

on indirect allocation. Our procedures, by separate expenditure category, are summarized below.

a. *General Government.* No direct allocation is possible here. Therefore, certain types of general government expenditures are allocated on a per capita basis, others on an income basis, and some others are allocated according to the percentage each locality receives of all state expenditure allocations.

b. *Courts and Corrections.* For the expenditures of the juvenile training schools, we were able to obtain data from the State Department of Juvenile Services concerning the location of the courts of commitment of the offenders and we use these percentages to allocate the expenditures. For the state penitentiaries, we use data from the *Maryland Statistical Abstracts* on the jurisdiction from which committed persons were received. Court expenditures are allocated locally according to the total number of cases filed in trial courts in each county as a percentage of the statewide total.

c. *Education.* Direct information is available concerning disbursements to localities. Percentages obtained from such direct allocations are also used to allocate the various administrative expenditures of the State Department of Education. State teacher retirement contributions are attributed to the localities according to their percentage of the total number of public school teachers in the state. This information is available from the State Department of Education.

A somewhat more complicated procedure is necessary to allocate higher education expenditures. This is due to the differential state/out-of-state tuition charges. Expenditures for each college, net of all nontuition charges, were divided into two parts—those for state students and those for out-of-state students. From these two "net" expenditure figures we deducted the appropriate tuition charges. The resulting net figures were then allocated to the localities according to the residence of the students. Information for the allocation comes from the Council on Higher Education in Maryland and the State Council on Higher Education in Virginia. The tuition information comes from the *College Handbook* and *American Colleges.*

d. *Health and Hospitals.* Through personal correspondence, information on county of residence of the patients was obtained. It is used to allocate the expenditures of the chronic disease, mental, and tuberculosis hospitals. For the rest of state health expenditures, the only percentages which could be obtained were those for Medicaid disbursements to physicians by county of practice. We use these percentages to allocate all state expenditures in this category.

e. *Social Services.* Data on public assistance payments by jurisdiction is available in the *Report of the Comptroller* and the expenditures could be obtained directly. Administrative costs are allocated using the direct percentages.

f. *Recreation and Cultural.* These expenditures are basically outlays for state parks and are allocated to the counties according to the location of the specific parks.

g. *Transportation.* This category includes the Department of Motor Vehicles, the State Highway Commission, and a portion of the State Police expenditures. The Department of Motor Vehicle expenditures are allocated to the localities according to vehicle registration percentages. The maintenance expenditures of the State Highway Commission allocated to the localities reflect actual disbursements. In addition, the *Report of the Comptroller* gives statistics for direct state-to-local grants. We were unable to obtain a functional breakdown of state police expenditures in Maryland so we are limited to applying the State of Virginia functional percentages to the Maryland totals. The traffic-related police expenditure component is then allocated to the localities according to vehicle registration percentages.

h. *Public Safety.* These expenditures are minimal at the state level. The nontraffic component of the state police expenditures was allocated to the localities using the FBI crime index and the small civil defense expenditures were allocated on a per capita basis.

i. *Public Works.* These expenditures are nonexistent at the state level. Expenditures for the State Board of Public Works are included under general government.

B. Virginia

Roughly the same procedures for allocating state revenues and expenditures to the Northern Virginia counties are used as are used in Maryland. Brief descriptions of the procedures are sketched out below.

1. Revenues. Direct allocations can be made for the state sales tax, the state income tax, and several small, locally-collected taxes such as the capitation tax, the tax on capital not otherwise taxed, the bank stock tax, and the taxes on wills, suits, deeds and contracts. Information for these allocations comes from the *Report of the Comptroller* and the *Report of the State Department of Taxation.* The major other revenues are allocated as follows:

a. The various alcoholic beverage taxes are allocated using information in the *Annual Report* of the State Alcoholic Beverage Control Board concerning sales at stores located in each jurisdiction. The profits of the state system are treated as taxes.

b. The various motor vehicle related taxes are allocated on the basis of motor vehicle registration. The fuel is an exception and is allocated in proportion to vehicle miles traveled driven in the localities. As is the case in Maryland, these revenues are mostly earmarked for the Highway Commission and thus a separate adjustment to account for capital and debt service expenditures is made.

c. The tobacco tax in Virginia is allocated in proportion to total sales by locality in 1971. Comparable data is unavailable for 1970.

d. The various agricultural and oyster taxes are not allocated as the Northern Virginia area because it is neither a major farm area nor an oyster harvesting region.

e. The corporate income tax is allocated using the same procedures as in Maryland.

f. The inheritance and estate tax in Virginia is allocated by using national data to derive a state wealth distribution by income class, computing the proportion of total state wealth held in these counties (based on their income distribution) and applying the proportion to the total state tax.

g. The taxes on railroad, car line, and express companies are allocated to the localities on a per capita basis.

h. The taxes on utility companies are allocated according to the proportion of state assessments on public utilities in those counties.

i. The taxes on Public Service Corporations are allocated to the localities according to property assessment figures found in the *Report of the Department of Taxation*.

j. The tax on the gross premiums of insurance companies is allocated to the localities according to income.

k. The wrestling and boxing exhibition gross receipts tax is allocated to the localities on a per capita basis.

l. The tax on motor vehicle carriers is allocated to the localities according to trucking and warehouse employment data from the *County Business Patterns*.

m. The various business and professional license taxes are allocated, where possible, according to percentages obtained from *County Business Patterns*. Many of these are agriculturally-oriented licenses and permits and thus no allocation is made to Northern Virginia.

n. The corporate franchise and charter fees are allocated to the localities according to the number of reporting units found in the *County Business Patterns*.

o. The fees for miscellaneous services are allocated to localities on the basis of total reporting units found in the *County Business Patterns*.

p. The special assessments to insurance companies and banks are allocated according to income.

2. Expenditures.

a. *General Government.* All figures in this category are allocated to the localities indirectly in the same general ways as in Maryland.

b. *Courts and Corrections.* Alexandria and Arlington constitute separate judicial circuits in Virginia while the other three jurisdictions in our study along with Prince William County form a third circuit. The Attorney General's Office has supplied us with information on courts of record by circuit and percentages compiled from these figures are used to allocate state judicial expenditures to the localities. The figures for Fairfax County and the cities of Falls Church and

Fairfax are computed by using their respective populations as a percentage of that for the entire circuit.

Correctional institution expenditures are allocated to the localities according to the location of the court of commitment. This information is available in the *Annual Statistical Report of Felons and Misdemeanants* and the *Annual Report of the Department of Welfare and Institutions.*

c. *Education.* Direct allocations are possible here for sales tax distributions earmarked for public schools and for direct state-to-local grants. Administrative expenditures of the state board are allocated to the localities based on the grant percentages.

The allocation for the various state colleges and universities are made using procedures identical to those discussed above for Maryland.

d. *Health and Hospitals.* The net expenditures for all hospitals (mental, tuberculosis, university) are allocated to the localities generally according to the geographical distribution of the patients. This information was obtained through personal communication with several hospitals. Other health expenditures are allocated in a variety of ways. For example, expenditures for legal medicine, postmortem examination, and the collection and publication of vital statistics are all allocated on a per capita basis, while the expenditures for tuberculosis prevention are allocated using the geographical distribution of tuberculosis hospital patients. Direct allocations are possible only with Medicaid payments and the local health department reimbursements.

e. *Social Services.* These expenditures are largely public assistance payments and the *Annual Report* of the Department of Welfare and Institutions gives figures for direct allocations. Expenditures of the Commission for the Visually Handicapped are allocated using the percentages from the public assistance payments to the blind and expenditures for vocational rehabilitation are allocated as are education administrative expenditures.

f. *Recreation and Council.* Unlike the suburban Maryland counties, those in Virginia contain no state parks. The small allocation to Northern Virginia reflects mainly per capita allocations of the expenditures of the various historical and art commissions. Expenditures for state-operated museums located outside our study area are not allocated to our localities.

g. *Transportation.* Division of Motor Vehicles expenditures, highway safety expenditures, and the traffic-oriented expenditures of the state police are all allocated to the localities according to passenger car registration percentages. The State Highway Commission supplied us with information which permitted direct allocations for highway maintenance payments to localities, state highway maintenance expenditures in the localities, and the earmarked fuel tax distribution to Arlington County. State contributions to the Washington Metropolitan Area Transit Authority are allocated on the basis of each Northern Virginia locality's own contribution.

h. *Public Works.* At the state level this category consists mainly of the State Water Control Board and these expenditures are allocated on a per capita basis.

i. *Public Safety.* Civil air patrol expenditures and civil defense expenditures are allocated to the localities on a per capita basis, while nontraffic state police expenditures are allocated according to percentages computed from the FBI crime index.

VI. Special Local Government Considerations

A. Adjustments to Include the
Sub-County Governments

As noted above, the revenues and expenditures of fifty-two small city and town governments are also included in our study. The yearly local revenues of these governments range from less than $4,000 for Oakmont in Montgomery County to more than $2,000,000 for Rockville in Montgomery County. The procedures used to obtain the revenues and expenditures for these areas are described below.

1. Suburban Virginia. For Vienna, we use a complete financial statement and proceed just as we did with the independent governments. For Herndon, we have only a statement of total revenues and total expenditures and no complete breakdown by revenue source or expenditure function. Lacking this breakdown, we compute the revenue and expenditure percentages by category in Vienna and apply these percentages to the adjusted Herndon total.

2. Suburban Maryland. Due to the large number of local governments in Maryland, the computation proved to be more difficult here. Time constraints and difficulty in obtaining the necessary documents precluded looking at each locality individually. *Local Government Finances in Maryland,* published by the Department of Fiscal Services, does give summary data on all local governments in Maryland, however, the breakdowns are incomplete for our purposes. In addition, due to the number of adjustments which we have made, these figures are not directly comparable with ours. Those localities shown by *Local Government Finances in Maryland* to have greater than $100,000 of locally-generated revenues in fiscal year 1970 are included directly in the study. We examined the audit report for each one and adjusted the figures just as we did with the counties and independent cities. There are twenty-two such governments. The remaining twenty-eight are treated indirectly. First, a correction was made for debt service and capital expenditures based on the findings for the twenty-two larger jurisdictions. The resulting revenue and expenditure categories are presumed distributed in the same proportions as in the larger jurisdictions.

Appendix B
Expenditure Incidence Assumptions

B.1 The income distribution used for the areas is obtained from the 1970 Census. Household income is the amount of money income received by each person fourteen years of age or older in a household in the previous year from each of the following sources: (1) money wages or salary; (2) net income from nonfarm self-employment; (3) net income from farm self-employment; (4) social security, veterans' payments, or other government or private pensions; (5) interest (on bonds or savings), dividends, and income from annuities, estates, or trusts; (6) net income from boarders or lodgers, or from renting property to others; (7) all other regular sources such as unemployment benefits, public assistance, alimony, etc. Irregular sources of income due to capital gains are not included. The amounts received represent income before deductions for personal taxes, social security, etc. In statistics on *family income* the combined incomes of all members of each family or household are treated as a single amount. For *unrelated individual income* the classification is by the amount of their own (individual) total income.

B.2 For each of the seven major jurisdictions which comprise the three areas we obtained a 25 percent sample of all Census tracts. An estimate of the income characteristics of school children is made by distributing the total number of school children in each tract by the income distribution of that tract. Tract data is summed by jurisdiction and then weighted by 1970 Census data on mean number of children per family by income class. The distribution of public school children by income class obtained from the sample of tract data for the seven jurisdictions, the data on mean family size by income class in the District and in the suburbs and the resulting distribution of public school children by income class by jurisdiction are presented in table B-1. This table also contains many other distributive series which are discussed subsequently in this appendix.

B.3 To assign benefits from higher education it is necessary to identify separately net higher education expenditures (expenditures less tuition) for both residents and nonresidents. Because of the substantial differentials in tuition rates charged to these two groups, a failure to do this would result in an overstatement of benefits to out-of-state students and an understatement of benefits to in-state students. Most of the larger institutions provided us with actual data on these tuition differentials. In the remaining cases we estimate these differentials.

The computation of net expenditures requires information on expenditures, tuition payments, and student residency characteristics. Expenditures in D.C. are

Table B-1
Distributive Series Employed

	Percentages Attributed to Income Brackets							
	Below $3,000	$3,000-$3,999	$4,000-$5,999	$6,000-$7,499	$7,500-$9,999	$10,000-$14,999	$15,000-$25,000	$25,000 and above
1. Distribution of Public School Children (D.C.)	.1291	.0460	.1358	.1143	.1677	.2381	.1255	.0435
2. Distribution of Public School Children (Montgomery)	.0299	.0142	.0325	.0395	.0958	.2294	.3532	.2055
3. Distribution of Public School Children (Prince Georges)	.0350	.0187	.0504	.0643	.1388	.3230	.3020	.0678
4. Distribution of Public School Children (Arlington)	.0333	.0148	.0517	.0489	.1050	.2267	.3684	.1512
5. Distribution of Public School Children (Fairfax)	.0309	.0120	.0396	.0424	.1013	.2627	.3659	.1452
6. Distribution of Public School Children (Alexandria)	.0748	.0330	.0893	.1125	.1887	.2799	.1776	.0442
7. Distribution of Public School Children (Fairfax City)	.0273	.0131	.0370	.0570	.1143	.2565	.3792	.1156
8. Distribution of Public School Children (Falls Church City)	.0361	.0283	.0393	.0534	.1389	.2704	.3093	.1243
9. Mean* Children Per Family (city)	1.6600	1.7580	1.6800	1.5270	1.4110	1.2860	1.6870	.9829
10. Mean Children Per Family (suburbs)	1.3760	1.1350	1.2030	1.4560	1.4590	1.5390	1.6080	1.4540
11. Weighted distribution of Public School Children (D.C.)	.1521	.0569	.1605	.1228	.1664	.2153	.0959	.0301
12. Weighted distribution of Public School Children (Montgomery)	.0273	.0107	.0259	.0380	.0924	.2333	.3751	.1974
13. Weighted distribution of Public School Children (Prince Georges)	.0309	.0142	.0410	.0622	.1343	.3298	.3221	.0655
14. Weighted distribution of Public School Children (Arlington)	.0309	.0111	.0413	.0471	.1014	.2308	.3919	.1455
15. Weighted distribution of Public School Children (Fairfax)	.0286	.0090	.0274	.0408	.0978	.2675	.3893	.1396
16. Weighted distribution of Public School Children (Alexandria)	.0688	.0254	.0726	.1120	.1881	.2940	.1951	.0440
17. Weighted distribution of Public School Children (Fairfax City)	.0247	.0098	.0294	.0546	.1097	.2598	.4014	.1106
18. Weighted distribution of Public School Children (Falls Church City)	.0320	.0215	.0325	.0518	.1348	.2767	.3306	.1201
19. Distribution of Families (D.C.)	.1062	.0440	.1190	.1029	.1513	.2263	.1708	.0801
20. Distribution of Families (Montgomery)	.0285	.0140	.0348	.0399	.0872	.2334	.3614	.2003
21. Distribution of Families (Prince Georges)	.0396	.0205	.0587	.0705	.1489	.3179	.2832	.0605
22. Distribution of Families (Arlington)	.0384	.0224	.0632	.0663	.1289	.2398	.2982	.1425
23. Distribution of Families (Fairfax)	.0316	.0130	.0405	.0427	.0945	.2505	.3804	.1464
24. Distribution of Families (Alexandria)	.1324	.0517	.1133	.1089	.1596	.2105	.1652	.0581
25. Distribution of Families (Fairfax City)	.0285	.1345	.0383	.0605	.1220	.2628	.3666	.1078

26. Distribution of Families (Falls Church City)	.0343	.0264	.0387	.0507	.1361	.2674	.3141	.1320
27. Distribution of families and unrelated individuals (D.C.)	.2445	.0612	.1371	.1066	.1382	.1574	.1075	.0470
28. Distribution of families and unrelated individuals (Montgomery)	.1040	.0272	.0562	.0529	.0966	.2083	.2944	.1600
29. Distribution of families and unrelated individuals (Prince Georges)	.1268	.0346	.0782	.0782	.1445	.2666	.2230	.0478
30. Distribution of families and unrelated individuals (Arlington)	.1420	.0448	.1031	.0935	.1436	.1913	.1957	.0856
31. Distribution of families and unrelated individuals (Fairfax)	.0767	.0243	.0595	.0572	.1050	.2290	.3248	.1231
32. Distribution of families and unrelated individuals (Alexandria)	.1324	.0517	.1133	.1099	.1596	.2105	.1652	.0581
33. Distribution of families and unrelated individuals (Fairfax City)	.0642	.0221	.0533	.0693	.1265	.2444	.3252	.0949
34. Distribution of families and unrelated individuals (Falls Church City)	.0992	.0393	.0668	.0696	.1408	.2321	.2501	.1018
35. Distribution of higher education benefits (D.C.)		.1056	.2852	.2466	.3626	—	—	
36. Distribution of higher education benefits (Maryland)	.0228	.0098	.0435	.0717	.1783	.2011	.2935	.1793
37. Distribution of higher education benefits (Virginia)	.0500	.0600	.1200	.1200	.1500	.2600	.1850	.0550
38. Average number of family visits to Alexandria health clinics	.6596	.5965	.5247	.4770	.4811	.4000	.3259	.3606
39. Distribution of users of health facilities (D.C.)	.3219	.0717	.1434	.1014	.1325	.1255	.0698	.0338
40. Distribution of users of health facilities (Maryland)	.1750	.0423	.0810	.0718	.1333	.2180	.1931	.0855
41. Distribution of users of health facilities (Virginia)	.1542	.0475	.0963	.0833	.1388	.1998	.1966	.0835
42. Distribution of welfare payments (D.C.)	.5970	.1256	.1312	.0559	.0426	.0222	.0182	.0073
43. Distribution of welfare payments (Maryland)	.4566	.1133	.1175	.0710	.0757	.0643	.0773	.0243
44. Distribution of welfare payments (Virginia)	.4318	.1166	.1257	.0685	.0720	.0608	.0931	.0312
45. Distribution of expenditures on books (D.C.)	.0189	.0162	.0680	.0920	.1369	.2250	.2730	.1700
46. Distribution of expenditures on books (Maryland)	.0050	.0050	.0210	.0370	.0780	.2210	.4110	.2220
47. Distribution of expenditures on books (Virginia)	.0060	.0060	.0260	.0419	.0789	.1960	.4162	.2288
48. Distribution of recreation benefits (D.C.)	.1515	.0633	.1711	.1479	.3692	.0849	.0080	.0037
49. Distribution of recreation benefits (Maryland)	.0763	.0389	.1058	.1255	.4583	.1632	.0231	.0089
50. Distribution of recreation benefits (Virginia)	.0853	.0426	.1172	.1266	.4413	.1507	.0256	.0102
51. Distribution of housing units by Income (D.C.)	.1437	.0466	.1132	.0902	.1429	.2005	.1749	.0877
52. Distribution of housing units by Income (Prince Georges)	.0524	.0183	.0519	.0469	.0972	.2491	.3422	.1415
53. Distribution of housing units by Income (Montgomery)	.0555	.0195	.0480	.0497	.1020	.2502	.3366	.1383
54. Distribution of housing units by Income (Arlington, Fairfax City and County)	.0506	.0174	.0428	.0458	.0959	.2521	.3501	.1453
55. Distribution of housing units by Income (Falls Church)	.0490	.0167	.0411	.0446	.0943	.2526	.3542	.1474

*The numbers for classes one and three are the average values of smaller intervals.

obtained directly through budget documents. In the suburban jurisdictions, higher education expenditures are defined to include local expenditures on community colleges plus some part of state expenditures on *all* colleges and universities in the state. Thus, for higher education we depart from our general procedure for estimating state expenditures for suburban jurisdictions. This procedure would consider only those expenditures which are made at facilities located within the suburban jurisdictions. Since the main campus of the University of Maryland is located in our study area, while the main campus of the University of Virginia is not, use of this procedure would grossly understate benefits to Virginia suburban residents from expenditures on higher education. Thus, expenditures which benefit residents of our study area from all state colleges and universities are considered and expenditures on state education in the suburban counties are defined as the sum of benefits to suburbanites from their attendance at these state institutions.

The allocation of benefits from higher education expenditures to the members of the Maryland and Virginia suburban jurisdictions requires information on the residency of students by county of origin. Certain institutions, for example, Washington Technical Institute, provided a classification of students by zip code which makes it relatively easy to identify Maryland and Virginia students from the suburban areas. For the most part in Maryland and Virginia less precise estimates are employed. The Council on Higher Education in Maryland and the State Council on Higher Education in Virginia provided us with residency data for each of the schools. It details residency characteristics by county within the state, but only by state for out-of-state students. Data from the Annual Report of the State of Maryland Department of Education allow us to estimate the number of suburban Maryland students attending Virginia schools given the assumption that the propensity was the same in 1970 as in 1968. Information on the attendance by suburban Virginia residents at Maryland institutions could only be computed by a fairly indirect method which derived from information on attendance of suburban Maryland residents at Maryland institutions.[a]

B.4 The information to distribute the expenditures by income class in Maryland comes from a questionnaire survey conducted by the University of

---

[a]We began by assuming that the percentage of Maryland students at Maryland institutions who came from the Maryland suburban counties could serve as a proxy for the proportion of total Virginia students from the Virginia suburban counties at Maryland institutions once the percentage had been weighted to account for the larger population of the Maryland suburbs. Thus, the total value of benefits to suburban Virginia residents equals:

Total Virginia Benefits [Proportion of Maryland students from suburban Maryland] = [Suburban Virginia population as a percentage of total Virginia population / Suburban Maryland population as a percentage of total Maryland population]

Maryland requesting the income class of each student's family. In Virginia, this same information is available from the State Council of Higher Education.[1] While the Maryland figures reflect just University of Maryland students, the Virginia figures are for all students in state-controlled four-year schools. It is unfortunate that a breakdown for all students in all Maryland schools is unavailable. The error introduced by using the University of Maryland figures for all the state schools is not great because expenditures for the University of Maryland constitute more than 75 percent of our "net" Maryland higher education expenditures.

For D.C. we obtained a printout from Washington Technical Institute which gave student residency by zip code area. Only zip code areas with one hundred or more students are considered. For each of these areas the income distribution of these students is assumed the same as the income distribution of the zip code area. Zip code area data on students is aggregated and a total distribution of students by income class is obtained.

In certain cases, the income groupings for which data are available do not exactly match the ones adopted for the study. In these cases, we decomposed certain income classes, allocating the sum between classes by the distribution of families and unrelated individuals, and then reaggregated to form the desired income distributions. The distributions we used are shown in table B-1.

B.5 No direct information could be obtained on the proportion of total hours spent and the proportion of total miles driven by residents and nonresidents of the metropolitan area and so an estimate is made using a variety of separate data sources.[b] The general procedure used is to study twenty-four-hour vehicle patterns, by state of registration of the vehicle, and classify the vehicles by trip purpose, using supplementary information on tourism and on commutation patterns from the 1970 Census.[2] Once the trip purpose is determined, the average number of hours spent and the average number of miles spent in a jurisdiction is assigned. The basic data source for this analysis is the D.C. Cordon Study,[3] which observed vehicles *entering* the District of Columbia. This provided good information on travel flows into the District by non-District residents and information on travel patterns by District residents in the suburbs.

A basic requirement for this calculation is information on the travel patterns of nonresidents. To derive estimates, we examine nonresident travel in the District, where nonresidents of the metropolitan area and nonresidents of the balance of the nation are separately identified.[c]

---

[b]A complete appendix with full documentation of procedures may be obtained upon request from the authors.

[c]Information on travel patterns in the suburban areas is available in less detail; in particular, there are limited observations on trips that originate outside the metropolitan area and which terminate in the suburban jurisdictions.

Table B-2

Summary Table of Distribution of Hours Spent and Miles Traveled for the District of Columbia, Suburban Maryland, and Suburban Virginia

	Distribution of VMT (Percentage)			Distribution of Hours Spent (Percentage)		
	D.C.	Maryland Suburbs	Virginia Suburbs	D.C.	Maryland Suburbs	Virginia Suburbs
Maryland Residents	27.1	67.18	15.76	9.4	92.87	4.11
Virginia Residents	10.14	12.41	67.05	4.5	1.75	89.62
D.C. Residents	51.47	7.81	3.47	81.33	2.65	1.29
Balance of the Nation	11.29	12.6	13.72	4.77	2.73	4.98

Travel patterns of a week day and weekend are estimated and then weighted to obtain an estimate of patterns on a typical day.

Table B-2 shows the distribution of hours spent and vehicle miles traveled by residents and nonresidents of the metropolitan area.

B.6 Since the beneficiaries of the expenditures on traffic-related services by the police department are the users of the roads, we chose to consider these expenditures under transportation expenditures. The benefits from these expenditures are allocated according to the proportion of total vehicle miles traveled by residents and nonresidents.

The value of services which benefit the federal government are measured and the benefits are assigned to individuals outside the metropolitan area. For the District of Columbia an estimate was supplied to us by the police department. For the suburban jurisdictions, we estimate the value of services to the federal government under the assumption that proportion would be the same if government employment were the same percentage of total employment as in the District.

B.7 Total fire protection benefits are set equal to total expenditures. The proportion of benefits which is assumed to accrue to property and people is 90 percent to property and 10 percent to people. Before calculating the dollar value of people and property benefits, expenditures which benefit the federal government are estimated. This estimate is made by applying the proportion of all fire calls which are made to federal government property to total expenditures.[d] Once the value of total federal government benefits are computed, these benefits are sub-

---

[d]The proportion was computed from a one-month sample of calls to federal property in D.C. for October 1970. An estimate of the proportion of expenditures benefiting the federal government in the suburbs was made under the assumption that the proportion would be the same if the federal government proportion of total employment were the same.

divided into benefits to property and people. The property component accrues to all U.S. citizens in the form of lower federal taxes and is assigned to the residents of the balance of the nation. The remaining expenditures (net of federal government benefits) are divided into people and property benefits using the appropriate proportions. Then federal government benefits to people are combined with other benefits to people.

Benefits which accrue to people are assigned, when measured on a cost-of-service basis, simply according to the proportion of total time spent in the jurisdiction by residents and nonresidents. Cost-of-service measurement of benefits to residents of the metropolitan area is distributed by a series on families and unrelated individuals by income class from the *1970 Census of Population and Housing.*[e]

Rather than making the assumption that the cost of protecting one dollar of residential property is equal to that of protecting one dollar of commercial property, and simply dividing total property benefits on the basis of relative property values, an effort is made to measure the differential. We do not know a priori whether one would expect higher costs for the protection of residential or commercial property. While some economies can be obtained in protecting high density business areas, the equipment required to respond to such fires is often more costly. Using data provided to us by the D.C. fire department, fire expenditures for the central business district are estimated.[f] The assumption is made that total fire expenditures for the central business district represent the cost of protection to business property and that the remainder represents expenditures for the protection of residential property. The relative costs of providing protection to a dollar of business and residential property in D.C. is used to weight the relative improvement values of business and residential property in the suburban jurisdictions in order to divide total property benefits into residential and commercial categories. Since fire services are an intermediate product to business (and the federal government), total business (and nonowner-occupied residential) property benefits are the same regardless of the particular definition of benefits which is adopted. The measurement of benefits on a welfare basis rather than on a cost-of-service basis does affect the distribution of the total benefits for residential property among income classes, since use of a welfare

---

[e]Cost-of-service benefits to residents of the rest of the world are distributed among income classes using national data on the distribution of trips among income classes in 1960. The distribution is adjusted to 1970 by assuming that the proportion of total trips taken by a particular class in a relative income distribution remains constant; i.e., the fraction of total trips made by the poorest 10 percent of the population is assumed to be the same in 1970 as in 1960. It is assumed that the income distribution of suburban visitors to the city and city visitors to the suburbs is the same as the total income distribution of the jurisdiction in which they reside. A limited sampling at the tract level of the income distribution of commuters confirmed this assumption to be a good one.

[f]This estimate is obtained by summing total costs for those fire stations which overlay the business district. A separate allocation of the expenditures of the ambulance and rescue squads is made on a per capita basis.

basis rather than a cost-of-service basis yields different benefits to owner-users of non-income producing residential property.

Whenever benefits intitially accrue to property, we assume that 75 percent of benefits go to users of property and 25 percent go to owners. The distribution of the benefits to owners of commercial and industrial property by income class is accomplished by using a series on dividend income by income class. Benefits to owners of apartments are distributed by income class according to a weighted series on rental income, dividend income, and "other" income. Benefits to users of business property are assigned to various jurisdictions like a negative business cost tax. The assumption is made that business cost taxes are passed forward to ultimate consumers.[g] An adjusted BLS Series of total consumption expenditures by income class is used as a basis for distributing benefits across income classes. Naturally benefits to users of apartments are distributed by rental payments by income class.

Since businesses are considered to evaluate their benefits at cost, no distinction is made in computing benefits using a cost-of-service or a benefit measure. Since these benefits reduce operating costs and increase profits and taxes it is necessary to determine the appropriate offset rates to apply. Estimates of profits by industrial category are made for the study area and then national data on the corporate income tax is used to determine the proportion of net profits subjected to each marginal rate (22 percent and 48 percent).[h]

Like benefits to business property, benefits to single-family residential property are assumed to accrue 75 percent to users and 25 percent to owners, for all three measures of benefits. Benefits to owners of residential property are first divided into those which accrue to owner-occupied and nonowner-occupied housing. Owner-occupied benefits are distributed by a series on the distribution of housing units by income class. Benefits to owners of renter-occupied, single-family residential property are allocated in the same way as benefits to owners of business (i.e., income-producing) property.

Benefits to users of single-family residential property accrue on a cost-of-service basis equally to each household unit. Benefits are distributed by income class using the distribution of families and unrelated individuals by income class. User benefits, using the benefit measure, are assumed to be equal to the value of property protected. Thus the benefits are distributed according to a series on house values by income class. Benefits measured by value for residential property, other than single-family homes, is distributed according to a series on rental payments by income class. Table B–3 summarizes the different ways in which various kinds of people and property benefits are computed using three separate benefit measures.

---

[g]It is assumed that customers of incorporated and unincorporated businesses have the same locational characteristics as customers of firms paying the corporate income tax.

[h]The estimates of the average marginal tax rate is 45 percent. Thus 45 percent of these benefits are assumed absorbed by increased federal tax payments of the beneficiaries.

Table B–3

Summary of Procedures Used for Computing Fire Protection Benefits on a Cost-of-Service Basis and on a Welfare Basis (After Offsets)

Recipient of Benefit	A Benefits Cost-of-Service Basis	B Benefits Welfare Basis
To Federal Government	Based on proportion of total calls to federal government property; property benefits go to residents of the balance of the nation, people benefits allocated by general procedure.	Same as A.
To People	Benefits allocated by proportion of total hours spent in jurisdiction by residents and non-residents.	Benefits weighted by income under the assumption that the marginal utility of income declines proportionately.
To Owners of Commercial Property	Survey of pattern of ownership by residents of various jurisdictions.	Same as A, but offsets are computed.
To Users of Commercial Property	Benefits allocated like a negative business cost tax.	Same as A.
To Owners of Residential Property	Allocated using data on ownership characteristics for owner- and nonowner-occupied housing.	Same as A, except offsets are applied to owners of renter-occupied housing.
To Users of Residential Property	Allocated equally to all units; benefits distributed by series on families and unrelated individuals by income class.	Benefits to owner- and renter-occupied separated; former distributed by an income series and the latter by a rental payment series.

B.8 Information on the distribution of users of health and hospital facilities in the various jurisdictions is based on data on the utilization of health clinics by Census tracts of residents of Alexandria during January-March 1971.[i] Those Census tracts in which residents made more than one hundred visits to the health clinic during the three month period were selected. The total number of visits were distributed among income classes using information on the income distribution of the tract from the *1970 Census of Population and Housing.* The resulting tract data were summed by each income class to obtain an average number of visits per family by income class. These numbers were considered average propensities for a particular income class to utilize health and hospital facilities. To

---

[i]Both the average number of visits per family in Alexandria and the resulting distribution of users of health facilities by income class for our three areas are shown in table B–1.

obtain a distribution of users of health and hospital facilities for each jurisdiction, the average propensity for specific income classes is multiplied by the number of families and unrelated individuals in that class, the results are summed over all classes and then used to compute a distribution by income class in the District, in suburban Maryland and in suburban Virginia respectively .

B.9 The distribution of welfare payments by income class is derived separately for the seven major jurisdictions using national data on average welfare payments for both families and unrelated individuals by income class. For all income classes in each jurisdiction, the average payment for families and unrelated individuals is multiplied by the number of individuals in the class to form an estimate of total payments to the class. The resulting estimates of payments are summed over income classes and a distribution of payments by income class is computed and shown in table B-1.

B.10 In the District of Columbia an estimate of the proportion of benefits to nonresidents on a cost-of-service basis is assumed equal to the percentage of total borrowers' cards held by nonresidents in 1970. A sample of borrowers' cards was conducted for us by the department of library services in the District of Columbia. Officials of suburban jurisdictions indicated that nonresident usage of libraries is negligible; hence, it is assumed to be zero for purposes of our study. An adjusted BLS series on average expenditures on books and technical journals by income class is applied to the income distribution of our areas to estimate a distribution of benefits from library expenditures by income class (see table B-1).

B.11 Benefits to nonresidents from park expenditures are estimated on cost-of-service basis using survey information on nonresident usage. In most cases license plate surveys were made as a means of obtaining the distribution of users by jurisdiction. The Smithsonian Institution provided user data for the zoo, the D.C. government provided us with surveys of out-of-state usage of D.C. parks and playgrounds. Heavy reliance was placed on extensive survey data of parks in the metropolitan area, which was prepared by Theodore Ehrlich and presented in "Specialized Trip Distribution Study: Metropolitan Recreation," prepared at the Urban Transportation Center Consortium of Universities. In addition, we surveyed a number of park facilities.[j] Survey results show that the highest proportion of nonresident usage occurs in D.C., and the lowest proportion occurs in metropolitan Virginia.

---

[j] As expenditure data for each park facility was not available, it was difficult to assign weights to the various observations which were made. Based on information on the characteristics of the various facilities for which surveys were available, weights were assigned so as to yield the average rates of resident and nonresident usage shown in table B-1. Benefits from park expenditures are assigned to income classes in the same way as recreation expenditures (see below).

While we find substantial utilization of parks by nonresidents, there is very little utilization of recreation services. Thus, it is assumed that all private benefits from recreation accrue to residents of the jurisdiction making the expenditures. Very little information is available on the income characteristic of the users of recreation facilities. Information does exist, however, on the swimming pool service population by income class.[k] The ratio of service population per family unit in D.C. is used as a proxy for average expenditure per income class in the suburbs. When combined with data on the number of families by income class in the suburbs, a separate distribution of benefits by income class is derived.

B.12 See B.5 for a discussion of the methods used to determine the proportion of total vehicle miles traveled by residents and nonresidents.

B.13 The use of public refuse collection services is not made available to all types of housing units. Practice varies throughout the study area; for example the District of Columbia, Prince Georges County and the City of Alexandria restrict the service to housing structures with three units or less. In Fairfax County, Fairfax City, Falls Church, and Arlington only one- and two-family homes are eligible, while in Falls Church City only single-family homes are serviced. Only Montgomery County's policy is somewhat more liberal in that structures containing five or less units are serviced.

Since refuse collection services are treated as pure private goods and the assumption is made that the cost of service per residential unit is constant, benefits on a cost-of-service basis are assigned by income class according to the distribution of housing units by income class.

For this purpose we use data from the *1970 Census of Housing, Metropolitan Housing Characteristics, Washington, D.C.,* which shows occupied housing units both by the number of units in a structure and by Census money income class of the inhabitant. Published data exists for D.C., for Alexandria, and for the SMSA. We use the direct data for D.C. and Alexandria, but for each of the other suburban jurisdictions we use data on the SMSA less housing units in the District of Columbia.

---

[k]The service population is defined as the number of children living within .75 miles of a pool.

Appendix C
Tax Incidence Assumptions

C.1 Two types of offsets are calculated. The first refers to those taxes that are deductible under the federal personal income tax. Here the size of the offset depends upon both the marginal tax rate of the individual and whether or not he itemizes his deductions. To determine the tax offset rate for each income class, we turned to the *1969 Statistics of Income, Individual Income Tax Returns,* and for the following adjusted gross income classes, multiplied the weighted marginal tax rate by the weighted percentage of taxpayers itemizing deductions in order to obtain the offset rate.

For the corporate income tax offset, we first estimated corporate profits by industrial category in Washington, D.C., suburban Maryland, and suburban Virginia. Using national statistics we estimated for each category the average marginal tax rate. This depends on the percentage of firm profits subject to the lower 22 percent federal tax rate. We then calculated the overall average marginal tax rate. The results were so close to 45 percent in each case that we assume that 45 percent is the offset rate in each jurisdiction.

Table C-1
Individual Income Tax Offset Rates

Income Class	Offset Rate
below $3,000	.0065
3,000–3,999	.0384
4,000–5,999	.0662
6,000–7,499	.0884
7,500–9,999	.1158
10,000–14,999	.1455
15,000–24,999	.2323
25,000 and above	.3924

C.2 The house value and renter payment series are estimated separately for the District and the suburbs by using data on house values and rent payments by income class contained in *U.S. Bureau of the Census, Metropolitan Housing Characteristics for Washington, D.C.,* Washington, 1972. The data for the suburban series were assumed equal to the difference between the data for the entire SMSA and the data for the central city, Washington. The distribution of this series by income bracket as well as other series used in our calculations is contained in table C-2.

Table C-2
Distributive Series Employed

Name of Series	Percentages Attributed to Income Bracket							
	Below $3,000	$3,000–$3,999	$4,000–$5,999	$6,000–$7,499	$7,500–$9,999	$10,000–$15,000	$15,000–$25,000	$25,000 and above
1. House Values (City)	.0720	.0240	.0590	.0540	.0910	.1900	.2500	.2600
2. House Values (Suburbs)	.0330	.0100	.0240	.0300	.0580	.2110	.4030	.2310
3. Rent Payments (City)	.1610	.0550	.1370	.1200	.1660	.1840	.1230	.0540
4. Rent Payments (Suburbs)	.0780	.0350	.0960	.1020	.1580	.2700	.2070	.0550
5. Total Consumption (D.C.)	.0659	.0291	.0904	.0894	.1421	.2126	.2115	.1590
6. Total Consumption (Md.)	.0227	.0107	.0321	.0398	.0900	.2304	.3530	.2213
7. Total Consumption (Va.)	.0210	.0120	.0381	.0455	.0916	.2045	.3577	.2296
8. Rental Income (D.C.)	.1054	.0318	.0812	.0871	.1089	.1650	.1944	.2262
9. Rental Income (Md.)	.0351	.0115	.0283	.0382	.0679	.1762	.3197	.3231
10. Rental Income (Va.)	.0355	.0127	.0331	.0433	.0686	.1550	.3211	.3307
11. Dividend Income (D.C.)	.1622	.0323	.1021	.0677	.1170	.1372	.1172	.2643
12. Dividend Income (Md.)	.0586	.0127	.0387	.0323	.0793	.1590	.2094	.4100
13. Dividend Income (Va.)	.0523	.0141	.0454	.0366	.0802	.1402	.2107	.4205
14. Money Income (D.C.)	.0342	.0217	.0739	.0772	.1298	.2111	.2308	.2213
15. Money Income (Md.)	.0108	.0075	.0237	.0310	.0740	.2062	.3471	.2997
16. Money Income (Va.)	.0107	.0086	.0286	.0362	.0769	.1867	.3589	.2934
17. Personal Income Taxes (D.C.)	.0011	.0044	.0314	.0495	.0998	.2109	.2957	.3072
18. Personal Income Taxes (Md.)	.0006	.0018	.0114	.0228	.0602	.1872	.3557	.3603
19. Personal Income Taxes (Va.)	.0004	.0003	.0140	.0308	.0712	.1948	.3784	.3091
20. Taxable Purchases (D.C.)	.0270	.0310	.0940	.0930	.1470	.2150	.2070	.1430
21. Taxable Purchases (Md.)	.0160	.0100	.0300	.0380	.0870	.2270	.3660	.2260
22. Taxable Purchases (Va.)	.0150	.0110	.0340	.0430	.0880	.2060	.3750	.2280
23. Meals at Works (D.C.)	.0080	.0180	.0770	.0760	.1320	.2410	.2800	.1680
24. Meals at Work (Md.)	.0030	.0060	.0250	.0300	.0740	.2320	.4190	.2100
25. Meals at Work (Va.)	.0030	.0060	.0270	.0350	.0770	.2120	.4270	.2130
26. Alcohol Expenditures (D.C.)	.0320	.0280	.0990	.0930	.1410	.2150	.2250	.1670
27. Alcohol Expenditures (Md.)	.0110	.0100	.0340	.0400	.0870	.2260	.3660	.2260
28. Alcohol Expenditures (Va.)	.0110	.0110	.0380	.0450	.0880	.2030	.3670	.2370
29. Tobacco Expenditures (D.C.)	.0600	.0410	.1310	.1280	.1820	.2230	.1610	.0740
30. Tobacco Expenditures (Md.)	.0230	.0170	.0530	.0640	.1300	.2720	.3050	.1360

31. Tobacco Expenditures (Va.)	.0230	.0190	.0590	.0720	.1310	.2450	.3050	.1460
32. Sundry Expenditures (D.C.)	.0640	.0360	.1030	.0970	.1550	.2240	.2000	.1210
33. Sundry Expenditures (Md.)	.0230	.0140	.0380	.0450	.1020	.2520	.3490	.1770
34. Sundry Expenditures (Va.)	.0220	.0150	.0420	.0520	.1050	.2300	.3550	.1790
35. Business Income (D.C.)	.0690	.0260	.0730	.0700	.1210	.1950	.2100	.2360
36. Business Income (Md.)	.0220	.0090	.0240	.0290	.0710	.1980	.3280	.3190
37. Business Income (Va.)	.0210	.0090	.0290	.0330	.0730	.1750	.3310	.3290
38. Gasoline Expenditures (D.C.)	.0180	.0230	.0910	.1090	.1840	.2640	.2200	.0910
39. Gasoline Expenditures (Md.)	.0060	.0080	.0320	.0490	.1170	.2870	.3700	.1310
40. Gasoline Expenditures (Va.)	.0060	.0090	.0370	.0550	.1190	.2590	.3730	.1420
41. Gas & Electric Expenditures (D.C.)	.1060	.0410	.1120	.1050	.1570	.2060	.1730	.1000
42. Gas & Electric Expenditures (Md.)	.0410	.0170	.0440	.0520	.1120	.2510	.3250	.1580
43. Gas & Electric Expenditures (Va.)	.0380	.0190	.0530	.0600	.1140	.2230	.3290	.1640
44. Telephone & Telegraph Expenditures (D.C.)	.0770	.0390	.1070	.0960	.1510	.2000	.1890	.1410
45. Telephone & Telegraph Expenditures (Md.)	.0290	.0150	.0400	.0450	.1010	.2300	.3350	.2050
46. Telephone & Telegraph Expenditures (Va.)	.0270	.0170	.0470	.0520	.1020	.2040	.3390	.2120
47. Wealth (U.S.)	.0010	.0010	.0030	.0020	.0050	.0080	.0170	.9630
48. Expenditures on Motor Vehicles (D.C.)	.0070	.0080	.0700	.1050	.1650	.2470	.2950	.1030
49. Expenditures on Motor Vehicles (Md.)	.0030	.0030	.0230	.0430	.0950	.2460	.4500	.1370
50. Expenditures on Motor Vehicles (Va.)	.0030	.0030	.0280	.0490	.0980	.2190	.4580	.1420
51. Life Insurance Premiums (D.C.)	.0230	.0180	.0610	.0750	.1290	.1990	.2220	.2730
52. Life Insurance Premiums (Md.)	.0070	.0060	.0190	.0300	.0730	.1950	.3370	.3330
53. Life Insurance Premiums (Va.)	.0070	.0070	.0230	.0350	.0760	.1800	.3470	.3250
54. Auto Insurance Premiums (D.C.)	.0230	.0180	.0850	.0980	.1630	.2600	.2370	.1150
55. Auto Insurance Premiums (Md.)	.0070	.0070	.0290	.0410	.0970	.2660	.3770	.1770
56. Auto Insurance Premiums (Va.)	.0070	.0070	.0340	.0500	.1050	.2550	.4030	.1390
57. Auto Registrations (D.C.)	.0930	.0340	.1110	.1110	.1640	.2120	.1910	.0840
58. Auto Registrations (Md.)	.0340	.0140	.0430	.0540	.1150	.2540	.3520	.1340
59. Auto Registrations (Va.)	.0310	.0150	.0520	.0620	.1170	.2260	.3580	.1390
60. Auto Ownership (D.C.)	.1230	.0440	.1350	.1260	.1720	.2000	.1390	.0610
61. Auto Ownership (Md.)	.0520	.0200	.0590	.0690	.1350	.2680	.2880	.1090
62. Auto Ownership (Va.)	.0480	.0220	.0710	.0790	.1370	.2380	.2920	.1130
63. Automobile Purchases (Va.)	.0060	.0050	.0270	.0490	.0930	.2740	.4140	.1320
64. Number of Individuals Over Twenty One (Va.)	.0740	.0280	.0670	.0670	.1200	.2310	.2960	.1170

C.3 The survey of office building usage in the District of Columbia found the following: 35 percent of the value of office space was occupied by organizations which serve the District of Columbia's market area, 29 percent serve the metropolitan area, and 36 percent serve the nation as a whole.

The percentage distribution of customers of the first two categories can be deduced from the sales tax allocations. The ultimate users of the service provided in the third class was divided between all jurisdictions in the nation in the same way as personal income. Thus only .48 percent, .72 percent, and .5 percent are attributed to D.C., suburban Maryland, and suburban Virginia. The incidence of these taxes by income class within a jurisdiction is assumed the same as the distribution of total consumption.

In the suburbs, no additional surveys were made. The percentages in the three categories were assumed to be 40 percent local market-oriented, 30 percent metropolitan market-oriented, and 30 percent national market-oriented.

C.4 The distribution between income classes of the taxes passed forward by both commercial and industrial establishments is assumed to be the same as the distribution of total consumption within the consumer's place of residency.

The distribution of the tax passed forward by commercial establishments between jurisdictions was assumed the same as the distribution of the sales tax of that jurisdiction, corrected for the presence of motel and hotel room payments in the sales tax base.

C.5 The percentage of homes not occupied by residents is obtained from the 1970 *Census of Population, Social and Economic Characteristics, District of Columbia, Maryland, Virginia.* Assuming that owner-occupied homes have the same average values, we estimate the following percentages of house values owned by nonresidents: D.C., 32.7 percent; Montgomery County, 12.8 percent; Prince Georges County, 13.9 percent; Arlington, 22.9 percent; Alexandria, 35.1 percent; Fairfax City, 17.2 percent; Fairfax County, 14.7 percent; Falls Church, 28.0 percent. Relative to the national average these percentages are quite high. The explanations are manifold. The Washington area is a booming area, the purchase of single-family homes has proved attractive to outside investors, there are many military people on duty elsewhere who maintain their homes in anticipation of returning, and there are many professional people on temporary assignment there.

In any case, when part of this tax is distributed to owners, the allocation between jurisdictions is made in a rather arbitrary fashion. Fifteen percent of the owners are assumed to live outside the area, the remainder are assumed distributed between jurisdictions in the same way as rental income. When the tax is distributed between income classes, it is done so in the same proportions as rental income by money income class.

C.6 Thus, for instance, we find in the District of Columbia that the breakdown of the ownership of income-producing property is as shown in table C–3.

Reasonable assumptions are then made to attribute the ownership of these properties to residents of various jurisdictions. We assume that the owners of national corporations are distributed throughout the nation in proportion to dividend income. For local corporations, we assume that 20 percent are owned nationally and the rest are divided between jurisdictions according to estimated dividend income in the various jurisdictions. Thus 15.8 percent is attributed to D.C. residents, 37.9 percent to Maryland residents, and 26.3 percent to Virginia residents. The owners of noncommercial organizations serving Washington are assumed to be all Washingtonians. The owners of those noncommercial organizations serving the metropolitan area are assumed distributed between jurisdictions in proportion to personal income within the study area. The owners of those noncommercial organizations serving the nation are assumed distributed like personal income in the nation as a whole.

Income-producing properties owned by individuals or partnerships, whose legal addresses are within the metropolitan area, are assumed owned 20 percent by people outside the area with the remainder allocated between jurisdictions on the basis of the distribution of income in the $15,000 and above class. Properties owned by individuals or partnerships outside the area are assumed fully owned by those outside the area. The owners of regional corporations are assumed to be one-third national. The remainder are divided between jurisdictions in proportion to dividend income.

When these taxes are borne by owners offset rates may apply. For categories A, B, and H the corporate income tax offset is applied. For categories C and D

Table C–3
Distribution of the Value of Income-Producing Property in the District of Columbia

A. National Corporations	21.89%
B. Local Corporations	20.91%
C. Noncommercial Organizations Serving Interests of D.C.	4.69%
D. Noncommercial Organizations Serving Metropolitan Interests	.99%
E. Noncommercial Organizations Serving National Interests	5.97%
F. Single Individuals or Partnerships with mailing addresses in the metropolitan area	38.09%
G. Single Individuals or Partnerships with mailing addresses in the rest of the world	3.11%
H. Regional Corporations	4.35%
Total	100.00%

no offset is applied. For categories E and F the personal offset attributed to those with incomes in excess of $15,000 is applied.

Similar procedures are employed in the suburbs.

C.7 Each of the states possesses data on the distribution of tax payments by adjusted gross income class. Such data also exists at the county level and for county income taxes in Maryland.

The difficulty with such a distribution is that the Census definition money income differs substantially from adjusted gross income. The basic differences are that transfer payments, including public assistance and social security payments and disability payments, are not included as part of the adjusted gross income but are money income. On the other hand, realized capital gains are not part of money income because of their irregular nature, but one-half of them are part of adjusted gross income (AGI). There are also some minor differences such as the fact that income in kind would be included as part of AGI, but not as part of money income, and that interest income from state securities would be included as part of money income but not as part of the states' AGI.

We attempt to correct for the worst discrepancies in the distinction between AGI and money income by using a rather involved procedure to estimate the distribution of income tax burdens by money income class. In the case of the District of Columbia and the Maryland counties, we possess data on taxes paid by AGI class. In Virginia such data could be obtained only for the state as a whole. The first step is to calculate a mean money income for each money bracket. Then from unpublished data supplied to us by the Bureau of the Census, we are able to estimate mean transfer payments for both families and individuals by income class. Using a weighted average of these, we obtain an estimate of the amount by which mean income exceeds mean adjusted gross income because of transfer payments in each money income class.

We then turn to *The Statistics of Income: Individual Tax Returns* to obtain an estimate of the mean amount of short-term and long-term capital gains in each AGI bracket. We simply assume that mean capital gains by money income bracket will be the same. Adding mean short-term capital gains and 1/2 of mean long-term capital gains, we estimate for each money income bracket the mean excess of AGI over money income because of such gains. Subtracting mean transfer payments and adding the mean of short-term and 1/2 the mean of long-term capital gains to mean money income in each bracket gives us estimated mean adjusted gross income by money income bracket.

The next step is to turn to the relevant distribution of taxes by adjusted gross income bracket. Taking nontaxable returns into consideration, we estimate the average tax paid by a return with average adjusted gross income in each bracket. This gives us a series of readings which show the tax rates imposed on an AGI of, for instance, $2,347 and on an AGI of $3,469. If, for instance, these are 1.62 percent and 1.83 percent respectively, then we assume that an average

return with an average AGI of $3,000 would pay [1.62 percent + (1.83 - 1.62) percent (653/1,122)] , or 1.74 percent. Given that we have an estimated average adjusted gross income corresponding to the average money income in each income class, we can calculate the average tax rate and hence the average tax on this average AGI. Given this and the number of families plus individuals in any money income class, we calculate estimated income tax paid in any money income class. Then we proceed to the sole purpose of our exercise, the estimation of the percentage distribution of the burden of the income tax by money income class. The methodology is a bit crude and approximate but it surely results in a better estimate than simply using raw data on the distribution of the taxes by adjusted gross income class.

The resulting percentage distributions are contained in the table C-2.

C.8 In the following discussion the numbers presented refer to total sales tax collections in the District of Columbia. Since we are analyzing only the portion of these taxes raised for current expenditures, the totals attributed to residents of the various jurisdictions in table 6-5 are slightly smaller and equal to the numbers presented below multiplied by one minus the percentage of current expenditures which were incurred for debt services and capital expenditures.

We discuss our methodology in four major sections. Only the District of Columbia sales tax collections are presented. The methodology employed in the suburbs is the same. A few minor technical differences are noted.

A. Sales to Businesses

Although many studies of the state and local fiscal structure have recognized that a substantial portion of the sales tax is paid for by business, usually they do not make allowance for this in their estimates. The usual assumption, with a reference to the *locus classicus,* John Due, *Sales Taxation,* (Champaign, Illinois, 1957), is that roughly 20 percent of the tax is paid for by business.

In this study, however, we have followed the analysis of Richard F. Fryman, "Sales Taxation of Producers' Goods in Illinois."[1] Fryman surveyed five major types of business firms (retailers, wholesalers, mining and manufacturing firms, contractors and service and leasing firms) to obtain the portion of their taxable sales made to other business firms. Using estimates of the portions of the retail sales tax collections which came from these five industrial categories, he was able to deduce what portion of the sales tax was levied on business purchases. His conclusion was that 23.72 percent of the Illinois sales tax in 1964 was paid by businesses.

Naturally, there are a variety of definitions of sales tax bases across the United States and their impingement on business sales differ as a result. There are basically three types of sales tax states as far as business taxation is concerned.

There are physical component states in which only things which physically become part of the purchaser's product are exempt. There are direct-use states where business purchases that are directly used in production, like machinery, but not typewriters, are exempt. There are intermediate states. Both the District of Columbia and Maryland fall into the last class but are close to the physical component end of the spectrum, exempting fuels used in production. Illinois, at the time of Fryman's study, was a physical component state, but the minor difference that fuels were taxable under the Illinois tax implies that Fryman's methodology, if not his statistics, are applicable.

In the District we break down the sales tax receipts into those obtained from manufacturing, service, construction, wholesale, and retail firms. Within the retail category we break down sales by type of firm using Fryman's findings that different retailers have substantially different percentages of sales to businesses. We then apply Fryman's findings about the portion of sales of various types of firms going to business in order to arrive at our own estimate of the percentage of the District of Columbia's sales tax which was levied on purchases of businesses.

We estimate that 15.7 percent of the District of Columbia sales tax receipts were from business purchases. Our failure to correct for the fact that industrial fuel (not sold to public utilities) is taxable under the Illinois but not under the District tax results is at most a miniscule error. Of the estimated 15.7 percent paid for by business our statistics attribute less than 1 percent of this to fuel

Table C-4
Calculation of Percentage of District of Columbia Sales Tax Paid by Businesses, 1970

(1) Industrial Group	(2) % of Sales Tax Receipts	(3) % of Sales Tax to Business	(2 X 3)
1. Retail	76.7*	4.43**	3.3978
2. Wholesale	7.6	82.08	6.2381
3. Mining and Manufacturing	2.1	89.74	1.8845
4. Service and Leasing	12.5	30.68	3.8350
5. Contractors	1.1	32.66	0.3593
Total	100.0		15.7147

*Given D.C.'s records of sales tax receipts we are not able to distinguish wholesale from retail submitters of the tax. We assume the relative breakdown was the same as in Fryman's sample.

**The percentage of sales made to businesses by these firms is considerably lower than Fryman's findings because we utilize Fryman's results on what portion of sales are made to businesses by different types of retailers. Retailer types with small portions of sales to businesses (like groceries) weight very heavily in the D.C. statistics.

dealers so that if all sales of any fuel to business were totally exempt our estimate would be off by only around .15 percent. In light of this, and in order to
avoid appearances of false accuracy, we round off our estimate to 15.5 percent.
Because we have no breakdown of sales tax receipts by industrial class of sub-
mitting firms in the suburbs we are forced to rely on the D.C. estimates. We
reduce, however, the suburban estimate still further. The ratio of business payrolls to retail sales in the suburbs is roughly one-half the ratio in the city.
Therefore, we assume sales to businesses are 7.75 percent of taxable sales in the
suburbs. In any event the following applies in the District:

Total D.C. Sales Tax Collections	$71,270,000
Paid by Businesses	$11,046,850
Paid by Ultimate Consumers	$60,223,150

B. Sales to Tourists

Our purpose now is to apportion the remaining $60.2 million of the sales
tax among D.C. residents, suburban residents, and residents of the outside world.
The first step in this procedure is to estimate tax payments by tourists. Here we
utilize data prepared for a study of the metropolitan area made by Zinder
Associates, Inc.[2] *The Future of Tourism in the District of Columbia–Financial
Approach,* Washington, 1967.
     We will not explain here the detailed analysis that led to their conclusions.
The interested reader is referred to the Zinder report for this data. Table C-5
presents a breakdown of the types of expenditures made by tourists in D.C. in
1967.
     The Zinder study calculates that the rate of growth in tourist expenditures in
D.C. in the period 1960–1967 was at an average annual rate of 7 percent. In the
intervening years we have witnessed some apprehension that tourist growth has

Table C-5
**Tourist Expenditures and Sales Tax Payments in Washington, D.C.,
in 1967**

Type of Expenditure	$ (000)	% Taxable	Rate	Tax (Rounded to Nearest $10,000)
Room Payments	55,900	100	.05	2,800,000
Shopping	100,000	75	.04	3,000,000
Food and Beverage	175,000	100	22% at .02 78% at .05	7,650,000
Other	100,000	25	.04	1,000,000
Total				14,450,000

fallen off because of the bad publicity generated by the 1968 riots. On the other hand, the rate of inflation accelerated in the period 1968–1970 and for this reason we would expect the rate of growth in tourist expenditures to accelerate. As a result, we assume that the average annual growth in tourist expenditures in the period was simply the past growth rate of 7 percent per annum. Therefore estimated total sales tax payments by tourists in D.C. amounted to $17,484,500.

C. Sales to Suburban Residents in the District of Columbia

Naturally, the next step is to divide the remaining $42,739,150 of sales tax payments between the residents of the suburban area and the residents of the taxing jurisdiction, the District. The procedure is to estimate the proportion of the tax paid by suburbanites, leaving the remainder as the portion paid by residents. Initially, therefore, we estimate taxable purchases and hence tax payments by commuters. To this we add an estimate of tax payments by suburban shoppers.

The commuter expenditures are assumed to be in four basic categories:

a.   lunch expenditures;
b.   alcohol expenditures;
c.   tobacco expenditures; and
d.   sundry expenditures which basically consist of personal care expenditures such as razor blades and hair cuts.

Undoubtedly there are some other minor taxable purchases. Some commuters undoubtedly buy candy bars that they eat on the way home. But these other types of expenditures excluded here are likely to be miniscule.

In order to calculate lunch expenditures, we estimate the expected average lunch expenditure at work using a revised BLS series and assuming that commuters possess the same income distribution as the locality from which they come. (Except in the case of those from the outlying parts of the SMSA in Virginia; there it is assumed that they have the same income distribution as other Virginia commuters, rather than the distributions of the fairly rural counties from which they come.) Note should be made that in table C-5 the assumed average lunch expenditures made by a commuter is not at all unreasonable. It would imply, for instance, that if two-thirds of the Maryland commuters eat in commercial establishments each day, then those that did eat out would spend on the average around $1.30 per working day.

The next question is the very complicated one of how much we would expect commuters to spend on alcohol, tobacco, and sundries in the jurisdiction where they work. Search of the relevant marketing literature revealed no sys-

Table C-6
Lunch Expenditures by Commuters in the District of Columbia

State	Number of Commuters	Average Annual Expenditures or Meals at Work	Total Expenditures	Taxes at the Rate of 4.67%
Maryland	178,145	$204.59	36,446,686	1,700,845
Virginia	107,192	204.15	21,883,247	1,021,219
Outside the Study Area	5,437	204.15	1,109,964	51,798
Total			59,439,897	2,773,862

tematic study of this question. As a result we are forced to fall back on an assumption that in the absence of price differentials the commuter is likely to make one-quarter of the family's total expenditures on these items in the jurisdiction where he works. In the case of tobacco expenditures, this assumption may be justified by arguing that the purchase of cigarettes may be proportional to the time spent in a jurisdiction. The commuter spends somewhat less than one-half his waking hours in the place where he works, thus somewhat less than one-quarter of potential smoker's time is spent there. On the other hand, the average number of commuters per family unit would be slightly in excess of one. The justification of the assumption for liquor and sundries is based on the proposition that roughly one-quarter of the family's shopping hours are spent by the commuter at his place of work.

In fact, however, there are substantial differences in tobacco and liquor prices in the Washington metropolitan area. We surveyed area liquor stores and concluded that prices in 1972 were approximately 10 percent higher in Virginia, 8 percent higher in Montgomery County where there is a county monopoly, and 7 percent higher in Prince Georges County, which operates a license system. We also deduce, however, that part of the higher price differential in Virginia was caused by an increase in the tax rate which occurred in 1970 and which was effective for only one-half the fiscal year we studied. Taking this into account we infer that liquor prices were around 7.2 percent higher in Virginia in fiscal year 1970.

The prices of cigarettes also differed substantially. Information obtained from the Tobacco Tax Council indicates that cigarette prices were approximately 5 percent lower in 1970 in Virginia than in D.C. and approximately 10 percent higher in Maryland than in D.C.

What alteration of our base assumption about the proportion of family expenditures made by the commuter should be made in light of these price differentials? Studies by Hamovitch,[3] Levin,[4] and Mikesell [5] have examined

the question of the loss of taxable sales to neighboring jurisdictions when a locality has a higher price level due to tax rate differentials. Although their methods differ, they each reach the conclusion that each percentage point increase in prices leads to approximately a six-percentage point decrease in what otherwise would be the expected level of sales tax receipts. We interpret this to mean that taxable purchases will be 6 percent below what they would otherwise be for each 1 percent price differential. If commuters ordinarily make 25 percent of family cigarette purchases at their place of work, but if prices there are 10 percent lower than in the home jurisdiction, we assume they make 40 percent (.25 + .6 [.25]) of the purchases at work. Table C-7 presents the relevant data from which we estimate commuter expenditures in the District.

The remaining $38,199,268 of sales tax payments must be made either by city residents or by shoppers. We proceeded to attempt to deduce the sales to suburban shoppers in the manner described below. Parking lot surveys and customer surveys supplied by Woodward and Lothrop, one of the area's leading department stores, are used to deduce the percentage of sales made to residents of the District and residents of the suburbs. Estimates are prepared for each of the major retail centers and the Central Business District. (Major retail centers are defined by the Census Bureau as those concentrations of retail stores having at least $5 million in retail sales and at least ten retail establishments, one of which is a department store. See 1967 Census of Business, *Major Retail Centers* for a description of the geographical boundaries of these centers.)

We then use *Sales Management* estimates of total 1970 sales and apportion them among the retail centers in the same proportion as they were apportioned in the 1967 *Census of Business.* This creates some difficulty for several newly created shopping centers for which 1967 sales statistics did not exist. We assume that the sales growth rate during the period 1963–1967 once corrected for increased inflation persisted in established shopping centers in the period 1967–1970. The excess of estimated sales over projected sales by older shopping centers is presumed generated by the new shopping centers. It is apportioned among them on an equal square footage basis. The sales per square foot thus calculated are quite close to comparably sized centers in the shopping areas which were able to supply us with sales per square foot data.

Before the estimated percentages of sales to various groups is applied to the estimated total retail sales data in the major retail centers, several subtractions from this total are made to avoid double counting. We subtract sales to businesses, tourists and commuters. The subtraction for sales to businesses is rather haphazard. We note from previous calculations that while 15.5 percent of the retail sales subject to tax are made by businessmen, only around 45 percent of such sales are made by firms that are of the type whose sales can be classified as retail. Therefore, we simply assume that in each business district 7 percent of sales are made to businesses. The Central Business District (CBD) contains the bulk of attractions for tourists and so we assume that 75 percent of their pur-

Table C–7
Sales Tax Payments by Commuters in the District

Residency	Number	Mean Family Expenditure	% Spent by Commuter	Mean Commuter Expenditure	Total Commuter Expenditure	Tax at 4.667%
Alcoholic Beverages:						
Montgomery Co.	72,020	198.48	37.0%	73.44	5,289,143	246,828
Prince Georges Co.	106,125	198.48	35.5%	70.46	7,407,108	345,668
Virginia	107,192	201.22	36.0%	72.44	7,764,988	362,366
Outside	5,437	201.22	36.0%	72.44	393,856	18,380
Total					20,855,095	973,242
Tobacco:						*Tax at 4%*
Maryland	178,145	151.94	40.0%	60.78	10,827,653	433,106
Virginia	107,192	153.98	17.5%	26.95	2,888,824	115,553
Outside	5,437	153.98	17.5%	26.95	146,527	5,861
Total					13,863,004	554,520
Sundry:						
Maryland	178,145	81.75	25.0%	20.44	3,641,284	145,651
Virginia	107,192	81.61	25.0%	20.40	2,186,717	87,469
Outside	5,437	81.61	25.0%	20.40	110,915	4,437
Total					5,938,916	237,557

chases were made in the CBD and 25 percent in other areas (between those areas in proportion to their retail sales). Commuters to the Central Business District (who constituted approximately 29.4 percent of all commuters) are assumed to make all their purchases therein. Other commuters were assumed to make one-quarter of their purchases in the CBD and the rest of their purchases in the various retail areas in proportion to the total retail sales in the various areas. Thus 64.7 percent of all commuter expenditures are assumed made in the Central Business District.

We summarize our calculations in table C-8.

D. The Use Tax

Although we calculate total taxable sales made in each jurisdiction by residents of other jurisdictions in this manner, account has to be made of the use tax. In some cases these taxable sales resulted in tax receipts not for the jurisdiction of sale but for the jurisdiction of residency of the purchaser. The District of Columbia received approximately $1,840,000 in use taxes in fiscal year 1970. After allowing for payment by business firms ($285,200) we divide these between suburban Maryland and Virginia in proportion to estimated resident D.C. sales tax payments in those jurisdictions. Thus 21.6 percent ($337,996) is attributed to D.C. purchases in Virginia and 78.4 percent ($1,226,803) to D.C. purchases in Maryland. In turn, although use tax figures are not available by county in the suburban states, we assumed that the same portion of total suburban taxable purchases in D.C. were subject to use tax.

C.9   This is an appropriate place for describing our method of estimating various distributions of purchases by income class. Series such as taxable retail

Table C-8
Payments of D.C. Sales Tax

Total Tax	$71,270,000
Less Tax Payments by Businesses	$11,046,850
	$60,223,150
Less Tax Payments by Tourists	$17,484,500
	$42,738,650
Less Tax Payments by Commuters (including some from outside our study area)	$ 4,539,181
	$38,199,469
Less Tax Payments by Suburban Shoppers (including some from outside our study area)	$ 4,389,000
Tax Payments by D.C. Residents	$33,810,469

purchases, lunch expenditures at work, expenditures on alcohol, tobacco, gasoline, etc., are estimated using the same methodology.

We use the Department of Commerce's Bureau of Labor Statistics *Survey of Consumer Finances For Urban Places in the Northeast Region,* May 1966. The Northeast is chosen rather than the Southeast because we feel that Washington more closely resembles urban places in the Northeast than the Southeast. Its housing prices are high like Northeastern cities. Its climate, and hence, fuel consumption more nearly resembles Philadelphia, New York, etc., than Atlanta, Miami, etc. It must be admitted, however, that we faced a second best choice.

From the 1960–61 data contained in this survey we are able to estimate the average propensity to spend on various commodities, for example alcohol, at particular before-tax money income levels. We then assume that an individual with the same real income in 1970 would have the same average propensity to spend. (The person with the same real income would make the same real purchase of alcohol.) Using the rate of inflation in the consumer price index we then deflate mean 1970 incomes in each of our income classes (the uppermost and open-ended bracket's mean income is estimated by a Pareto distribution). Using simple linear interpolation of the 1960–1961 figures, we estimate the average propensity to spend for this particular income level. (The only exception made to linear interpolation was in the lowest and highest brackets, where we assume the same elasticity of average propensities prevail as actually do prevail between those brackets and the next to the lowest and the next to the highest brackets respectively.) We then apply this average propensity to 1970 mean income to arrive at estimated 1970 average expenditures on, for instance, alcohol. The percentage distribution of alcoholic expenditures in each jurisdiction is estimated by applying the jurisdiction's own income distribution to these average expenditures.

C.10 Since we assume that the geographical distribution of customers is the same as that of corporate and unincorporated firms, some method of weighting the portion of the tax paid by corporate as opposed to unincorporated businesses is necessary. The District of Columbia levied the same tax rate on the net income of corporate and unincorporated businesses. Of the total taxes raised from these two sources, 88 percent was generated by the corporate income tax. We use this as a way to weight the customers of corporate and unincorporated firms in both the city and the suburbs.

C.11 The lack of any detailed input-output type of analysis for the area hampered us in our attempt to determine the locational characteristics of the customers of area corporations. Perhaps even a greater handicap to our efforts was the inability of the District of Columbia to supply us with any breakdown on corporate income tax payments by class of industry. Some knowledge of the type of firm paying the tax is essential for answering the question of the residency of its customers.

Table C-9
Customers of Business Firms of Various Jurisdictions

	Corporate	Unincor-porated	Weighted Average
District of Columbia			
D.C. Residents	34.8	53.5	37.00
Suburban Md. Residents	23.7	8.8	21.90
Suburban Va. Residents	15.4	4.2	14.10
Others	26.1	33.5	27.00
Suburban Maryland			
D.C. Residents	9.0	6.3	7.65
Suburban Md. Residents	53.0	89.5	71.25
Suburban Va. Residents	13.2	2.5	7.85
Others	24.8	1.7	13.25
Suburban Virginia			
D.C. Residents	8.9	2.7	5.80
Suburban Md. Residents	18.4	4.2	11.30
Suburban Va. Residents	47.2	87.8	67.50
Others	25.5	5.3	15.46

Lacking direct information, we proceed as follows. We estimate profits in each industrial category in D.C., suburban Maryland, and suburban Virginia by using county payroll statistics (U.S. Bureau of the Census, *County Business Patterns,* 1970) and by assuming that the ratio of profits to wages in each category is the same as in the nation as a whole. From the Internal Revenue Service's *Corporation and Business Income Tax Returns,* 1968, we estimate the proportion of profits in each industrial category earned by corporations. Applying these proportions gives estimated profits by industrial category. The corporate profit taxes are distributed between industrial categories in the same proportions.

What little tax estimated to be paid for by mining and agriculture is assumed borne by customers within the metropolitan area. The same is held true for the goods and services of construction, wholesale and retail, and service firms. Similarly, the firms in the finance, insurance, and real estate areas are assumed to make their sales within the metropolitan area. Within the transportation, communication and public utility fields, allowance is made for exporting of 25 percent of the transportation services to external markets.

For manufacturing, we classify certain manufacturing industries into what we consider to be clearly, wholly, metropolitan-oriented industries. These are basically dairy products, bakery products, lumber and wood products, newspapers, and sand, stone and gravel. It is assumed that the profits of these firms are proportional to their payrolls. Of the remaining corporate profits, we assume that 50 percent are on sales within the metropolitan market and 50 per-

cent are on exports. The net result is to estimate that 66 percent, 55 percent, and 54 percent of the manufacturing firm sales of firms located in D.C., suburban Maryland, and suburban Virginia respectively, are made within the metropolitan market.

Before the sales taking place within the metropolitan area are divided between residents of the different jurisdictions, allowances are made for sales to governments. If taxes related to such sales are fully passed forward, then they lead either to higher federal or state-local taxes. The former is thus assumed fully shifted out of the area. The latter already is embodied in the taxes that we are allocating.

We assume that the government makes at most an infinitesimal portion of the purchases from firms in mining, finance, real estate, and insurance, and the service sector and from those firms in the transportation, communication and public utility field that are subject to the corporate income tax. Governments are assumed to purchase nothing at the retail level, but their purchases at wholesale are assumed equal to the ratio of government employment to total business and government employment in the area.

Government is also likely to be a substantial purchaser in the construction field. We assume that construction in the private versus public sector is such as to maintain the same relative proportions of government and private property values. So for instance, since the D.C. Department of Finance and Revenue estimated that 36 percent of the value of improvements was located on government property, we assume that government makes 36 percent of the construction purchases from D.C. firms. In the suburbs, data on the value of government property as a percentage of the total could be obtained only from Prince Georges County. This ratio was assumed to prevail elsewhere in the suburbs.

The sales made within the area to nongovernment purchasers were divided up into two categories: (a) those simply made to any customer within the metropolitan market and (b) those made solely to residents of the metropolitan area. In the latter category we include the sales of firms in finance and real estate. Few tourists would be likely to purchase services in this latter category. Sales in the first category are divided between residents of various localities in the same way as total retail sales to final consumers; sales in the latter category in the same way as total retail sales to final consumers who live in the study area.

This, however, raises the question of whether one ought to assume that the firm producing in Washington, for the metropolitan market, sells its entire output in Washington or whether its sales are evenly distributed over the metropolitan area. In the first case, we would distribute the taxes in the same way as the sales in D.C. to nonbusiness customers. In the other case, they should be distributed in the same way as such sales in the entire area. We feel that reality falls somewhere in between. Exactly where is unknown and so the midpoint seems the best estimate. Table C-10 summarizes the resulting assumptions about corporate customers.

Table C-10
Geographic Location of Corporate Customers

Jurisdiction of Firm:	D.C.	Md.	Va.
Jurisdiction of Customer:			
D.C.	36.30	9.0	8.9
Md.	24.85	53.0	18.4
Va.	16.05	13.2	47.2
Other	22.80	24.8	25.5

The portion of the tax shifted forward is assumed distributed between income classes in the same way as total consumption.

The part borne by owners is distributed between jurisdictions in the same way as the owners of income producing property within the jurisdiction. The resulting distributions are summarized in table C-11. This part of the tax is distributed by income classes in the same way as dividends.

C.12   The District of Columbia labor force breakdowns are: 48 percent D.C. residents, 32 percent suburban Maryland residents, 19 percent suburban Virginia residents, and 1 percent from outside the study area. These statistics are derived from commutation data provided in The Bureau of the Census, *Social and Economic Characteristics: The District of Columbia.*

Since the firms subject to the unincorporated income tax are overwhelmingly in the retail and service field and since many service fields serving basically only local clientele such as doctors and lawyers are excluded from the tax, we assume that the tax is distributed among residents of various jurisdictions in proportion to total retail sales made to such residents in D.C. Thus we estimate that 53.5 percent of these taxes are shifted forward to D.C. residents, 8.8 percent to residents of suburban Maryland, 4.2 percent to residents of suburban Virginia, and 33.5 percent to residents of other parts of the world.

While the tax borne by consumers is distributed by income class in proportion to total consumption, that borne by owners is distributed by gross business income.

Table C-11
Geographic Location of Corporate Owners

Jurisdiction of Firm:	D.C.	Md.	Va.
Jurisdiction of Owners:			
D.C.	8.4	10.0	10.0
Md.	20.0	24.2	23.6
Va.	14.0	16.8	16.4
Other	57.6	49.0	50.0

C.13 Our attempt to determine the residency of those who bear the motor fuel excise tax was facilitated somewhat by the identity of tax rates in the study area. A deduction is made for payment by business. Commercial vehicle miles traveled as a fraction of total vehicles miles traveled within the jurisdiction multiplied by 10 percent (to account for greater fuel consumption per mile) is assumed equal to the percentage of the burden borne by business. Given this, a first approximation of the geographic distribution can be made by assuming that people buy their gasoline where they drive and by utilizing our data on vehicle miles driven within a jurisdiction by residents of various areas.

This would tend, however, to overestimate nonresident gasoline purchases because people tend to patronize automobile repair shops close to home. They try to build up goodwill in anticipation of the snowy morning when their car doesn't start by buying their gas at a particular station close to home. Moreover, the purchase of gasoline within the jurisdiction of employment often would require the motorist to exit from the main arteries causing considerable delay. On the other hand, there is little reason to believe that the percentage of retail sales of gasoline within a given jurisdiction that are sold to residents of other jurisdictions should be much less than the percentages of total retail sales in the jurisdictions made to these nonresidents. Thus this may be taken as a lower limit. In the face of our ignorance, our best guesstimate lies halfway between these and the vehicle-miles driven percentages.

C.14 The number of gallons of liquor sold in each jurisdiction was deduced from its per gallon tax rates and its tax collections. The results are shown in table C-12.

Estimates of the number of man-days spent by tourists in the different jurisdictions are multiplied by twice the average annual consumption of alcohol per person eighteen years of age and over. This is based on the supposition that

Table C-12
Sales of Liquor in the Different Jurisdictions

	Gallons	Gallons per person 18 years of age and older
District of Columbia	5,640,000	10.61
Montgomery County	730,353	2.19
Prince Georges County	1,208,457	2.91
Alexandria	182,553	2.27
Arlington	213,379	1.61
Fairfax County	528,633	1.91
Fairfax City	80,467	6.17
Falls Church City	58,268	7.90

tourists with much leisure time are apt to consume alcohol at higher than normal rates. If they consume at 300 percent the national rate but one-third are under eighteen, then our use of twice the national average is appropriate.

Given the estimate of tourist purchases we can deduce total consumption by area residents. Deducting tourist purchases of 250,813 gallons from total sales in the area gives us a total consumption of 8,391,297 gallons by residents of the area. Per person eighteen years of age and older this is 4.69 gallons per capita.

It is then assumed that residents of the various jurisdictions consume the same amount of alcohol. Our estimated alcoholic beverage expenditures indicate that suburban residents spend on the average over 45 percent more on alcohol. But we are interested not in purchases, but in physical consumption because we are dealing with a per unit excise tax. Most of the spending differential may be explained by the purchase of more expensive liquor. Washingtonians may on the average buy a $5.00 quart of gin and suburbanites may buy a $7.25 quart of scotch. If residents of different jurisdictions do consume the same amount, table C-12 indicates that suburbanites consume much more than they purchase in their own jurisdictions.

We estimate D.C. resident purchases in D.C. by assuming that except for commuters to the suburbs (25,000 gallons) all D.C. resident purchases are made in D.C. Subtracting both the estimated sales to tourists, 177,867 gallons, and the estimated sales to residents, 2,477,304 gives purchases by other residents of the SMSA of 2,984,829 gallons.

These gallons are divided between suburban Maryland and suburban Virginia by assuming that all purchases in the suburbs, except for tourist purchases and minor amounts by reverse commuters, are made by residents. Applying our consumption of 4.69 gallons per year gives total estimated consumption by residents of suburban Maryland and suburban Virginia. Subtracting purchases made in the consumer's own jurisdiction from total consumption, gives purchases in D.C. by Maryland and Virginia suburbanites. The portion of Virginia suburban purchases made in D.C. by residents of Loudon and Prince William counties is assumed equal to their share of commuters. Table C-13 presents the estimated percent-

Table C-13
Percentage of Liquor Purchases by Residency of Purchaser

Jurisdiction	Residents of			
	D.C.	Md.	Va.	Other
D.C.	44.2	28.5	23.1	4.2
Md.	.3	97.7	.7	1.3
Va.	.5	2.5	92.1	4.8

ages of liquor purchases made by residents of various areas. It is assumed that these percentages also apply to wine purchases and hence the taxes on wine.

Unfortunately data on per capita beer consumption in the area could not be deduced from existing excise tax figures. As a result a third best solution was used to allocate these taxes across jurisdictions.

Beer is a commodity whose weight/value ratio is rather high. Moreover, since beer prices do not vary substantially between jurisdictions in the Washington area, little cross-hauling of beer would be expected. Basically, beer is likely to be consumed where purchased and consumption is likely to be proportional to leisure time spent in the area. Therefore, we allocated beer consumption by man-hours spent in a jurisdiction by residents of various jurisdictions, once these hours had been corrected for the portion spent at leisure. Resident hours are assumed to be 3/7 leisure. Nonresidents who live in neighboring jurisdictions spend 1/6 of their time in the jurisdiction they are visiting at leisure, and those not residents of the area spend about 1/3 of their time at leisure.

C.15 A breakdown for the sales of gas by jurisdiction by class of user was made available by the sole supplier in the area, Washington Gas and Light. Thus the percentage of gas sales to business, to government and to residencies is established.

In the electric utility field, only the Virginia Electric and Power Company would give us a useful breakdown by sales by type of customer. In light of this, in the other jurisdictions, we assume that the ratio between the percentage of electric sales to residencies and the percentage of gas sales to residencies was the same as the ratio in Virginia. Likewise, the ratios for sales of electric and gas to business and government were assumed the same as in Virginia.

Attempts to secure the cooperation of the telephone company in deducing the portions of their sales which go into different uses proved futile. In light of this, we are forced to make arbitrary assumptions about these proportions. Data on phones in use in D.C. secured from the Chesapeake and Potomac Telephone Company reveals that 52 percent of the phones are residential. Giving weight to greater usage of nonresidential phones we assumed that 50 percent of sales are nonresidential. We assume commercial sales are half this proportion, or 25 percent, in the suburbs. Commercial sales are divided between government and business on the basis of the ratio of civilian government employment to private employment in the respective areas. The revised Bureau of Labor Statistics series to distribute the taxes borne directly by individuals are contained in table C-2.

C.16 In calculating the federal offset for the death and gift taxes we are limited, because of the relatively small number of federal returns, to solely national data. From the Internal Revenue Service, *Estate Tax Returns, 1969,* we calculate that of the total state estate and inheritance tax returns around 34.3

percent are credited against the federal death taxes. We round this to 35 percent and also assume that the same offset applies to the gift tax.

We chose to distribute the tax by income class by net wealth. We use the distribution of such wealth appearing in Dorothy S. Projector and Gertrude S. Weiss, *Survey of Financial Characteristics of Consumers,* Board of Governors of the Federal Reserve System, table 18. Their data apply to 1963. We assume that the relative distribution of wealth remained unchanged between 1963 and 1970 so that a Gini coefficient measure of the distribution would be unchanged. The resulting distribution for the United States as a whole, which is assumed applicable in each of the jurisdictions, is contained in table C-2.

C.17   In 1970, the District of Columbia collected $5.5 million in cigarette excise taxes. The rate of 3.5 cents per pack implies sales of 157.1 million packs. Presuming an average price per pack of 30 cents implies sales of $47.13 million.

If tourists maintained the average national rate of consumption of 131.8 packs per capita per year they would purchase 4,473,819 packs or 2.8 percent of the total in Washington. Our estimated BLS series predicts tobacco expenditures of $39,265,305 by D.C. residents. Of this approximately 10 percent will be on noncigarette tobacco (given national consumption patterns and assuming an average price of cigarettes of 30 cents per pack, cigars of 12-1/2 cents per cigar and tobacco of $1.25 per pound). Also 5 percent of these total expenditures will be made elsewhere. Thus D.C. residents are estimated to spend about $34,844,000 on cigarettes or 73.9 percent of the total spent within their own jurisdictions. The remaining 23.3 percent is assumed spent by suburbanites.

In the suburbs we estimate tourist purchases and purchases by commuters from D.C. The remainder is assumed purchased by residents. The resulting percentage distribution of cigarette sales is contained in table C-14.

C.18   Data on the residency of those paying D.C. fines were available in police records. In the suburbs the lack of such data forced us to distribute the fines by vehicle miles traveled within the jurisdiction by residents of various jurisdictions on the presumption that the probability of being fined was proportional to vehicle miles traveled. Parking fees were always distributed in this fashion.

C.19   The percentage of the tax paid for by business purchasers is assumed equal to the percentage of vehicle registration fees paid for by business.

C.20   Table C-15 summarizes the taxable insurance premiums by type of policy. The only categories that can result in the flow of burdens between jurisdictions are the commercial and group life policies. The group life policies are assumed divided among jurisdictions according to the origin of the work force of the jurisdiction. The percentages of the work force coming from various juris-

Table C–14
Distribution of Cigarette Purchases by Place of Residency

Taxing Jurisdiction	Percentage Purchases by Residents of:			
	D.C.	Md.	Va.	Other
D.C.	73.9	14.5	8.4	3.2
Md.	1.1	98.0	.2	.7
Va.	3.7	7.8	87.0	1.5

Table C–15
Percentage Distribution of Insurance Premiums by Category

	Jurisdiction		
	D.C.	Md.	Va.
Commercial	19	15	10
Ordinary Life	19	28	29
Group Life	42	23	29
Automobile	16	27	24
Homeownership	4	7	8

dictions are weighted by the average expenditures on life insurance of the people in the jurisdiction from which they come.

Life insurance premium taxes are distributed between classes by a series on life insurance expenditures by income class. The automobile insurance premium taxes are allocated by a series on automobile insurance premiums. Finally, the burden passed forward in homeownership premiums is distributed by house values by income class.

C.21 Through unpublished data supplied to us by the Comptroller of the Currency, we are able to estimate the types of loans made by commercial banks located in the District of Columbia, suburban Maryland and suburban Virginia. Data on the loan patterns of savings and loan institutions could not be found at less than national level. We therefore, rely on national data summarized in the *United States Savings & Loan League Savings and Loan Fact Book '72.* These data, together with the assumption that each dollar lent includes the same proportion of shifted forward tax, enable us to estimate the percentage of the bank tax borne by different types of borrowers, as shown in table C–16.

Substantial research failed to discover any relevant data on the location of the properties on which D.C. and suburban banks issue mortgage loans. Since the overwhelming majority of new housing construction in the D.C. area is located in the suburbs, we arbitrarily assume that 50 percent of the loans made

Table C-16
Percentage of Bank Taxes Paid by Class of Borrower

	D.C.	Md.	Va.
Mortgage Loan	61.2	35.3	41.3
Security Loan	1.2	.4	.7
Personal Loan	14.4	33.2	35.5
Business Loan	23.2	31.1	22.5

by D.C. banks are on suburban properties. None of the loans made by suburban banks is assumed issued on D.C. property. The distribution between Maryland and Virginia and between houses and apartments of the D.C. loans is made on the basis of estimated market values of the properties in each jurisdiction and category. The part on home mortgages is distributed by the series on house values by income class. The part on apartment house mortgages is distributed by the series on rental payments by income class.

As for the tax on security loans, all of the suburban taxes are assumed paid for by suburbanites. However, since the overwhelming majority of such loans are made by D.C. banks, it is apparent that the D.C. security loan market is an areawide market. Therefore, the loans made by D.C. banks are distributed among residents of the various jurisdictions in proportion to the dividend receipts of those with income in excess of $10,000. The distribution by income bracket within a jurisdiction is on the basis of dividends received by those with income in excess of $10,000 in that jurisdiction.

The part of the tax paid by people taking out consumer loans is assumed distributed among jurisdictions in the same proportions as nontourist retail purchases in any given jurisdiction. They are divided by income class by the series on total consumption expenditures.

C.22   While data existed on commercial vehicle registration fees in Maryland and Virginia, in the District we are forced to add an estimate of automobiles owned by business firms to data on the percentage of registration fees paid for by trucks and buses to arrive at this figure. The latter is obtained from the U.S. Department of Transportation, *Highway Statistics 1970*. The estimate of automobile ownership by commercial interests is assumed equal to the national average as reported in *Automobile Facts and Figures 1971*.

Motor vehicle license fees are distributed according to a series on automobile ownership by income class. This is national data obtained from the Survey Research Centers *The Survey of Consumer Finances 1970*. Given the percentage that owned cars in any given income class we are able to deduce the percentage distribution of license ownership. The data present one difficulty. Data are available for only the above $15,000 group. Therefore, we assume that the percentage that owned cars in this group, 97 percent, was the same as the

percentage in the $15,000–$24,999 and the $25,000 and above classes. Since the corresponding percentages in the $10,000–$14,999 income bracket was 95 percent, this assumption is likely to create little distortion.

Registration fees paid by individuals are distributed using the same data source's report on the number of cars owned by income class. Again the data presents a slight difficulty. It shows only the percentage in each income class that owned zero, one, two, or three or more cars. We are forced to assume that those who owned three or more on the average owned only three. Moreover, data are available only for those with income above $15,000. We assume the incidence of car ownership is the same in the $15,000–$25,000 and the $25,000 and above brackets.

C.23 In Virginia only one of the counties, Fairfax, could provide data on the portion of the personal property tax paid for by business. In Fairfax, this amounts to 27.2 percent. The other counties are likely to derive a somewhat greater percentage of their revenues from business because of their greater extent of commercial and industrial development. Therefore, we assume that these counties collect a third of their personal property tax from business property.

C.24 License plate surveys at Bowie, based on the assumption that one-fifth of the Maryland licenses came from counties other than those under study, estimated attendance as 51 percent from suburban Maryland, 7 percent from suburban Virginia, 13 percent from the District of Columbia and 29 percent from the rest of the world.

Surveys at the two smaller tracks (Rosecroft and Marlboro) were not undertaken. A substantial utilization by residents of the rest of the world seems unlikely. We assume that they contribute 10 percent of the handle. The remainder is distributed among the jurisdictions under the study in the same proportions estimated for Bowie. In summary, we estimate that 55 percent of this tax is paid for by suburban Maryland residents, 8 percent by suburban Virginia residents, 14 percent by residents of the District of Columbia and 23 percent by the rest of the world.

C.25 The distribution used for the capitation tax is the distribution in the Virginia study area of the sum of (a) the number of single individuals less the approximately 10 percent of single individuals below the age of twenty-one and (b) twice the number of families by income class. This would tend to slightly overstate the tax paid for by the lowest income classes because single individuals under twenty-one years of age are likely to be concentrated quite heavily in the lower-income classes. Without a distribution of individuals both by income level and by age by income level, we are not able to do any better.

The data used are from the *U.S. Bureau of Census, General Population Characteristics, Virginia.*

Notes

Notes to Chapter 1
Metropolitan Fiscal Flows

1. For a recent formulation of the interdependent utility phenomenon, see Harold M. Hochman and James D. Rodgers, "Pareto Optimal Redistribution," *American Economic Review* 59 (September 1969): 542–57.
2. For a detailed discussion of the differences between the District tax structure and that of other areas see L.L. Ecker-Racz, *Financing the District of Columbia,* a report prepared for the District of Columbia, August 1968; and Department of Finance and Revenue, Government of the District of Columbia, "Major State and Local Tax Burdens in Washington Compared with those in the 30 Largest Cities," and "Comparison of Major State and Local Tax Burdens in Selected Washington Metropolitan Area Jurisdictions," Washington, D.C., 1973.

Notes to Chapter 2
Public Sector Exchanges in a Metropolitan Area

1. For a review of the literature since 1920 which comments on metropolitan problems, see Robert O. Warren, *Government in Metropolitan Regions* (Davis, California: Institute of Governmental Affairs, 1966), pp. 5–48.
2. Charles M. Tiebout, "A Pure Theory of Local Expenditures," *Journal of Political Economy* 64 (1956): 416–24.
3. Wallace E. Oates, "The Effects of Property Taxes and Local Public Spending on Property Values: An Empirical Study of Tax Capitalization and the Tiebout Hypothesis," *Journal of Political Economy* 77 (1969): 957–71. Hamilton has pointed out that, while the Oates results contradict the hypothesis that citizens ignore fiscal variables in their location decisions, they do not necessarily follow from the Tiebout hypothesis. For example, logically there is no reason why higher property values cannot be found in low-expenditures cities if these cities are in short supply due to zoning restrictions. Bruce M. Hamilton, "The Effects of Property Taxes and Local Public Spending on Property Values: A Theoretical Comment," *Journal of Political Economy,* forthcoming. For a critique of Oates' statistical techniques, see Harry O. Pollakowski, "The Effects of Property Taxes and Local Public Spending on Property Values: A Comment and Further Results," *Journal of Political Economy* 81 (1973): 994–1003.
4. William J. Baumol, "Urban Services: Interactions of Public and Private Decisions," in Howard G. Shaller (ed.), *Public Expenditures Decisions in the Urban Community* (Washington: Resources for the Future, 1963), pp. 11–14.

5. Baumol, "Urban Services," p. 13.
6. William J. Baumol, "The Macroeconomics of Unbalanced Growth," *American Economic Review* 57 (1967): 414–26.
7. Peter S. Albin, "Unbalanced Growth and Intensification of the Urban Crisis," *Urban Studies* 8 (1971): 139–46.
8. James M. Buchanan, "Principles of Urban Fiscal Strategy," *Public Choice* 11 (1971): 1–16. While discussing the implications of their dynamic model of urban development, Oates, Howrey, and Baumol quite correctly point out that ". . . while a specific program may induce well-to-do families to live in the cities (and this may well be of importance to the mayor of a city who is worried about his own fiscal problems), such a program is not necessarily in the national interest." W.E. Oates, E.P. Howrey, and W.J. Baumol, "The Analysis of Public Policy in Dynamic Urban Models," *Journal of Political Economy* 79 (1971): 153. The level of poverty in the nation, for example, is not reduced simply by keeping high income residents in the central city and poor people in rural areas. However in terms of the relative fiscal burdens borne by central city and suburban residents, it is of some little importance whether the central city must attempt to finance growing expenditures for poverty-related services by taxing its own residents, whose income is low relative to suburban levels.
9. The extent to which economies of scale exist in the provision of public services remains problematic despite several empirical studies. For a summary of this literature, see Werner Z. Hirsch, *The Economics of State and Local Government* (New York: McGraw-Hill, 1970), pp. 273–74.
10. For a discussion of city-county consolidations in the United States, see *American County* 37 (1972): 9–19. There have also been numerous consolidations in Canada, the most notable being Toronto, Winnipeg, and Vancouver.
11. Five different structures of metropolitan consolidations can be identified: (1) the consolidated city-county government as in Jacksonville-Duval County, Florida; (2) the urban county in Dade County (Miami), Florida; (3) the federated two-tiered structure in Toronto, Canada; (4) the multi-function special purpose district in Portland, Oregon; and (5) the third tier of government in the Twin Cities, Minnesota. The experience of metro government as found in these five areas has been judged, on balance, to be positive by Melvin B. Mogulof, *Five Metropolitan Governments* (Washington: The Urban Institute, 1972), 145 pp.
12. For a discussion that is generally skeptical of the value of political unification, see Vincent Ostrom, Charles Tiebout, and Robert Warren, "The Organization of Government in Metropolitan Areas: A Theoretical Inquiry," *American Political Science Review* 55 (1961): 831–42; Vincent Ostrom, "Operational Federalism: Organization of Public Services in the American Federal System," *Public Choice* 7 (1969): 1–17; Kenneth V. Greene, "Some Institutional Considerations in Federal-State Fiscal Relations," *Public Choice* 9 (1970): 1–18; and Robert L. Bish, *The Public Economy of Metropolitan Areas* (Chicago: Markham, 1971), pp. 148–58.
13. From a significant analysis of the whole question of the optimal provision

of local public services in the face of fragmentation, Rothenberg concludes that political consolidation ". . . is not likely to be voluntarily accepted because the very incentives that led to jurisdictional fragmentation (the self-interest of small, homogeneous groups) would make it unattractive to the beneficiaries of that fragmentation." Jerome Rothenberg, "Local Decentralization and the Theory of Optimal Government," in Julius Margolis (ed.), *The Analysis of Public Output* (New York: National Bureau of Economic Research, 1970), p. 63.

14. Alan W. Evans, "Public Goods and Metropolitan Consolidation," *Proceedings of 28th Congress of the International Institute of Public Finance, New York, 1972.*

15. Koleda, using assumptions that are closer to those employed by Tiebout, for example, that goods provided by local public sector are public within a jurisdiction but private between jurisdictions, also shows under what conditions consolidation is likely to occur. Michael S. Koleda, "A Public Good Model of Governmental Consolidation," *Urban Studies* 8 (1971): 103–110.

16. For confirmation by voter and survey data of the hypothesis that citizens of higher income communities are expected to oppose proposals for financing services through a metropolitan-wide jurisdiction that embraces a taxing area with a mean income lower than their own community, see William B. Neenan, *Political Economy of Urban Areas* (Chicago: Markham, 1972), pp. 91–116.

17. Ellickson concludes from his model of residential choice that metropolitan fragmentation tends to increase the welfare of residents in wealthy suburbs and decrease the welfare in less wealthy suburbs. Bryan Ellickson, "Jurisdictional Fragmentation and Residential Choice," *American Economic Review* 61 (1971): 338.

18. Evans, "Public Goods."

19. Amos H. Hawley, "Metropolitan Population and Municipal Government Expenditures in Central Cities," *Journal of Social Issues* 7 (1951): 107. Kasarda reports that between 1950 and 1970 the suburban population in general and the commuting population in particular for 168 SMSAs is positively correlated with central city expenditures, even when controls are introduced for such variables as central city size and age, per capita income of central city, and percentage of central city population that is nonwhite. However, he also found that the commuting population has a significant impact on city retail and wholesale trade, among other activities. See John Kasarda, "The Impact of Suburban Population Growth on Central City Service Functions," *American Journal of Sociology* 77 (1972): 1123. As will be discussed below, Vincent, among others, contends that the commuter impact generates gains for the central city which offset the cost of commuters to the central city.

20. Julius Margolis, "Metropolitan Finance Problems: Territories, Functions, and Growth," in James M. Buchanan (ed.), *Public Finances: Needs, Sources, and Utilization* (Princeton, N.J.: Princeton University Press, 1966), p. 258.

21. Ibid., p. 259.

22. Harvey E. Brazer, *City Expenditures in the United States* (New York:

National Bureau of Economic Research, 1959), p. 58. See also "Some Fiscal Implications of Metropolitanism," in Guthrie S. Birkhed (ed.), *Metropolitan Issues: Social, Governmental, Fiscal* (Syracuse: Maxwell Graduate School, 1962), pp. 61–82.

23. Woo Sik Kee, "Suburban Population Growth and Its Implications for Core City Finance," *Land Economics* 43 (1967): 202–211. Two other multivariate regression studies by Kee are relevant to the suburban-central city question: "Central City Expenditures and Metropolitan Areas," *National Tax Journal* 18 (1965): 337–53, and "City-Suburban Differentials in Local Government Fiscal Effort," *National Tax Journal* 21 (1968): 183–89.

24. Samuel H. Book, "Costs of Commuters to the Central City as a Basis for Commuter Taxation," Ph.D. dissertation, Columbia University, 1970, p. 201.

25. Phillip E. Vincent, "The Fiscal Impact of Commuters," in Werner Z. Hirsch, Phillip E. Vincent, Henry S. Terrell, Donald C. Shoup, and Arthur Rosett, *Fiscal Pressures on the Central City* (New York: Praeger, 1971), pp. 95–96.

26. Ibid., p. 112.

27. Just as central city property values are enhanced through suburban contacts, so suburban property values reflect their proximity to a population concentration. "What would the Kenilworth house be worth if it suddenly were transported to the real estate market of Watertown, South Dakota?" Theodore Lowi, *The End of Liberalism* (New York: Norton, 1969), p. 195.

28. Vincent, "Fiscal Impact," p. 110. This finding is consonant with other studies. For example, even though Neenan found that the Detroit suburban area as a whole received net uncompensated benefits from interaction with the Detroit public sector, commuters were found to more than compensate for the benefits they received *qua* commuters. See Neenan, *Political Economy*, pp. 148–49.

29. R.F. Smith, "Are Nonresidents Contributing Their Share to Core City Revenues," *Land Economics*, 1972, p. 242.

30. Ibid., p. 245.

31. Ibid.

32. James M. Banovetz, *Government Cost Burdens and Service Benefits in the Twin Cities Metropolitan Area* (Minneapolis: Public Administration Center, University of Minnesota, 1965).

33. Ibid., p. 29.

34. Shoup and Rosett have examined fiscal exploitation by overlapping government in the case of Los Angeles County. They find that the provision of police services by the Los Angeles County Sheriff's Department is the source of two forms of exploitation. They estimate that in 1968 the unincorporated areas of the county received a subsidy of $6.1 million from the incorporated areas and that the cities which contracted for police services from the Sheriff's Department enjoyed a subsidy of $5.1 million resulting from payments of less than the marginal cost of the services. Donald C. Shoup and Arthur Rosett, "Fiscal Exploitation by Overlapping Governments," in Werner Z. Hirsch, Phillip E. Vincent, Henry S. Terrell, Donald C. Shoup, and Arthur Rosett, *Fiscal Pressures on the Central City* (New York: Praeger Publishers, 1971), pp. 241–301.

35. William B. Neenan, *Political Economy of Urban Areas* (Chicago: Markham, 1972), pp. 53–139.
36. Ibid., p. 137.
37. David D. Ramsey, "Suburban-Central City Exploitation Thesis: Comment," *National Tax Journal* 25 (1972): 602.
38. Ibid., p. 600. For a discussion of this issue, see Kenneth V. Greene and Claudia D. Scott, "Suburban-Central City Spillovers of Tax Burdens and Expenditure Benefits," *Northeast Regional Science Review* 3 (1973).
39. D.A.L. Auld and Gail C.A. Cook, "Suburban-Central City Exploitation Thesis: A Comment," *National Tax Journal* 25 (1972): 597.
40. David F. Bradford and Wallace E. Oates, "Suburban Exploitation of Central Cities and Governmental Structure," in Harold M. Hochman and George E. Peterson (eds.), *Redistribution Through Public Choice* (New York: Columbia University Press, 1973), pp. 9–10.

Notes to Chapter 3
Measurement of Benefits from
Government Services

1. Some major benefit incidence studies are: Charles Stauffacher, "The Effects of Governmental Expenditures and Tax Withdrawals Upon Income Distribution, 1930–39," *Public Policy* 2 (1941): 232–62; Tibor Barna, *Redistribution of Incomes Through Public Finance in 1937* (Oxford, 1945); Rufus S. Tucker, "The Distribution of Government Burdens and Benefits," *American Economic Review, Papers and Proceedings* 43 (1953): 518–43; Alfred H. Conrad, "Redistribution Through Government Budgets in the United States," in Alan T. Peacock (ed.), *Income Redistribution and Social Policy* (London: Cape, 1954), pp. 178–263; Allen M. Cartter, *The Redistribution of Income in Postwar Britain* (New Haven: Yale University Press, 1955), Chapter 5; Richard A. Musgrave and Darwin W. Daicoff, "The Incidence of Michigan Taxes," *Michigan Tax Studies: Staff Papers* (Michigan Secretary of Finance 1958), pp. 131–84; O.H. Brownlee, "Estimated Distribution of Minnesota Taxes and Public Expenditure Benefits," *Studies in Economics and Business*, No. 21 (University of Minnesota, 1960), 38 pp.; W. Irwin Gillespie, "Effect of Public Expenditures on the Distribution of Income," in Richard A. Musgrave (ed.), *Essays in Fiscal Federalism* (Washington: The Brookings Institution, 1965), pp. 122–86; and *Tax Burdens and Benefits of Government Expenditures by Income Class, 1961 and 1965* (New York: Tax Foundation, Inc., 1967).
2. James M. Buchanan, *Fiscal Theory and Political Economy* (Chapel Hill: University of North Carolina Press, 1960), pp. 11–12.
3. J.B. Say, *A Treatise on Political Economy* (Philadelphia: J.B. Lippincott and Company, 1855), p. 413.
4. Weisbrod discusses the question of whose welfare should be consulted in designing redistributive programs. For him the resolution of this problem involves a balancing of both "taxpayer" sovereignty and "consumer" sovereignty with the "consumer" being the recipient of redistributional

expenditures. Presumably therefore both "taxpayer" and "consumer" benefit from the expenditure. See Burton A. Weisbrod, "Collective Action and
Distribution of Income: A Conceptual Approach," in Robert A. Haveman
and Julius Margolis (eds.), *Public Expenditures and Policy Analysis* (Chicago:
Markham Publishing Company, 1970), pp. 130–31.

5. As Haveman and Krutilla have pointed out, the opportunity cost of a
government project is less than its budgetary cost to the extent it draws
upon otherwise unemployed resources. For an elaboration of this problem
and some calculations for the American economy for 1957–1964, see
Robert Haveman and John Krutilla, *Unemployment, Idle Capacity, and the
Evaluation of Public Expenditures* (Baltimore: The Johns Hopkins Press,
1968), pp. 65–86.

6. Most benefit incidence studies, however, consider total interest payments
as "benefits" to the bondholders. For example, W. Irwin Gillespie, "Effect
of Public Expenditure on the Distribution of Income," in Richard A. Musgrave (ed.), *Essays in Fiscal Federalism* (Washington: The Brookings Institution, 1965), pp. 157–58; and Allen M. Cartter, *The Redistribution of_
Income in Postwar Britain* (New Haven: Yale University Press, 1955), p. 49.
Cartter does enter the full value of interest payments in his benefit calculations, but he does not consider them to be source-of-income benefits, as
Gillespie does. Rather he suggests that interest payments are ". . . general
governmental expenses representing the cost of certain benefits which are
being paid for in installments," (p. 49) and thus are equivalently use-of-
income benefits, as will be discussed below.

7. This conclusion is similar in spirit to Lampman's discussion of redistribution
wherein an individual's receipt of "consumer-power income" from a trans-
fer program is greater than his "producer-contribution" to finance it. See
Robert J. Lampman, "Transfer and Redistribution as Social Process," in
Shirley Jenkins (ed.), *Social Security in International Perspective* (New
York: Columbia University Press, 1969), pp. 35–36.

8. For example, Gillespie, "Effect of Public Expenditures."

9. M. Schmundt, E. Smolensky, and L. Stiefel, *The Evaluation by Recipients
of In-Kind Transfers* (Madison: University of Wisconsin, Institute for
Research on Poverty), p. 3.

10. Ibid., p. 15.

11. From a two commodity model (housing and all other services) Aaron and
von Furstenberg show that, with plausible assumptions regarding the elasticity of substitution between housing and all other services, the inefficiency
of housing subsidies will range from only 3.4 to 10.0 percent. In other
words, in-kind public housing subsidies would be evaluated by recipients at
close to their cost. See Henry Aaron and George von Furstenberg, "The
Inefficiency of Transfers in Kind: The Case of Housing Assistance," *Western
Economic Journal* 9 (1971): 189.

12. Gillespie disregards the impact of government outlay on factor income in
computing benefits. "Their [public expenditures on goods and services]
effect upon the distribution of factor earnings will be disregarded under the

assumption that money incomes before taxes are disregarded." Gillespie, "Public Expenditures," p. 130. Gillespie, however, does distribute payments under the various transfer programs to the direct recipients. See Gillespie, "Public Expenditures," pp. 150–52. Similarly, Banovetz, in his study of the Minneapolis-St. Paul metropolitan area, allocates the costs of all poverty-related expenditures as "benefits" to the recipients and the recipients alone, thus implicitly assuming that they generate no use-of-income benefits. See James M. Banovetz, *Governmental Cost Burdens and Service Benefits in the Twin Cities Metropolitan Area* (Minneapolis: Public Administration Center, University of Minnesota, 1965).

13. This "individualistic" approach to public sector analysis has largely carried the field among economists. A representative sample of the principal contributions in this tradition would include the following: Richard A. Musgrave, "The Voluntary Exchange Theory of Public Economy," *Quarterly Journal of Economics* 38 (1943): 27–48; Paul A. Samuelson, "The Pure Theory of Public Expenditure," *Review of Economics and Statistics* 36 (1954): 387–89; Anthony Downs, *An Economic Theory of Democracy* (New York: Harper and Row, 1957), 310 pp.; Richard A. Musgrave, *A Theory of Public Finance* (New York: McGraw-Hill, 1959), 628 pp.; some essays of James M. Buchanan dealing with many aspects of the "individuistic" approach and published as *Fiscal Theory and Political Economy* (Chapel Hill: University of North Carolina Press, 1960), 197 pp.; as well as two other books by Buchanan: *Public Finance in Democratic Process* (Chapel Hill: University of North Carolina Press, 1967), 307 pp., and *The Demand Supply of Public Goods* (Chicago: Rand McNally and Company, 1968), 214 pp.; and one by Buchanan and Gordon Tullock, *The Calculus of Consent* (Ann Arbor: University of Michigan Press, 1962), 361 pp.

There is an opposing tradition which contends that public sector decisions reflect more than the preferences of individuals qua individuals. Steiner terms this the "public interest" tradition in contrast with the "individualistic" tradition. Its principal base of support is among political scientists although there have been notable contributions by economists. For a sampling of this viewpoint see Charles E. Lindblom, "The Science of Muddling Through," *Public Administration Review,* 1959: 79–88; and "Decision-Making in Taxation and Expenditures," in James M. Buchanan (ed.), *Public Finances: Needs, Sources and Utilization* (Princeton: Princeton University Press, 1961), pp. 296–336; Gerhard Colm, *Essays in Public Finance and Fiscal Policy* (New York: Oxford University Press, 1955), pp. 3–43; Peter O. Steiner, *Public Expenditure Budgeting* (Washington: The Brookings Institution 1969), 117 pp.; and Aaron Wildavsky, *The Politics of the Budgetary Process* (Boston: Little Brown, 1964). For an excellent critical review of both the individualistic and the public interest viewpoints see Jesse Burkhead and Jerry Miner, *Public Expenditure* (Chicago: Aldine-Atherton, 1971), pp. 145–71.

14. Richard A. Musgrave, "Provision of Social Goods," in J. Margolis and H. Guitton (eds.), *Public Economics* (London: Macmillan, 1969), p. 125.

15. Paul A. Samuelson, "Pure Theory of Public Expenditure and Taxation," in Julius Margolis and Henri Guitton (eds.), *Public Economics* (London: Macmillan, 1969), p. 108.
16. Duncan MacRae, Jr., "Normative Assumptions in the Study of Public Choice," *Public Choice* 16 (Fall 1973): 33.
17. Recent major contributions to the discussions of income distribution include Martin Bronfenbrenner's compendious *Income Distribution Theory* (Chicago: Aldine-Atherton, 1971), 487 pp; as well as the contributions of many others, including notably Henry Aaron, Martin David, Robert Lampman, Martin McGuire, Benjamin Okner, Lester Thurow, and Burton Weisbrod. For a sampling of this literature in the context of the "grants economy," see Kenneth E. Boulding and Martin Pfaff (eds.) *Redistribution to the Rich and Poor* (Belmont: Wadsworth, 1971), 390 pp.; and Kenneth E. Boulding, Martin Pfaff, and Anita Pfaff (eds.), *Transfers in an Urbanized Economy* (Belmont: Wadsworth, 1973), 376 pp.
18. Kenneth E. Boulding, "Notes on a Theory of Philanthropy," in Frank G. Dickinson (ed.), *Philanthropy and Public Policy* (New York: National Bureau of Economic Research, 1962), p. 59.
19. Ibid., p. 61.
20. Ibid.
21. Ibid.
22. Thomas R. Ireland, *The Economics of Charity* (Blacksburg: Center for the Study of Public Choice, 1970), p. 22.
23. See Edward C. Banfield, *The Unheavenly City* (Boston: Little, Brown and Company, 1968), pp. 250–51.
24. Frances Fox Piven and Richard A. Cloward, *Regulating the Poor* (New York: Pantheon Books, 1971), p. xiii.
25. Thus Vickrey contends ". . . it is no longer necessary to say that a donation by A, designed to increase the standard of living of X, Y, and Z, must yield A as much utility through this effect as it would if spent to raise A's own standard of living. A will expect that B and C may also be induced by his gift to contribute to the same or similar objectives. The combined effects of A's original gift plus that of the induced gifts on the standard of living of X, Y, and Z will provide for A a level of satisfaction equal to what he would have obtained had he kept the amount of his contribution for himself." William S. Vickrey, "One Economist's View of Philanthropy," in Frank G. Dickinson (ed.), *Philanthropy and Public Policy* (New York: National Bureau of Economic Research, 1962), p. 41.
    Marglin employs much the same argument in contending that an individual in this generation is more willing to forego consumption in order to increase the income of a subsequent generation if he knows others are willing to do the same. See Stephen A. Marglin, "The Social Rate of Discount and the Optimal Rate of Investment," *Quarterly Journal of Economics* 77 (1963): 95–111.
26. For a discussion of this point in terms of some game experiments by RAND, see Vickrey, "One Economist's View of Philanthropy," pp. 41–42.
27. For an attempt to measure the impact of a community's dispersion of in-

come as well as other variables, on charitable giving, where dispersion is defined as the sum of the percentage of sample families with income less than 50 percent of the recorded mean and the percentage with incomes more than 50 percent above this level, see Harold M. Hochman and James D. Rodgers, "Utility Interdependence and Income Transfers Through Charity," in Kenneth E. Boulding, Martin Pfaff and Anita Pfaff (eds.), *Transfers in an Urbanized Economy* (Belmont: Wadsworth, 1973), pp. 63–77.

28. Pauly has discussed the question of the optimal supply of income redistribution under various assumptions including variations in the "spatial dimension in the motivation for redistribution." See Mark V. Pauly, "Income Redistribution as a Local Public Good," *Journal of Public Economics* 2 (1973): 35–58.

29. This discussion does not allow us to draw inferences whether support for redistribution in favor of central city poor, for example, is stronger among high income central city residents than among high income suburbanites. However, Watts and Free have found from a national survey that "suburb" and "city" attitudes do not vary notably concerning federal redistributional programs. William Watts and Lloyd A. Free, *State of the Nation* (New York: Universe Books, 1973), pp. 320–33.

30. Harold M. Hochman and James D. Rodgers, "Pareto Optimal Redistribution," *American Economic Review* 61 (1969): 543. The four motives for transfers discussed above, the "silent trade," philanthropic, Kantian, and regulatory motives, can all be subsumed under the Pareto criterion since, in all these instances, the handing over of income is a source of utility for the donor. For further discussion of interdependent utility functions, see Robert Haney Scott, "Avarice, Altruism, and Second Party Preferences," *Quarterly Journal of Economics* 86 (1972): 1–18; and Laurence D. Shall, "Interdependent Utilities and Pareto Optimality," *Quarterly Journal of Economics* 86 (1972): 19–25.

31. Of course "utility interdependence" can also mean that low-income people get utility from the increased welfare of higher-income individuals. There may be some such interdependence operative in the apparently widespread opposition among low income individuals to confiscatory taxes on inheritances above a certain level. Vickrey allows for such a possibility ". . . to cover the case of the charwoman who knits a shawl for a princess, or more generally of the MP who as her representative votes for a substantial civil list. . . ." William S. Vickrey, "One Economist's View of Philanthropy," p. 44. Of course, low-income people may oppose confiscatory taxes simply on the grounds that they intend to be wealthy themselves someday. They oppose such taxes for the same reason that they might buy lottery tickets. There is a very small chance that they might lose if confiscation were instituted.

32. Hochman and Rodgers, "Pareto Optimal Redistribution," p. 553.

33. Ibid., p. 555.

34. Henry Aaron and Martin C. McGuire, "Public Goods and Income Distribution," *Econometrica* 38 (1970): 907–920. In an attempt to introduce

explicit utility values into benefit estimation Neenan constructed "willing-ness-to-pay" multipliers to adjust government services measured by cost-of-service to a welfare basis in his study of fiscal flows in the Detroit metropolitan area. See William B. Neenan, *Political Economy of Urban Areas* (Chicago: Markham, 1972), pp. 81–118.

35. Schlomo Maital, "Public Goods and Income Distribution: Some Further Results," *Econometrica* 41 (1973): 561–568; and "Is Redistributive Taxation a Myth?" Discussion Paper No. 122, Institute of Economic Research, Queens University, Kingston, Ontario, 1973.
36. See Kazuo Sato, "Additive Utility Functions with Double-Log Consumer Demand Function," *Journal of Political Economy* 80 (1972): 102–124.
37. Maital, "Public Goods and Income Distribution," p. 567.
38. See William Fellner, "Operational Utility: The Theoretical Background and a Measurement," in *Ten Economic Studies in the Tradition of Irving Fisher* (New York: Wiley, 1967), pp. 39–74; A.A. Powell, Tran Van Hoa, and R.H. Wilson, "A Multi-sectoral Analysis of Consumer Demand in the Post-War Period," *Southern Economic Journal* 34 (1968): 109–120; and Koichi Mera, "Experimental Determination of Relative Marginal Utilities," *Quarterly Journal of Economics* 83 (1969): 468–74.
39. Maital, "Is Redistributive Taxation a Myth?", p. 17.
40. Fellner, "Operational Utility"; and Powell, Tran Van Hoa, and Wilson, "A Multi-sectoral Analysis of Consumer Demand."
41. Mera, "Experimental Determination."
42. Fellner, "Operational Utility," pp. 48–49.
43. For survey and voting data which support the hypothesis that citizen support for public expenditures would be fairly constant across income classes if tax incidence were proportional, see William B. Neenan, *Political Economy of Urban Areas* (Chicago: Markham, 1972), pp. 81–118.

Notes to Chapter 4
Optimal Supply of Public Output
in a Metropolitan Area

1. Prest's comment on this procedure is terse and to the point: "In principle the valuation of public expenditure by reference to costs of inputs is wrong: what is really needed is a system of valuing outputs." Alan R. Prest, "The Budget and Interpersonal Distribution," in *The Budget and the Distribution of National Income,* Proceedings of 1967 Congress of International Institute of Public Finance, Prague, 1968, p. 86.
2. On this point see Kenneth V. Greene, "Collective Decision Making Models and the Measurement of Benefits in Fiscal Incidence Studies," *National Tax Journal* 26 (1973): 177–88.
3. The assumption that the good is purely public is made solely for purposes of simplification. A mixed public-private good may be analyzed within the same framework. See James M. Buchanan, *The Demand and Supply of Public Goods* (Chicago: Rand McNally, 1968); and Mark V. Pauly, "The Mixed

Private-Public Financing of Education," *American Economic Review* 57 (1967): 120–30.

4. This diagram (fig. 4–2) is used in James M. Buchanan, *Public Finance in Democratic Process* (Chapel Hill: University of North Carolina Press, 1967).

5. As Barlow has pointed out, if the median voter's share of total benefits is greater (less) than his share of costs, then the level of provision chosen will be greater (less) than the social optimum. Robin Barlow, "Efficiency Aspects of Local School Finance," *Journal of Political Economy* 78 (1970): 1028–40.

6. Buchanan has made the same observation. See James M. Buchanan, *Finance in Democratic Process* (Chapel Hill: University of North Carolina Press, 1967).

7. Estimated income elasticities from recent cross-sectional studies of city and state expenditures lead us to suspect that primary education, police and fire protection, and parks and recreation have the greatest likelihood of underprovision; while sanitary services, highway expenditures, and health and hospital services are most likely overprovided. See Thomas E. Borch-erding and Robert T. Deacon, "The Demand for the Services of Non-Federal Government," *American Economic Review* 62 (1972): 891–901; and John C. Weicher, "Determinants of Central City Expenditures: Some Overlooked Factors and Problems," *National Tax Journal* 23 (1970): 379–96.

8. For a discussion of this general equilibrium question, see Harry G. Johnson, *The Two Sector Model of General Equilibrium* (Chicago: Aldine-Atherton, 1971); and Hirofumi Shibata, "Public Goods, Increasing Cost and Monopsony," *Journal of Political Economy* 81 (1973): 223–30.

9. McKean has argued that due to the activity of organized pressure groups, there is a tendency for public expenditures to be greater than socially optimal. Niskanen infers similar results from his model of government agencies as monopsonists who milk the consumer of his taxpayer's surplus. He sees bureaucratic suppliers of public services and the owners of factors supplied to the government enjoying a symbiotic relationship.

Downs comes to just the opposite conclusion, namely, that there is a tendency for government expenditures to be less than socially optimal. He argues that benefits from government services are diffused over a large population and so may be unnoticed, whereas taxes are very visible and painful. In the framework of the analysis employed here, Downs can be said to argue that the use-of-income benefits are so invisible that citizens' rates of substitution between private and public expenditures are very low whereas the slopes of the relevant budget lines are at least as steep as the actual tax price lines.

See Roland N. McKean, *Public Spending* (New York: McGraw-Hill, 1968); William Niskanen, *Bureaucracy and Representative Government* (Chicago: Aldine-Atherton, 1971); and Anthony Downs, "Why the Government Budget is too Small in a Democracy," in Edmund S. Phelps (ed.), *Private Wants and Public Needs* (New York: W.W. Norton, 1972).

10. On a point related to this Frey offers an explanation for the observed correlation between participation in the political process and income. He says

this correlation can be understood as the result of the interaction of two factors: (1) the opportunity costs of the time expended and (2) the productivity of the time used in performing political activities. The opportunity costs of high-income individuals is higher than for lower-income people and on this basis alone we would expect them to have lower participation rates. However, he says this is not so because their productivity is greater than for lower-income people. "Citizens with high paying jobs are more used to dealing with political questions which are in principle of the same character as their daily work, and which are therefore done much more efficiently. Consider, e.g., writing a letter to a Congressman. Citizens with low income from manual work find it very difficult to formulate it, as it is completely outside their occupation. An executive, on the other hand, dictates it to his secretary along with the rest of his routine work." Bruno S. Frey, "Why Do High Income People Participate More in Politics," *Public Choice* 11 (1971): 103.

Undoubtedly the "productivity" of higher-income classes from political effort is higher than for lower-income classes but perhaps for reasons in addition to being able to formulate a cogent argument in a letter. Higher-income people have greater access to the center of the "system," and their opinion is taken more seriously than that of some unknown person with little resources. Surely a Lockheed or Litton executive can reasonably expect greater "productivity" from a letter to a government official than can a short-order cook in Boone, Iowa.

11. See Chapter 9 for a discussion of citizen attitudes toward welfare programs. We may infer that Tullock feels that opposition to transfer programs in favor of the poor is misplaced since in the final analysis they effect very little redistribution. He contends that most redistribution in our society takes place in favor of certain middle-income citizens with little transferred to the very poor. As he sees it, distribution does not take place along a one-dimensional income continuum. For him bargaining theory suggests that the dominant coalition made up of the bottom 51 percent of the population may provide as much to the top portion of this 51 percent, the lower middle, as to the bottom portion. Tullock asserts that this is close to what we observe. "These transfers do not meet any egalitarian criteria. Basically they are transfers from groups of people who, for one reason or another, are not politically powerful to people who are." See Gordon Tullock, "The Charity of the Uncharitable," *Western Economic Journal* 9 (1971): 385.

12. A vast literature has developed around the heading of political fragmentation. To capture only a bit of the flavor of this literature concerning the principal point being addressed here, see Alan Williams, "The Optimal Provision of Public Goods in a System of Local Governments," *Journal of Political Economy* 74 (1966): 18–33; and the Comments and Rejoinder found in *Journal of Political Economy* 75 (1967): 86–92.

Notes to Chapter 5
Estimates of Benefit Incidence of State
and Local Expenditures in the
Washington Metropolitan Area

1. For a summary of how this problem has been treated in some other benefit
    incidence studies, see *Tax Burdens and Benefits of Government Expenditures by Income Class,* 1961 and 1965 (New York: Tax Foundation, 1967),
    pp. 60–63.
2. For a fuller discussion of the external benefits from education, see Burton
    A. Weisbrod, *External Benefits of Public Education: An Economic Analysis*
    (Princeton, New Jersey: Princeton University, Department of Economics,
    1964).
3. Henry Aaron and Martin C. McGuire, "Public Goods and Income Distribution," *Econometrica* 38 (1970): 916.
4. For some attempts to quantify the dimensions of this problem, see Gary
    Becker, *Human Capital: A Theoretical and Empirical Analysis* (New York:
    Columbia University Press, 1964); Giora Hanoch "An Economic Analysis of
    Earnings and Schooling," *Journal of Human Resources* 2 (1967): 310–29;
    and Fred Hines, Luther Tweeten, and Martin Redfern "Social and Private
    Rates of Return to Investment in Schooling, By Race-Sex Groups and
    Regions," *Journal of Human Resources* 5 (1970): 318–40. For a discussion
    of these issues see also M. Blaug, *An Introduction to the Economics of
    Education* (Baltimore: Penguin, 1972), pp. 224–34.
5. William Watts and Lloyd A. Free, *State of the Nation* (Washington: Potomac
    Associates, 1973).
6. This detailed breakdown of the survey results was supplied by Potomac
    Associates.
7. Grubb defines benefits as the investment return from education. Since the
    returns are lower for poor children the degree of progressivity of local school
    expenditures would be considerably less than even our welfare estimates
    imply, to say nothing of the "progressivity" implied by the traditional cost
    of service estimates. See W.N. Grubb, "The Distribution of Costs and Benefits in an Urban Public School System," *National Tax Journal* 24 (1971):1–12.
8. Thus Aaron and McGuire assume as a high estimate that 70 percent of
    elementary and secondary educational benefits are public, while their high
    estimate for the public benefits from higher education is only 50 percent.
    Aaron and McGuire, "Public Goods," p. 916.
9. For an elaboration of this position, see Milton Friedman, *Capitalism and
    Freedom* (Chicago: University of Chicago Press, 1963).
10. W. Irwin Gillespie, "Effect of Public Expenditures on the Distribution of
    Income," in Richard A. Musgrave (ed.), *Essays in Fiscal Federalism*
    (Washington: Brookings Institution, 1965).

11. A. Thomas Eapen and Ann Navarro Eapen, *Incidence of Taxes and Expenditures of Connecticut State and Local Governments,* Fiscal Year 1967, Hartford, 1971.

12. Watts and Free, for example, report that in 1971, 87 percent of those with incomes over $15,000 would like to see the Medicaid program, which finances hospital and medical care for the medically indigent, either increased in scope or at least kept at its present size. Watts and Free, *State of the Nation,* p. 295.

13. Previous benefit incidence studies have uniformly considered that hospitalization services generate private benefits. See, for example, O.H. Brownlee, *Estimated Distribution of Minnesota Taxes and Public Expenditure Benefits* (Minneapolis: University of Minnesota Press, 1960); Eapen and Eapen, *Incidence of Taxes and Expenditures of Connecticut*; and Gillespie, "Effect of Public Expenditures."

14. The possible option demand for certain public services was pointed out by Burton A. Weisbrod, "Collective-Consumption Services of Individual Consumption Goods," *Quarterly Journal of Economics* 78 (1964): 471–77. For further discussion of the validity of the option demand concept, see D.R. Byerlee, "Option Demand and Consumer Surplus: Comment," and Charles J. Cicchetti and A. Myrick Freeman III, "Option Demand and Consumer Surplus: Further Comment," *Quarterly Journal of Economics* 85 (1971): 523–39.

Notes to Chapter 6
Estimates of Incidence of State and Local
Revenues in the Washington
Metropolitan Area

1. Among the most often cited incidence studies of state and local taxes are R.A. Musgrave and D.W. Daicoff, "Who Pays Michigan Taxes?" *Michigan Tax Study Staff Papers,* Lansing, 1958, pp. 131–84; *Wisconsin's State and Local Tax Burden,* Madison, 1959; and O.H. Brownlee, *Estimated Distribution of Minnesota Taxes and Public Expenditure Benefits,* Minneapolis, 1960.

   More recent studies include James A. Johnson, *The Incidence of Government Revenues and Expenditures,* Ottawa, no date; and A.T. Eapen and A.N. Eapen, *Incidence of Taxes and Expenditures of Connecticut State and Local Government Fiscal Year 1967,* Hartford, 1971.

2. One must admit that deductibility of state and local taxes means that federal tax rates must be higher for any given level of yield. But for any one jurisdiction, the federal tax structure is basically independent of the jurisdiction's tax decisions. Therefore the individual taxpayer will view the true subjective burden of a state or local tax to himself as the tax net of offset. For a theoretical treatment of the effects of such deductibility on local fiscal decisions, see Robert P. Inman, *Four Essays on Fiscal Federalism,* Ph.D. dissertation, Harvard, 1972.

3. See Peter Mieszkowski, "The Property Tax: An Excise Tax or a Profits Tax?" *Journal of Public Economics* 1 (1972): 73–96;
4. For a detailed discussion of the reasoning employed to arrive at these results, see ibid., pp. 81–90.

Note should be made here of some of the literature dealing with the incidence of the property tax. Dick Netzer, *Economics of the Property Tax* (Washington: The Brookings Institution, 1966), is generally considered a standard reference work. It contains a review of the literature published before it. Since that time there have been two significant lines of theoretical inquiry besides the publication of the Mieszkowski article.

Larry Orr, "The Incidence of Differential Property Taxes on Urban Housing," *National Tax Journal* 21 (1968): 253–62, argues that the housing stock is relatively fixed and cannot be augmented significantly except in the very long run. Since in a given housing market there may be a large number of differential taxing jurisdictions, the demand for housing services in any one district is likely to be quite elastic. The consequence is that the portion of a jurisdictions' property taxes that are above the lowest rate in the area is likely to be absorbed by the owners of the property. Raymond Richman, "The Incidence of Urban Real Estate Taxes Under Conditions of Static and Dynamic Equilibrium," *Land Economics* 43 (1967): 122–80, makes the same theoretical argument. This argument is similar to Mieszkowski's. However, Mieszkowski's reason for imputing some of the differential tax to land is the complete elasticity of supply of capital in the long run. Orr's reason is the elasticity in the demand for its services and the short-run inelasticity in its supply. It seems to us that when one considers that only mobility at the margin is required for substantial elasticity in the supply of capital, Mieszkowski's assumption is the more plausible one. Moreover, Mieszkowski's analysis is more general both because it admits of a wider capital market and because it refers to all taxes on improvements and not simply on housing. For debate about the validity of some of the Orr data, see J.D. Heinberg and W.E. Oates, "The Incidence of Differential Property Taxes on Urban Housing: A Comment and Some Further Evidence," *National Tax Journal* 23 (1970): 92; and Orr, "Reply," *National Tax Journal* 23 (1970): 99–101. Heinberg and Oates present data to indicate, however, that the full tax differential is capitalized. This would not be inconsistent with Mieszkowski's contention that only a quarter of any differential would be borne by land, because the data referred to by Heinberg and Oates analyze owner-occupied homes where the distinction between decreased land values and increased costs of services provided on the land blurs.

The other significant effort concerning the incidence of the property tax revolves around the question of the permanent income elasticity of demand for housing and the question of whether the ratio of market value to rental income increases for more expensive housing. Given reasonable estimates of the permanent income elasticity of demand for housing and the gross rent multiplier, George Peterson ("The Regressivity of the Residential Property Tax," *Journal of Public Economics,* forthcoming) concludes that

the residential property tax may well not be regressive. Robin Barlow and Richard Coe, however ("The Incidence of Selected Taxes by Income Classes," Institute for Social Research, Panel Study of Family Income Dynamics," forthcoming), find that the property tax on housing is only slightly less regressive if a five-year definition of both taxes and income is used than an annual definition. For a review of research on the demand for housing, see Frank deLeeuw, "The Demand for Housing: A Review of Cross-Section Evidence," *Review of Economics and Statistics* 53 (1971): 1–10. James N. Morgan, Martin H. David, Wilbur Cohen, and Harvey E. Brazer, *Income and Welfare in the United States* (New York: McGraw-Hill, 1962), pp. 288–301, found that property tax is a proportional incidence even when current income is used if a concept of "full income" is employed.

5. This debate centers around the work of Earl Rolph and George Break. A good summary of their position appears in Chapter 13 of their *Public Finance* (New York, 1961). Their argument draws on the work of Harry G. Brown, "The Incidence of a General Output or a General Sales Tax," *Journal of Political Economy* 48 (1939): 254–62.

6. Perhaps the most forceful presentation of orthodoxy's case is made by Richard A. Musgrave, *The Theory of Public Finance* (New York: McGraw-Hill, 1959), pp. 379–82. For the most extensive study of the sales tax, consult John Due, *Sales Taxation* (Champaign, Illinois, 1957). A summary of some of the important issues is found in Daniel Morgan, *Retail Sales Tax: An Appraisal of New Issues* (Madison: University of Wisconsin Press, 1964), pp. 194.

7. This term and much of the analysis employed is derived from Carl S. Shoup, *Public Finance* (Chicago: Aldine, 1969), p. 244. Shoup's analysis is noteworthy in that it is one of the few that considers taxes in an open-economy framework.

8. But sales taxes paid by business are treated as part of the jurisdiction's sales taxes. Practice differs here. In one of the few studies of a local tax system, Alan D. Donheiser, "The Incidence of the New York City Tax System," *Financing Government in New York City* (New York, 1966), pp. 153–207 include the part of the sales tax paid for by businesses as part of business cost taxes. This procedure results in an apparently more progressive sales tax. The reason is that these business cost taxes are presumed to be paid in proportion to total consumption which is distributed more regressively among income classes than taxable sales. We chose to include the part of the sales tax paid by business as part of the total incidence of the sales tax.

9. For a discussion of what is best assumed in areas with heavy exporting of locally produced commodities, see Charles E. McClure, "The Interstate Exporting of State and Local Taxes: Estimates for 1962," *National Tax Journal* 20 (1967): 49–77, especially pp. 57–59. For a more theoretical discussion, see McClure, "Commodity Tax Incidence in Open Economies," *National Tax Journal* 17 (1964): 187. For an earlier analysis that concentrates on tax differentials, see Robert H. Parks, "Theory of Tax Incidence: International Aspects," *National Tax Journal* 14 (1961): 190–97. Recently Donald Phares *State-Local Tax Equity* (Lexington, Massa-

chusetts: Lexington Books, D.C. Heath, 1973) has incorporated both the exporting and the importing of all state and local taxes into his attempt to measure the fiscal incidence of all fifty state and local structures.

10. *Corporate Tax Report,* 5th edition (Washington, 1971), p. 15.

11. Marian Kryzaniak and Richard Musgrave, *The Shifting of the Corporate Income Tax* (Baltimore: The Johns Hopkins University Press, 1963), have presented empirical estimates implying that the corporate income tax may be more than fully shifted forward to consumers. This result has largely been treated skeptically. For example, see Arnold C. Harberger, "The Incidence of the Corporate Income Taxation," *Journal of Political Economy* 70 (1962): 215–40; John G. Cragg, Arnold C. Harberger and Peter Mieszkowski, "Empirical Evidence on the Incidence of the Corporation Income Tax," *Journal of Political Economy* 75 (1967): 215–40, who present empirical data supporting the proposition that the tax is entirely borne by capital. Robert Gordon's model built upon a cost plus pricing rule implies that little of the tax is borne by consumers. Robert J. Gordon, "The Incidence of the Corporation Income Tax in U.S. Manufacturing," *American Economic Review* 57 (1967): 731–58; M. Kryzaniak and R.A. Musgrave, "Incidence of the Corporation Income Tax in U.S. Manufacturing: Comment," and R.J. Gordon, "Reply," *American Economic Review* 58 (1968): 1358–67. Further discussion of Musgrave and Kryzaniak's results is contained in Kryzaniak (ed.), *Effects of the Corporation Income Tax* (Detroit: Wayne State University Press, 1966).

Notes to Chapter 7
Interjurisdictional Fiscal Flows in
Metropolitan Washington

1. See, for example, Ramsey, "Suburban Central City Exploitation Thesis: Comment."
2. Neenan, *Political Economy of Urban Areas,* pp. 53–139.

Notes to Chapter 8
Fiscal Incidence of State and Local Public
Sectors in Metropolitan Washington

1. See James Buchanan, "Federalism and Fiscal Equity," *American Economic Review* 40 (1950): 170–89.
2. Anthony D. Scott, "Federal Grants and Resource Allocation," *Journal of Political Economy* 60 (1952): 534–36.
3. James M. Buchanan, "Federal Grants and Resource Allocation: Reply," *Journal of Political Economy* 60 (1952): 536–38.
4. Richard A. Musgrave, "Approaches to a Fiscal Theory of Political Federalism," *Public Finances: Needs, Sources and Utilization* (New York: National Bureau of Economic Research, 1961), pp. 97–112.

5. James M. Buchanan and Richard E. Wagner, "An Efficiency Basis for Federal Fiscal Equalization," Julius Margolis (ed.), *The Analysis of Public Output.*

6. Another consideration leading to inefficient incentives toward migration may be differing degrees of income redistributional activities in local government budgets. Incentives will be given to the poor to move into and for the rich to move out of those communities whose fiscal structures favor the poor. It was for this reason that George Stigler, for example, insisted that income redistribution is not within the tenable range of functions of state and local governments, "The Tenable Range of Local Government," in *Federal Expenditure Policy for Economic Growth and Stability* (U.S. Congress, Joint Economic Committee, 1957), pp. 213–19. James M. Buchanan and Charles G. Goetz, "Efficiency Limits of Fiscal Mobility: An Assessment of the Tiebout Model," *Journal of Public Economics* 1 (1972): 25–43, argue that overmigration will necessarily occur only in the case of purely public goods which must be supplied in equal amounts. Where the good is only partly public and supplied in different quantities, the theoretical result may be either over or undermigration. They contend, however, that real world circumstances imply overmigration.

7. See Bruce W. Hamilton, "Zoning and Property Taxes in a System of Local Governments," *Urban Studies,* forthcoming. The rights of communities to practice such "fiscal zoning" has come under increasing criticism.

8. For a fuller discussion of this point, see Kenneth V. Greene, "Some Institutional Considerations in Federal-State Fiscal Relations," *Public Choice* 9 (1970): 1–18.

9. Mark A. Haskell and Stephen Leshinski, "Fiscal Influences on Residential Choice: A Study of the New York Region," *Quarterly Review of Economics and Business* 9 (1969): 47–56.

10. David F. Bradford and Harry H. Kelejian, "An Econometric Model of the Flight to the Suburbs," *Journal of Political Economy* 81 (1973): 566–89.

11. It must be noted that they use a rather imprecise measure of fiscal residual. Basically they assume that ". . . a dollar of city government expenditure yields an equal benefit to all families on the average" and that ". . . an average nonpoor family pays roughly 2.5 times as much in local taxes as the average poor family . . ." Bradford and Kelejian, ibid., p. 577. Additional evidence on the locational response to differential tax expenditure levels is found in Wallace Oates, "The Effects of Property Taxes and Local Public Spending on Property Values: An Empirical Study of Tax Capitalization and the Tiebout Hypothesis," *Journal of Political Economy* 77 (1969): 957–71.

Notes to Chapter 9
Discussion of the Results

1. See Gillespie, "Effects of Public Expenditures," table 13.

2. The assumptions employed in this study are discussed in Chapter 6. For Gillespie, see ibid., pp. 132–34.

3. Ibid., table 14 and table 1.4.
4. For a review of other voting and survey studies which in general support the pattern of fiscal residuals that emerges from the welfare estimates of benefits, see Neenan, *Political Economy of Urban Areas,* pp. 96–116.
5. Edward C. Banfield and James Q. Wilson, "Voting Behavior on Municipal Public Expenditures: A Study of Rationality and Self-Interest," in Julius Margolis (ed.), *The Public Economy of Urban Communities* (Washington, D.C.: Resources for the Future, 1965), pp. 74–91.
6. William Watts and Lloyd A. Free (eds.), *State of the Nation,* (New York: Universe Books, 1973), p. 320.
7. Ibid.
8 Ibid.
9. For a thorough discussion of the issues involved in evaluating in-kind transfers, see M. Schmundt, E. Smolensky, and L. Stiefel, "The Evaluation by Recipients of In-kind Transfers," Conference on Income and Wealth, Ann Arbor, May 1974.
10. A recent national survey, however, reports that among those with $15,000 and over income there is little difference between central city and suburban attitudes toward "programs to help improve the situation of black Americans." While 86.7 percent of central city residents in that income class were in favor of either maintaining or increasing such programs, 83.3 percent of suburbanites were similarly inclined. See Watts and Free, *State of the Nation,* pp. 294 and 320–22.
11. On the basis of their national survey, Watts and Free find that there is little difference between central city and suburban attitudes toward income redistribution. Thus for central city residents in the $15,000 and over income class, 86.4 percent favored either maintaining or expanding five different income redistributional programs, while 83.3 percent of the suburbanites in that income class also favored maintaining or expanding the programs. See Watts and Free, *State of the Nation,* pp. 294 and 320–22.

Notes to Appendix A
Documentation of the Revenue and
Expenditure Data for the
Washington Metropolitan Area

1. The following documents form the basis for much of our revenue-expenditure data:
   1. District of Columbia
      a. *Justification for the 1972 Budget,* D.C. Budget Office
      b. *Financial and Statistical Report, 1970,* Government of the District of Columbia
   2. Maryland
      a. *Report of the Comptroller of the Treasury of Maryland 1970*
      b. *Local Government Finances in Maryland for the Fiscal Year Ended June 30, 1970,* Department of Fiscal Services, Division of Fiscal Research of the State of Maryland.

    c. *Annual Financial Report for the Fiscal Year July 1, 1969–June 30, 1970,* Montgomery County.

    d. *The Recommended Operating Budget FY 1971–1972,* Montgomery County, Maryland.

    e. *Annual Financial Report for the Fiscal Year July 1, 1969–June 30, 1970,* Montgomery County Public Schools.

    f. *Budget Request Operating Expenditures for the School and Fiscal Year Ending June 30, 1972,* Montgomery County Public Schools.

    g. *Operating Budget, 1971–1972,* Prince Georges County, Maryland

    h. *Report and Financial Statements, June 30, 1970,* Maryland National Capital Park and Planning Commission.

The various financial statements of the Maryland local town governments were also used. These are on file with the Division of Fiscal Research of the Department of Fiscal Services in Annapolis.

  3. Virginia

    a. *Report of the Comptroller,* 1970: State of Virginia

    b. *Report of the Department of Taxation,* 1970; State of Virginia

    c. *Arlington County Fiscal 1972 Budget*

    d. *County of Arlington, Virginia, Audited Financial Statements, 1970*

    e. *Advertised Fiscal Plan Fairfax County Fiscal 1972*

    f. *1971–1972 Annual Budget,* City of Alexandria

    g. *Report on Examination, 1970*; City of Fairfax

    h. *Budgets, 1971–1972,* Falls Church, Virginia

    i. *Town of Vienna, Virginia Auditor's Report,* 1970

    j. *Town of Herndon, Virginia Auditor's Report,* 1970

Notes to Appendix B
Expenditure Incidence Assumptions

1. State Council of Higher Education, A Study of Student Financial Aid in Virginia, Richmond, Virginia (1969).

2. H. Zinder and Associates, Inc. *The Future of Tourism in the District of Columbia–A Financial Approach,* Washington, 1967, 82 pp.

3. D.C. Department of Highways and Traffic, *D.C. Cordon Traffic Survey 1969.*

Notes to Appendix C
Tax Incidence Assumptions

1. Richard F. Fryman, "Sales Taxation of Producers' Goods in Illinois," *National Tax Journal* 22 (1969): 273–81.

2. H. Zinder Associates, Inc., *The Future of Tourism in the District of Columbia– Financial Approach,* Washington, 1967, 82 pp.

3. William Hamovitch, "Sales Taxation:: An Analysis of the Effects of Rate Increases in Two Contrasting Cases," *National Tax Journal* 19 (1966): 411–20.
4. Henry M. Levin, "An Analysis of the Economic Effects of the New York City Sales Tax," in *Financing Government in New York City* (New York: Graduate School of Public Administration, New York University, 1966), pp. 635–91.
5. John L. Mikesell, "Central Cities and Sales Tax Differentials: The Border City Problem," *National Tax Journal* 23 (1970): 206–213.

Index

Aaron, Henry, 42, 45, 62, 244, 246, 247, 251
Auld, D.A.L., 22, 23, 243
Albin, Peter S., 15, 240

Banfield, Edward C., 37, 180, 246, 257
Banovetz, James M., 21, 22, 242, 245
Barlow, Robin, 249, 254
Barna, Tibor, 243
Baumol, William J., 15, 239, 240
Becker, Gary, 62, 251
Benefits from government expenditures:
  cost-of-service basis, 61, 145, 146–147;
  individual basis of, 28; private, 29; public
  nonredistributive, 29, 34; public redis-
  tributive, 29, 35; source-of-income, 29;
  use-of-income, 29; welfare basis, 61,
  145, 146, 147–148
Birkhead, Guthrie S., 242
Bish, Robert L., 240
Blaug, M., 251
Book, Samuel H., 18, 19, 242
Borcherding, Thomas E., 249
Boulding, Kenneth E., 36, 37, 246, 247
Bradford, David F., 23, 159, 160, 161, 243, 256
Brazer, Harvey E., 18, 241, 254
Break, George, 254
Brown, Harry G., 254
Brownlee, O.H., 243, 252
Buchanan, James M., 15, 28, 157, 158,
  159, 240, 243, 245, 248, 249, 255, 256
Burkhead, Jesse, 245
Business cost taxes: incidence of, 126–127
Byerlee, D.R., 252

Cartter, Allen M., 243, 244
Cicchetti, Charles J., 252
Cloward, Richard A., 37, 38, 246
Coe, Richard, 254
Cohen, Wilbur, 254
Colm, Gerhard, 245
Commuters, impact on central city, 18,
  171
Conrad, Alfred H., 243
Cook, Gail C.A., 22, 23, 243
Corporate income tax: incidence of,
  130–131

Cost-of-service benefits, 61, 145, 146–147
Cragg, John G., 255
Daicoff, Darwin W., 243, 252
David, Martin, 246, 254
Deacon, Robert T., 249
deLeeuw, Frank, 254
Dickinson, Frank G., 246
Donheiser, Alan D., 254
Downs, Anthony, 245, 249
Due, John, 219, 254

Eapen, A. Thomas, 77, 252
Eapen, Ann Navarro, 77, 252
Ecker-Racz, L.L., 239
Ehrlich, Theodore, 210
Elementary and secondary education,
  40–43, 62–65, 190
Ellickson, Bryan, 241
Evans, Alan W., 16, 241
Exploitation thesis, surburban-central-
  city, 17–25

Federal payment to District of Columbia,
  6, 173, 174
Fellner, William, 47, 248
Fire protection service, 40, 71–78, 160,
  191
Fiscal flows, 2, 152–154
Fiscal incidence, 3, 160–168, 176–178
Fiscal residuals: and attitude toward gov-
  ernment expenditures, 178–180;
  definition of, 157–160; measurement
  of, 160–168; and optimal supply of
  public services, 172–175
Free, Lloyd A., 180, 183, 247, 251, 252,
  257
Freeman, A. Myrick III, 252
Frey, Bruno, 250
Friedman, Milton, 251
Fryman, Richard F., 219, 220, 258

Gillespie, W. Irwin, 39, 71, 77, 176, 178,
  243, 244, 245, 251, 256
Goetz, Charles G., 256
Gordon, Robert J., 255
Greene, Kenneth V., 159, 240, 243, 248,
  256
Grubb, W.N., 251

261

Guitton, Henri, 245, 246

Hamilton, Bruce M., 239, 256
Hamovitch, William, 233, 259
Hanoch, Giora, 251
Harberger, Arnold C., 255
Haskell, Mark A., 159, 160, 161, 256
Haveman, Robert A., 244
Hawley, Amos H., 17, 241
Health services, 42, 78–79, 190
Heinberg, John D., 253
Higher education, 40, 65, 71
Hines, Fred, 251
Hirsch, Werner Z., 240, 242
Hochman, Harold M., xvi, 39, 239, 243, 247
Howrey, E.P., 240

Income tax, individual: incidence of, 117, 120
In-kind transfers, 29
Inman, Robert P., 252
Ireland, Thomas R., 37, 246

Jenkins, Shirley, 244
Johnson, Harry G., 249
Johnson, James A., 252

Kasarda, John, 241
Kee, Woo Sik, 18, 242
Kelejian, Harry H., 159, 160, 161, 256
Koleda, Michael, 241
Krutilla, John, 244
Kryzaniak, Marian, 255

Lampman, Robert J., 244, 246
Leshinski, Stephen, 159, 160, 161, 256
Levin, Henry M., 233, 259
Libraries, 40–42, 90, 190
Lindblom, Charles E., 245
Lowi, Theodore, 242

McClure, Charles E., 254
McGuire, Martin C., 42, 45, 62, 246, 247, 251
McKean, Roland, 249
MacRae, Duncan Jr., 35, 246
Maital, Shlomo, 45, 46, 248
Marglin, Stephen, 246
Margolis, Julius, 18, 240, 241, 243, 245, 246, 256
Mera, Koichi, 248
Mieszkowski, Peter, 115, 253, 255
Mikesell, John L., 233, 259
Miner, Jerry, 245
Mogulof, Melvin B., 240
Money transfers, 29, 32

Morgan, Daniel, 254
Morgan, James N., 254
Musgrave, Richard A., 27, 33, 158, 243, 244, 245, 251, 252, 254, 255

Neenan, William B., 22, 23, 241, 242, 243, 248, 257
Netzer, Dick, 253
Niskanen, William, 249

Oates, Wallace E., 14, 23, 239, 240, 243, 253, 256
Okner, Benjamin, 246
Orr, Larry, 253
Ostrom, Vincent, 240

Parks, Robert H., 254
Pauly, Mark V., 247, 248
Peacock, Alan T., 243
Peterson, George E., 243, 253
Pfaff, Anita, 246, 247
Pfaff, Martin, 246, 247
Piven, Frances Fox, 37, 38, 246
Pollakowski, Harry O., 239
Police service, 40, 71, 78
Political fragmentation: controversy over, 14–17; impact on supply of services, 58–59
Political unification of metropolitan areas, 16
Powell, A.A., 248
Prest, Alan R., 248
Projector, Dorothy S., 234
Property tax: incidence of, 114–117
Private benefits, 40, 63
Public nonredistributive benefits, 29, 34, 39, 41, 63
Public redistributive benefits, 29, 35, 39, 42, 63

Ramsey, David D., 22, 243, 255
Recreation, 40, 96–97, 190
Redfern, Martin, 251
Richman, Raymond, 253
Rodgers, James D., 39, 239, 247
Redistributive programs: reasons for, 36–37; support for, 37–38
Rolph, Earl, 254
Rosett, Arthur, 242
Rothenberg, Jerome, 241

Sales tax: incidence of, 120–124
Samuelson, Paul, 27, 34, 245, 246
Sato, Kazuo, 45, 248
Say, J.B., 28, 243
Schmundt, M., 31, 244, 257
Scott, Anthony D., 158, 255

Scott, Claudia D., 243
Scott, Robert Hanley, 247
Shall, Laurence D., 247
Shaller, Howard G., 239
Shibata, Hirofumi, 249
Shoup, Carl S., 254
Shoup, Donald C., 242
Smith, R.F., 20, 21, 242
Smolensky, Eugene, 31, 244, 257
Stauffacher, Charles, 243
Steiner, Peter O., 245
Stiefel, L., 31, 244, 257
Stigler, George, 256
Source-of-income benefits: impact of
  government expenditures on, 55;
  nature of, 29
Suburban-central-city exploitation
  thesis, 17–25, 169–170, 171, 173

Taxes: alcoholic beverage excise, 131;
  bank, 133; business cost, 126–127;
  capitation, 135; corporate income, 130–
  131; death and gift, 132; individual income, 117, 120; insurance companies,
  133; motor fuel, 131; motor registration
  and license, 133; personal property, 134;
  property, 114–117; railroad, 134;
  sales, 120–124
Terrell, Henry S., 242
Thurow, Lester, 246
Tiebout, Charles M., 13, 14, 15, 183,
  239, 240
Transfers: in-kind, 31, money, 32
Transportation, 40, 103, 190
Tucker, Rufus S., 243
Tullock, Gordon, 245, 249
Tweeten, Luther, 251

Use-of-income benefits: imputations of,
  42–48, 63; nature of, 29, 33–48

Vickrey, William S., 246, 247
Vincent, Phillip E., 19, 20, 241, 242
von Furstenberg, George, 244

Wagner, Richard E., 159, 256
Warren, Robert O., 239, 240
Watts, William, 180, 183, 247, 251,
  252, 257
Weicher, John C., 249
Weisbrod, Burton A., 243, 244, 246,
  251, 252
Weiss, Gertrude S., 234
Welfare-basis for benefits, 61, 145, 146,
  147–148
Welfare services, 42, 79, 90, 190
Wildavsky, Aaron, 245
Williams, Alan, 250
Wilson, James Q., 180, 257
Wilson, R.H., 248

Zinder Associates, Inc., 221, 258

About the Authors

Kenneth V. Greene is assistant professor of economics at the State University of New York, Binghamton. A graduate of St. John's University and the University of Virginia, Dr. Greene's major interests are public finance, urban economics, and microeconomics.

William B. Neenan is associate professor of economics and social work at the University of Michigan; he received degrees from St. Louis University and the University of Michigan. He is a frequent contributor to journals on a wide range of fiscal and economic subjects, and is the author of *Political Economy of Urban Areas* (Markham, 1972). In addition to his academic endeavors, Dr. Neenan has conducted numerous evaluation and analytic projects for governmental and public interest organizations.

Claudia D. Scott joined the urban public finance research group at The Urban Institute in 1970. A graduate of Mt. Holyoke College and Duke University, Dr. Scott's major interests have been urban and regional economics and planning, and public finance. She is the author of *Forecasting Local Government Spending,* and has taught at George Washington University and Federal City College. She is a senior lecturer in economics at the University of Auckland, New Zealand.

Greene, Neenan, and Scott undertook the work for this book while members of the urban public finance research team at The Urban Institute. The study was funded by a grant from the National Science Foundation.

Published in cooperation with
The Urban Institute, Washington, D.C.

**Fiscal Interactions
in a
Metropolitan
Area**